P9-CKH-241

Also by Richard John Neuhaus

Appointment in Rome: The Church in America Awakening

America Against Itself: Moral Vision and the Public Order

Doing Well and Doing Good: The Challenge to the Christian Capitalist

The Naked Public Square

Dispensations: The Future of South Africa as South Africans See It

The Catholic Moment: The Paradox of the Church in the Postmodern World

Freedom for Ministry

Christian Faith and Public Policy: Thinking and Acting in the Courage of Uncertainty

Time Toward Home: The American Experiment As Revelation

Death on a Friday Afternoon

Richard John Neuhaus

BASIC
BOOKS

A Member of the Perseus Books Group

Death

on a

Friday

Afternoon

Meditations on the

Last Words of Jesus

from the Cross

Published by Basic Books,
A Member of the Perseus Books Group

Book design by Mark McGarry

Library of Congress Cataloging-in-Publication Data
Neuhaus, Richard John.
Death on a Friday afternoon : meditations on the last words of Jesus from the
cross / Richard John Neuhaus.— 1st ed.
p. cm.
ISBN 0–465–04932–X
1. Jesus Christ—Seven last words—Meditations. 2. Good Friday—Meditations.
I. Title.
BT456 .N48 2000
232.96'35—dc21
99–050283

First Edition
00 01 02 03 / 10 9 8 7 6 5 4 3 2 1

To

Matthew Berke, Davida Goldman, James Nuechterlein
loyal companions on the way from strength to strength, with detours

Contents

Preface

Good Friday is not just one day of the year. It is a day relived in every day of the world, and of our lives in the world. In the Christian view of things, all reality turns around the "paschal mystery" of the death and resurrection of Christ. As Passover marks the liberation from bondage in Egypt, so the paschal mystery marks humanity's passage from death to life. Good Friday cannot be confined to Holy Week. It is not simply the dismal but necessary prelude to the joy of Easter, although I'm afraid many Christians think of it that way. Every day of the year is a good day to think more deeply about Good Friday, for Good Friday is the drama of the love by which our every day is sustained.

I suppose I should not be surprised anymore, but I am. With remarkable frequency I run into people who admit that, when it comes to this business about the cross and crucifixion, they just don't "get it." Some of these people are lifelong and devout Christians, others are inquirers and still others are devout unbelievers for whom the bloodiness of Good Friday is just one more reason for not being a Christian.

I say it is surprising because there is nothing more central to Christianity than what happened on Good Friday. It is, if you will, crucial. In fact the word "crucial" comes from the Latin word *crux*, meaning "cross." Preachers, televangelists and billboards beyond number proclaim, "Jesus died for your sins." Christians piously nod their heads in assent, as well we should. But what does it *mean* to say that Jesus died for our sins? Why was it necessary? Or was it? And which sins in particular? And how can it really make any difference in the real world today that a good man died a horrible death two thousand years ago? What does it have to do with the lives *we* have to live and the deaths *we* have to die?

In the face of such questions, many of us become tongue-tied and quite incoherent. We mumble something about "atonement," a word we heard somewhere, or about Jesus "making up for" what we did wrong or about how Jesus set an example of love. Others think they know very well what Good Friday means, and they don't like it one bit. A while back an elderly man who lives next door here in New York told me it means that God killed his son. He could never respect a man who killed his son, he declared, and he certainly could not worship a God who did such a terrible thing.

This book does not claim to "explain" what happened on Good Friday. That would be unspeakably presumptuous. It does invite readers to explore the meanings that people have found in the crucifixion of Christ. It is an exploration into the meaning of suffering, of justice, of loss, of death and of whatever hope there may be on the far side of death. These pages are an exploration into mystery. The word "mystery" in this connection does not mean a puzzle, as in a murder mystery. It is not a thing to be solved, but an adventure into wonder, with each wonder that we encounter leading on to the next and greater wonder.

The book is in the form of a reflection or meditation. I hope speed-readers (I often wish I were one) will find themselves slowing down and maybe even putting the book aside from time to time just to think about the mystery. The book is not entirely meditative, however. Arguments are also advanced, and there is some vigorous wrestling with traditional doctrine—"doctrine" being just another word for "teaching"—about the death of Christ. And there are stories about people today who in their troubles find themselves, as they say, at the foot of the cross. Sometimes they find themselves there in anger, sometimes in joy, but always in a deeper awareness of the mystery of their lives within the mystery of life itself.

If what Christians say about Good Friday is true, then it is, quite simply, the truth about everything. I have written this for people who are convinced of that truth, for people who are open to thinking about whether it may be true and for people who are just curious about why so much of the world thinks Good Friday is the key to understanding what Dante called "the love that moves the sun and all the other stars."

Our exploring follows the path of what are called the "Seven Last Words" of Jesus from the cross. Actually, they are not seven single words but seven statements of quite different sorts. They are taken from the four Gospels in the New Testament—Matthew, Mark, Luke and John—each of which reports the death of Jesus from its own distinctive angle. The Good Friday meditation on the Seven Last Words became a very popular devotion among both Protestants and Catholics in the late eighteenth century. For most Christians today, the last words of Jesus from the cross are encountered in the liturgy of Holy Week, when the story of Jesus' suffering and death, known as the passion narrative, is read in its fullness. But thinking about Good Friday is not just for Holy Week. Good Friday, and this book about Good Friday, is for every day of every year, and all year round. The truth is that Good Friday forms the spiritual architecture of Christian existence. And the Seven Last Words embody the truth of Good Friday.

The Seven Last Words are these:

"Father, forgive them, for they know not what they do."

"Truly, I say to you, today you will be with me in paradise."

"Woman, behold your son. Son, behold your mother."

"My God, my God, why have you forsaken me?"

"I thirst."

"It is finished."

"Father, into your hands I commend my spirit."

I have devoted a chapter to exploring each "word," and I confess that at the end of each I realized the exploration had just begun. Numerous writers and composers have been captivated by the suggestiveness of the Seven Last Words. Haydn, Beethoven, Dubois, Gounod and Dvorák are among those who have composed major works around these texts. Saverio Mercadante's oratorio *The Seven Last Words of Our Savior* was published in 1882, the year that James Joyce was born, and received literary attention by occurring several times in Leopold Bloom's stream of consciousness in *Ulysses*. In 1630, in his very last sermon, the great John Donne spoke on "Death's Duel or a Consolation to the Soule, against the Dying Life, and Living Death of the Body." He drew a parallel between the Seven Words and the seven days of the week. "That which we call life is but *Hebdomada mortium*, a weeke of deaths, seaven dayes, seaven periods of our life spent in dying, a dying seaven times over." Pretty morbid stuff, you might think. But I think not, and hope you will remain open to persuasion on that score.

Gerard Manley Hopkins composed what he called seven "terrible" sonnets, trying to plumb the depths of each utterance from the cross. And once again, James Joyce, in *Stephen Hero*, an early version of *A Portrait of the Artist as a Young Man*, has his hero attending the "Three Hour" service on Good Friday, after which he wanders the streets for three hours in agonized reflection on the Seven Words before deciding to "regard himself seriously as a literary artist." In the 1950s, Dylan Thomas in "Altarwise by Owl-light" paraphrases the Seven Last Words, beginning with "This was the crucifixion on the mountain, / Time's nerve in vinegar" and ending with "Suffer the heaven's children through my heartbeat." Samuel Beckett (*Waiting for Godot*) insisted on Good Friday as his birthday, writing that his "birthmark" was his "deathmark." In the "single sentence" of his spiritual biography, "flesh becomes word" only to decline through a series of "last words" into sound, "a stain upon the silence."

By way of sharpest contrast, the opening of the Gospel according to St. John declares that the Word became flesh. In these last words of the Word in descent into death, we come upon the perfect sound of silence, a silence of the completion toward which all good words tend. "It is finished," Jesus said from the cross. It is finished, but it is not over. To accompany him to his end is to discover our beginning. At least, people beyond number have for two thousand years found that to be so. I hope this book will help readers understand why that has been the case. Even better is to discover why it may be the case also for you.

I am grateful to Monsignor Michael Wrenn, pastor of the Church of St. John the Evangelist in Manhattan, who invited me to preach the three-hour Good Friday meditation some six years ago, the occasion that prompted me to start writing a book that had been on my mind a long time. I have drawn extensively on Raymond E. Brown's *The Death of the Messiah* and am also indebted to Avery Dulles's work on the death of Jesus as sacrifice. The influence of the great Swiss theologian Hans Urs von Balthasar will be evident throughout, and I have also borrowed selectively from Edward Oakes's admirable synthesis of Balthasar's work, *Pattern of Redemption*. Those who detect also the presence of René Girard will not be mistaken. I thank Robert Louis Wilken, of the University of Virginia, for his critical reading of the manuscript,

and, as always, Davida Goldman and the staff of the Institute on
Religion and Public Life for their unstinting assistance. Loretta
Barret, my agent, and Don Fehr, my editor, have been
unfailingly helpful. The translation of the biblical texts is the
Revised Standard Version, except in a few instances where other
translations illuminate alternative interpretations. For easy
reference, the biblical texts are given in the Biblical References
at the back of the book.

Richard John Neuhaus
The Day of St. Thomas
New York City

Death on a Friday Afternoon

1
Coming to Our Senses

The First Word from the cross:

"Father, forgive them, for they know not what they do."

Perhaps you are reading this in the summertime, or in autumn, or in the dead of winter. It makes no difference. I do not ask you to forget the present and imagine that it is Holy Week. Rather, I invite you to be open to the thought that this time that you are now calling the present *is* Holy Week, for all time was there, *is* there, at the cross.

Christians call them the Triduum Sacrum, the three most sacred days of the year, the three most sacred days of all time when time is truly told. The first, Maundy Thursday, is so called because that night, the night before he was betrayed, Jesus gave the command, the *mandatum*, that we should love one another. Not necessarily with the love of our desiring, but with a demanding love, even a demeaning love—as in washing the feet of faithless friends who will run away and leave you naked to your enemies.

The second day is the Friday we so oddly call "good." And the third day, the great Vigil of Resurrection conquest. Do not rush to the conquest. Stay a while with this day. Let your heart be broken by the unspeakably bad of this Friday we call good. Some scholars speculate that "Good Friday" comes from "God's Friday," as "good-bye" was originally "God be by you." But it is just as odd that it should be called God's Friday, when it is the day we say good-bye to the glory of God. Wherever its name comes from, let your present moment stay with this day. Stay a while in the eclipse of the light, stay a while with the conquered One. There is time enough for Easter.

By these three days all the world is called to attention. Everything that is and ever was and ever will be, the macro and the micro, the galaxies beyond number and the microbes beyond notice—everything is mysteriously entangled with what happened, with what happens, in these days. This is the *axis mundi*, the center upon which the cosmos turns. In the derelict who cries from the cross is, or so Christians say, the Alpha and Omega, the beginning and the end. The life of all on this day died. Stay a while with that dying.

Every human life, conceived from eternity and destined to eternity, here finds its story truly told. In this killing that some call senseless we are brought to our senses. Here we find out who we most truly are, because here is the One who is what we are called to be. The derelict cries, "Come, follow me." Follow him there? We recoil. We close our ears. We hurry on to Easter. But we will not know what to do with Easter's light if we shun the friendship of the darkness that is wisdom's way to light.

In Good Friday's service of the Seven Words, alongside this

First Word from the cross, we read the parable of the prodigal son, the wayward son, the wastrel son. It is all there in the fifteenth chapter of Luke's Gospel. Determined to reach for the stars, to seize the light, to shatter the restraints of life, he went to his father and asked for all he could get. The father, with deep foreboding and a breaking heart, gave him what he asked for. So lightly, so eagerly did impetuous youth leave the love that gave him life. He rushed to the light.

And so the prodigal son went off to what we are told was a distant country. There he wasted his money, he wasted his energies, he wasted his youth. With what he had and with what he was he bought friends and pleasure, until he had no more and was no more what he had been. Destitute, he was reduced to feeding the pigs and envying the pigs for the slop they ate. And then, in the eclipse of the light, we encounter those abruptly wondrous words in the Gospel account: "He came to his senses." Other translations say, "he came to himself." I will return to that later—how we come to know our true selves when we are encountered by an "other" who defines who we are. But, for the moment, we stay with the simple telling of the tale.

He came to his senses. "What am I doing, what have I done, with my life?" From this madness, from the darkness of delusion, we are told that he turned his face homeward, homeward to the waiting father. The father saw him coming from afar. He was way off down the road, not even near the house yet. I suspect the father had been going out every day, month after month, maybe year after year, waiting for his son—this son so filled with promise, this son so filled with light—to return to the love that gave him life. Day after day, the father had slowly turned back to the house disappointed. This day he had gone out once again, hoping against hope, expecting against expectation, and this day, there in the distance, there just over the horizon—his son.

He saw him far off, coming home, coming home to the waiting father. Quickly—the fatted calf, the finest robe and shoes, the ring of fidelity! And the father forgave him everything, even the calculated confession by which he would win his father's favor. Of the son it is said, "He came to his senses," and coming to his senses he came to his father.

Good Friday brings us to our senses. Our senses come to us as we sense that in this life and in this death is our life and our death. The truth about the crucified Lord is the truth about ourselves. "Know yourself," the ancient philosophers admonish us, for in knowing yourself is the beginning of wisdom. To which the Psalmist declares, "The fear of the Lord is the beginning of wisdom." The beginning of wisdom is to come to our senses and know the fearful truth about ourselves, that we have wandered and wasted our days in a distant country far from home. We know ourselves most truly in knowing Christ, for in him is our true self. Or so Christians say. His cross is the way home to the waiting Father. "If you would come to your senses," he says, "come, follow me."

The ancient Christian fathers spoke of the Christ event as the "recapitulation" of the entire human drama. In this one life, all lives are summed up; in the eternal present of this one life, the past is encompassed, the future is anticipated and the life of Everyman and Everywoman is most truly lived. "I am the way, the truth, and the life," he said. Not a way among other ways, not a truth among other truths, not a life among other lives, but the way of all ways, the truth of all truths and the life of all lives. Recapitulation. It means, quite simply and solemnly, that this is your life, this is my life and we have not come to our senses until we sense ourselves in the life, and death, of Christ. This is the *axis mundi*.

"When I came to you," writes St. Paul to the Corinthians, "I did not come proclaiming to you the testimony of God in lofty words or wisdom. For I decided to know nothing among you except Jesus Christ and him crucified." Stay a while. Do not hurry by the cross on your way to Easter joy, for we know the risen Lord only through Christ and him crucified. The philosopher Alfred North Whitehead said that the only simplicity to be trusted is the simplicity to be found on the far side of complexity. The only joy to be trusted is the joy on the far side of a broken heart; the only life to be trusted is the life on the far side of death. Stay a while, with Christ and him crucified.

We contemplate for a time the meaning of Good Friday, and then return to what is called the real world of work and shopping and commuter trains and homes. As we come out of a movie theater and shake our heads to clear our minds of another world where we lived for a time in suspended disbelief, as we reorient ourselves to reality, so we leave our contemplation—we leave the church building, we close the book—where for a time another reality seemed possible, believable, even real. But, we tell ourselves, the real world is a world elsewhere. It is the world of deadlines to be met, of appointments to be kept, of taxes to be paid, of children to be educated. From here, from this moment at the cross, it is a distant country. "Father, forgive them, for they have forgotten the way home. They have misplaced the real world." Here, here at the cross, is the real world, here is the *axis mundi*.

Not long ago I was invited to lecture to a large group of clergy in the Midwest. They had for two days been studying sacramental and liturgical theology, and it came time for the bishop to introduce me. "It has been a rewarding two days," he said, "as we have been thinking about worship and the sacramental life, but now we have Father Neuhaus to return us to the real world as he addresses the subject of the Church and social responsibility."

Really? The real world? What then is that other world of worship, prayer and contemplative exploration into the mystery of Christ's presence, a presence ever elusive and disturbingly near? On the part of the bishop it was perhaps a slip of the tongue, but behind slips of the tongue are slips of the mind and sometimes slips of the soul. It happens among all Christians today, of whatever denomination or persuasion, that there is a great slippage of the soul. It is by this world, this world at the cross, that reality is measured and judged. That other world, the world we call real, is a distant country until we with Christ bring it home to the waiting Father.

We are bringing it home, dragging it all behind us: the deadlines and the duties, the fears of failure and hopes for advancement, the loves unreturned, the plans disappointed, the children we lose, the marriage we cannot mend. And so we come loping along with reality's baggage, returning to the real— the real that we left behind when we left for what we mistook as the real world. "I will arise and go to my father, and I will say to him, 'Father, I have sinned against heaven and before you; I am no longer worthy to be called your son.'" I am no longer worthy to be called your son. I am no longer worthy to be called your daughter. And Christ our elder brother takes the baggage and hoists it upon his shoulders, adding this to all that on the cross he is bearing and bringing home. "Father, forgive them, for they knew not what they were doing."

"Come to me," he had earlier said, "all you who are weary and heavy burdened, and I will give you rest." Bring me your baggage.

"Father, forgive them." For whom does he pray forgiveness? For the leaders of his own people, a fragile, frightened establishment that could not abide the threat of the presence of a love so long delayed. For pitiable Pilate, forever wringing his hands forever soiled. For the soldiers who did the deed, who wielded the whip, who drove the nails, who thrust the spear, it all being but a day's work on foreign assignment, far from home. And for us he asks forgiveness, for we were there.

On the Sunday that begins Holy Week we read the passion story and come to the part where the crowd shouts, "Crucify him! Crucify him!" That part is read by the entire congregation, for we were there. The old spiritual asks, "Were you there when they crucified my Lord?" Yes, we answer. Yes, we were there when *we* crucified our Lord.

Over the centuries theologians have contrived wondrously refined theories of the atonement: Why it is that this One had to die, why it is that his dying is for us death's death, why it is that his open tomb opens for every last child of earth the door

to tomorrows without end. And all the theories of atonement are
but probings into mystery, the mystery of a love that did not
have to be but was, and is. All the theories are intellectual
variations, imaginative riffs, on the assertion of St. Paul that
"God was in Christ reconciling the world to himself, not
counting their trespasses against them, and entrusting to us the
message of reconciliation." As the prodigal son was reconciled to
his father, but infinitely more so.

"Not counting their trespasses." Accountants reconcile the
books, and there is no doubt that the disordered books of our
lives need reconciling. But the books are disordered by our
disordered lives, and our lostness cannot be remedied by the
accountant's craft. Someone must go to the distant country
where we have strayed, as a good shepherd seeks a sheep that is
lost. Someone must go, but not just anyone. If we are to be
brought home, it has to be one who is, in the words of the
Nicene Creed, "God from God, Light from Light, true God from
true God."

Only he can bring us home who comes from home, who
comes from God. Coming from the very heart of God, he is
God. And so we say that God became man. It is the longest
journey, long beyond our ability to imagine. God became man.
We say it trembling, we say it puzzling, but more often we say it
rotely, counting on routine to buffer what we cannot bear. What
can we do with the burden of such a truth? This is the awful
truth: that we made necessary the baby crying in the cradle to
become the derelict crying from the cross. The awful truth—as
in awe-filled, filled with awe.

"Atonement." It is a fine, solid, twelfth-century Middle
English word, the kind of word one is inclined to trust. Think of

at-one-ment: What was separated is now at one. But after such a separation there can be no easy reunion. Reconciliation must do justice to what went wrong. It will not do to merely overlook the wrong. We could not bear to live in a world where wrong is taken lightly, where right and wrong finally make no difference. In such a world, we—what we do and what we are—would make no difference. Spare me a gospel of easy love that makes of my life a thing without consequence.

Again, St. Paul says God was in Christ "not counting their trespasses against them." Atonement is not an accountant's trick. It is not a kindly overlooking; it is not a not counting of what must count if anything in heaven or on earth is to matter. God could not simply decide not to count without declaring that we do not count.

But someone might say that, if God is God, he could do anything. Very well, then, God *would* not decide not to count, because he would not declare that we do not count. And yet God's "would" implicates and limits his "could." The God of whom we speak is not, in the words of Pascal, the God of the philosophers but the God of Abraham, Isaac and Jacob. He is the God of unbounded freedom who willed to be bound by love. God is what he wills to be and wills to be what he is. St. John tells us, "God is love," and love always binds. In the seminars of philosophical speculation, many gods are possible. In the arena of salvation's story, God is the God who is bound to love.

He does not count our trespasses against us because something has been done about them. He reckons us sinners to be righteous because sins have been set to right. Dorothy Day, founder of the Catholic Worker movement among the poor, spoke of a "harsh and dreadful love." It is the love of Christ's cross borne for us, and of the cross he calls us to bear. Dietrich Bonhoeffer, Lutheran pastor and martyr under the tyranny of the Third Reich, wrote against and lived against the "cheap grace" that devalues sin and forgiveness alike. Cheap grace is easy grace. Cheap grace does not reckon what went wrong; it requires no costly love.

We confess to hurting someone we love and she says, "Forget it. It's nothing. It doesn't matter." But she knows and we know that it is not nothing, it does matter and we will not forget it. Forgive and forget, they say, but that is surely wrong. What is forgotten need not, indeed cannot, be forgiven. Love does not say to the beloved that it does not matter, for the beloved matters. Spare me the sentimental love that tells me what I do and what I am does not matter.

Forgiveness costs. Forgiveness costs dearly. Some theories of atonement say that Christ paid the price. His death appeased God's wrath and satisfied God's justice. That way of putting it appeals to biblical witness and venerable tradition, and no doubt contains great truth. Yet for many in the past and at present that way of speaking poses great problems. The subtlety of the theory is overwhelmed by the cartoon picture of an angry Father who demands the death of his Son, maybe even kills his Son, in order to appease his own wrath. In its vulgar form—which means the form most common—it is a matter of settling scores, a drama vengeful and vindictive, more worthy of *The Godfather* than of the Father of whom it is said, "God is love."

And yet forgiveness costs. Forgiveness is not forgetfulness; not counting their trespasses is not a kindly accountant winking at what is wrong; it is not a benign cooking of the books. In the world, in our own lives, something has gone dreadfully wrong, and it must be set right. Recall when you were a little child and somebody—maybe you—did something very bad. Maybe a lie was told, some money was stolen or the cookie jar lay shattered on the kitchen floor. The bad thing has been found out, and now something must happen, something must be done about it. The fear of punishment is terrible, but not as terrible as the thought that nothing will happen, that bad things don't matter. If bad things don't matter, then good things don't matter, and then nothing matters and the meaning of everything lies shattered like the cookie jar on the kitchen floor.

Trust that child's intuition. "Unless you become as little children," Jesus said, "you cannot enter the kingdom of God." Unless we are stripped of our habits of forgetting, of our skillful making of excuses, of our jaded acceptance of a world in which bad things happen and it doesn't matter.

This, then, is our circumstance. Something has gone dreadfully wrong with the world, and with us in the world. Things are out of whack. It is not all our fault, but it is our fault too. We cannot blame our distant parents for that fateful afternoon in the garden, for we were there. We, too, reached for the forbidden fruit—the forbidden fruit by which we not only know good and evil, but, much more fatefully, presume to name good and evil. For most of us, our rebellion did not have about it the gargantuan defiance depicted in Milton's *Paradise Lost*. Most of us did not, as some do, stand on a mountain peak and shake a clenched fist against the storming skies, cursing God.

But, then, neither were Adam or Eve so melodramatic. On a perfectly pleasant afternoon in paradise, they did no more than listen to an ever so reasonable voice. "Did God really mean that? Surely he wants you to be yourself, to decide for yourself. Would he have made something so very attractive only to forbid it? The truth is he wants you to be like him, to be like gods." The fatal step was not in knowing the difference between good and evil. Before what we call "the fall" they knew the good in the fullest way of knowing, which is to say that they did the good, they lived the good. They knew the good honestly, straightforwardly, simply, uncomplicatedly, without shame.

Some thinkers have argued that "the fall" was really a fall up rather than a fall down. By the fall our first parents were raised, it is said, to a higher level of consciousness in the knowing of good and evil. Now they know no longer simply and directly, but reflexively; now they know in the consciousness of knowing. This, however, is but another conceit of our fallen nature. It is as though a paraplegic, marvelously skilled in the complex maneuvering of a wheelchair, were to despise the healthy as belonging to a lower order because they walk simply, in blithe ignorance of the complexity of movement that the paraplegic knows so well. The conceit is that our complicated way of knowing is superior because it is ours.

What we call our higher level of consciousness is but an instance of our calling evil good, of our priding ourselves on the consequence of the catastrophe that is our fall from the knowledge of the good. True knowledge of the good is a way of knowing that is, in the words of Jesus, loving the Lord our God with all our heart and all our soul and all our mind. The reflexive mind, the divided soul, the conflicted heart—these many take to be the marks of maturity and growth. To know the good simply, to love the good and do the good because it is self-evidently to be loved and to be done—that is taken to be the mark of those whom we condescendingly call simple. So it is that sin's injury is declared a benefit, our weakness a strength, and the fall of that dread afternoon a fall up rather than down. Of those who thus confound good and evil, St. Paul says "they glory in their shame."

If good would have come from eating of the Tree of Knowledge, God would not have forbidden it. Nor, contrary to popular myth, is the fatal knowledge the knowledge of sexuality, although God knows how large is the part of sexuality in our glorying in our shame. Yet the fall was not a fall into sexuality. Adam and Eve were created as sexual beings, and the Genesis account leaves no doubt that from the beginning they knew what this meant. "Therefore a man leaves his father and his mother and cleaves to his wife, and they become one flesh. And the man and his wife were both naked, and were not ashamed."

The shame came later, when they reached, when they overreached, for a different kind of knowledge. The Hebrew verb "to know," *yada*, is rich in meanings. In connection with what we call the fall, to know good and evil is to reach for a universal knowledge, to be unbounded by truth as it is presented to us, to aspire to create our own truth. I say we were there in the garden when humanity aspired to "be like gods" by knowing good and evil, by reaching to know the power to define what is good and what is evil.

This page of Genesis is rewritten every day in the living out of the human story. Each of us has been there when we, godlike, decided that we would determine what is good and what is evil—at least for our own lives. Perhaps we shied away from the godlike pretension of making a universal rule that applies to all. Modestly—or so we said—we limited ourselves to deciding "what is good for me" and "what is wrong for me." "I can speak only for myself," we say. We would not think of "imposing" our judgment upon others. Under the cover of modesty, we deny the truth about the good and the evil that does not require our permission to be true. Thus we would evade the truth of good and evil that brings us to judgment. The truth is that we do not judge the truth; the truth judges us.

"And they heard the sound of the Lord God walking in the garden in the cool of the day, and the man and his wife hid themselves from the presence of the Lord God among the trees of the garden." It was the cool of the day, toward evening, when the light was going out. "Where are you, Adam?" And Adam said, "I heard the sound of thee in the garden, and I was afraid, because I was naked; and I hid myself." And the Lord God said, "Who told you that you were naked? Have you eaten of the tree of which I commanded you not to eat?"

And so the questions come at us. Who told us we are naked? Who so complexified our existence? From where did we get this reflexive knowledge so that we no longer simply know, but know only our act of knowing? How did it happen that the simplicity of loving is now displaced by unending complexity over the meanings of love? And why are we ashamed of our nakedness, a nakedness that was once the sign of immediacy to the beloved but is now a sign of innocence lost, of ludicrous vulnerability in the face of our pretension to be our own god, a sign of our sad ending up as our own best beloved? Where are

you, my prodigal son Adam? Into what distant country have you
gone?

The questions come at each of us. Were you there when
they reached for an alien knowledge, turned away from the light
and hid themselves in shame? Of course we were there. Not
once, but many times we have been there, hiding from the voice
of the waiting Father who calls in the night, "Where are you?"

The First Word from the cross: "Father, forgive them."
Forgiveness costs. Whatever the theory of atonement, this is at
the heart of it, that forgiveness costs. Any understanding of
what makes at-one-ment possible includes a few simple truths.
First, like the child, we know that something very bad has
happened. Something has gone very wrong with us and with the
world of which we are part. The world is not and we are not
what we know was meant to be. That is the most indubitable of
truths; it is beyond dispute, it weighs with self-evident force
upon every mind and heart that have not lost the sensibility that
makes us human.

The something very bad that has happened takes the form of
the long, dreary list of history's horribles, from concentration
camps to the tortured deaths of innocent children. And it takes
the everyday forms of the habits of compromise, of loves
betrayed, of lies excused, of dreams deferred until they die. The
indubitable truth is illustrated in ways beyond number, from
Auschwitz to the shattered cookie jar on the kitchen floor.
Something very bad has happened.

Second—and here I simplify outrageously, but our purpose is
to cut through to the heart of the matter—we are complicit in
what has gone so terribly wrong. We have problems with that.

World-class criminals, murderers and drug traffickers, if they
know what they have done, may have no trouble with that, but
for many of us it may be a bit hard to swallow. I mean, we
haven't done anything *that* bad, have we? Surely nothing so bad
as to make *us* responsible for the death of God on the cross . . .
True, the writer of 1 Timothy called himself "the chief of
sinners," and St. Paul did do some nasty things to the Christians
in his earlier life as Saul of Tarsus. But then it would seem that
he made up for it with an exemplary, indeed saintly, life. Chief
of sinners? There would seem to be an element of pious
hyperbole there, perhaps even an unseemly boastfulness, a
reverse pride, so to speak.

It is difficult to face up to our complicity because the
confession of sins does not come easy. It is also difficult because
we do not want to compound our complicity by claiming sins
that are not ours. We rightly recoil from those who seem to
wallow in guilt. The story is told of the rabbi and cantor who,
on Yom Kippur, the Day of Atonement, lament their sins at
great length, each concluding that he is a nobody. Then the
sexton, inspired by their example, laments his sins and declares
that he, too, is a nobody. "Nuh," says the rabbi to the cantor.
"Who is he to be a nobody?"

Contemporary sensibilities are offended by what is dismis-
sively termed "guilt tripping." Some while ago I was on the same
lecture platform with a famous television evangelist from
California who is noted for accenting the positive and upbeat in
the Christian message. According to this evangelist, it is as with
Coca-Cola: Everything goes better with Jesus. He had built a
huge new church called, let us say, New Life Cathedral, and he

explained that during the course of the building there was a debate about whether the cathedral should feature a cross. It was thought that the cross might prompt negative thoughts, maybe even thoughts about suffering and death. "Finally, I said that of course there will be a cross," the famous evangelist said. "After all, the cross is the symbol of Christianity and we are a Christian church. But I can guarantee you," he declared with a triumphant smile, "there is nothing downbeat about the cross at New Life Cathedral!"

St. Paul said the cross is "foolishness to the Greeks" and a "stumbling block to the Jews" and seemed to think it would always be that way. Little did he know what gospel salesmanship would one day achieve. In the eighteenth century, Isaac Watts wrote the hymn words: "Alas! and did my Savior bleed, / And did my Sovereign die? / Would He devote that sacred head / For such a worm as I?" A worm? Really now. . . . A contemporary hymnal puts it this way: "Would he devote that sacred head / For sinners such as I?" Surely "sinners" is bad enough. Similarly with the much beloved "Amazing Grace." "Amazing grace, how sweet the sound / That saved a wretch like me." "Wretch" will never do. That is cleaned up in a contemporary version: "That loved a soul like me."

Examples can be multiplied many times over. Groveling is out, self-esteem is in. And if self-esteem seems not quite the right note for Good Friday, at least our complicity can be understood as limited liability. Very limited. Perhaps the changes in Christian thought are not all bad. There have been in Christian devotion excesses of self-accusation, of "scrupulosity," as it used to be called. Wallowing in guilt and penitential grandstanding are justly criticized. And yet . . . we cannot just take the scissors to all those Bible passages that say he died for us and because of us, that they were our sins he bore upon the cross. Yes, Christianity is about resurrection joy, but do not rush to Easter. Good Friday makes inescapable the question of complicity.

I may think it modesty when I draw back from declaring myself chief of sinners, but it is more likely a failure of imagination. For what sinner should I speak if not for myself? Of all the billions of people who have lived and of all the thousands whom I have known, whom should I say is the chief of sinners? Surely I am authorized, surely I am competent to speak only for myself? When in the presence of God the subject of sin is raised, how can I help but say that chiefly it is I? Not to confess that I am chiefly the one is not to confess at all. It is the evasion of Adam, who said, "It was the woman whom you gave to be with me." It is the evasion of Eve, who said, "The serpent beguiled me." It is not to confess at all, and by our making of excuses is our complicity compounded.

"Forgive them, for they know not what they do." But now, like the prodigal son, we have come to our senses. Our lives are measured not by the lives of others, not by our own ideals, not by what we think might reasonably be expected of us, although by each of those measures we acknowledge failings enough. Our lives are measured by who we are created and called to be, and the measuring is done by the One who creates and calls. Finally, the judgment that matters is not ours. The judgment that matters is the judgment of God, who alone judges justly. In the cross we see the rendering of the verdict on the gravity of our sin.

We have come to our senses. None of our sins are small or of
little account. To belittle our sins is to belittle ourselves, to
belittle who it is that God creates and calls us to be. To belittle
our sins is to belittle their forgiveness, to belittle the love of the
Father who welcomes us home.

From the same Latin root come "complicity" and
"complexity." Only the dulling of moral imagination prevents us
from seeing how we are implicated in the complex web of
human evil. The late Rabbi Abraham Joshua Heschel was fond
of saying, "Some are guilty, all are responsible." We rightly
condemn the great moral monsters of history—the Hitlers and
Stalins and Maos and lesser mass murderers. Justice requires the
gradation of guilt. Distinctions are in order. In important ways,
we are not like them, and they are not like us. Yet complicity
and complexity alert us to the ways in which their crimes find
corrupting correlates in our own hearts. "He who looks at a
woman to lust after her has already committed adultery with her
in his heart." Such words of Jesus encourage not scrupulosity,
but candor. Contemplating the unspeakable crimes of Stalin's
gulag archipelago, Alexander Solzhenitsyn wrote, "The line
between good and evil runs through every human heart."

We would draw the line between ourselves and the really
big-time sinners. For them the cross may be necessary. For us a
forgiving wink from an understanding Deity will set things to
right. But the "big time" of sinning is in every human heart. We
make small our selves when we make small our sins. Fearing the
judgment of great evil, we shrink from the call to great good.
Like Adam, we slink away to hide in a corner. Like the prodigal
son, we hunker down behind the swine's trough of our shrunken

lives. But then he came to his senses. He remembered who he was in his former life, in his real life. There is no way to have that dignity restored except through the confession of that dignity betrayed.

Still we hold back from confession, holding on to the tattered remnants of our former dignity. The more Adam hides from his shame, the more he proclaims his shame. What ludicrous figures we sinners cut. It is all so unnecessary; it only increases the complicity that we deny. We act as though there is not forgiveness enough. There is more than forgiveness enough.

Were you there when they crucified my Lord? Yes, we were there when we crucified our Lord. Recognizing the line that runs through every human heart, no longer do we try to draw the line between "them" and "us." Who can look long and honestly at the victims and the perpetrators of history's horrors and say that this has nothing to do with me? To take the most obvious instance, where would we have taken our stand that Friday afternoon? With Mary and the Beloved Disciple or with the mocking crowds? "Know thyself," the philosophers said, for this is the beginning of wisdom. "The fear of God is the beginning of wisdom," wrote the Psalmist. Knowing myself and fearing God, knowing a thousand big and little things that I have done and failed to do, I cannot deny that I was there. In ways I do not fully understand, I know that I, too, did the deed, wielded the whip, drove the nails, thrust the spear.

About chief of sinners I don't know, but what I know about sinners I know chiefly about me. We did not mean to do the deed, of course. The things we have done wrong seemed, or mostly seemed, small at the time. The word of encouragement withheld, the touch of kindness not given, the visit not made, the trust betrayed, the cutting remark so clever and so cruel, the illicit sexual desire so generously entertained, the angry answer, the surge of resentment at being slighted, the lie we thought would do no harm. It is such a long and tedious list of little things. Surely not too much should be made of it, we thought to ourselves. But now it has come to this. It has come to the cross. All the trespasses of all the people of all time have gravitated here, to the killing grounds of Calvary.

Not only about our entanglement in the loss of each but also in the consequence of our deeds, John Donne was right: "No man is an Island, entire of itself; every man is a piece of the continent, a part of the main." It was not only for our sins, but surely for our sins too. What a complex web of complicity is woven by our lives. Send not to know by whom the nails were driven; they were driven by you, by me.

Is there a perverse presumption in confessing that we did the deed? There could be, I suppose. But there is also prudence, and an irrepressible awareness of John Donne's truth about our entanglement with the whole. We pray with the Psalmist, "Who can discern his errors? Cleanse me from my secret faults." Foolishly we hold back from the admission, separating ourselves from the full burden of common deed. We do not know the measure of our trespass, whereas we know God's mercy is beyond measure. Be grateful that forgiveness is not limited to the sins that we know. "Father, forgive them, for they know not what they do."

These, then, are the truths at the heart of atonement. First, something has gone terribly wrong. We find ourselves in a distant country far from home. Second, whatever the measure of our guilt, we are responsible. Then, third, something must be done about it. Things must be set right. We cannot go on this way. False gospels of positive thinking or stoic exhortations to make the best of it are worse than useless—they are obscene. They are invitations to make our peace with a corruption at the core of everything. Better that Job and all the Jobs on the long mourning bench of history should curse God and die than that they should make their peace with the evil that they know. Such a peace is the peace of the dead, of those who are already spiritually and morally dead. The religious marketplace is crowded with the peddlers of peace of mind and peace of soul. But the narcotic of denial or pretense is too high a price to pay. Better to rage against the night.

Something must be done about what has gone wrong. Things must be set to right. And this brings us to the fourth great truth of atonement: Whatever it is that needs to be done, we cannot do it. Each of us individually, the entirety of the human race collectively—what can we do to make up for one innocent child tortured and killed? Never mind making up for Auschwitz, or the killing fields of Cambodia, or the coffin ships of traffickers in human slavery or the slaughter beyond number of innocents in the womb. We chatter on about modernity and progress while King Herod reigns secure. "A voice was heard in Ramah, wailing and loud lamentation, Rachel weeping for her children; she refused to be comforted, for they were no more."

Rightly does Rachel refuse to be comforted. Something must be done. It started long before Rachel and her children. From far back in the mists of our beginnings, the blood of Abel has been crying from the ground; and along the way we have allowed ourselves to be comforted by the counsel of Cain, advising us to get over it, to get on with our lives, for, after all, are we our brother's keeper? But we know we are. We don't know what to do about it, but we know that if we lose our hold on that impossible truth, we have lost everything. Something must be done. Justice must be done. Things must be set to right.

But what can *we* do? We cannot even put our own lives in order, never mind setting right a radically disordered world. The Apostle Paul declares, "I can will what is right, but I cannot do it. For I do not do the good I want, but the evil I do not want is what I do. . . . Wretched man that I am! Who will deliver me from this body of death?" There is an answer to that question, but do not rush to the answer. Stay with the question for a time if you would understand why the derelict hangs there on the cross.

If things are to be set to right, if justice is to be done, somebody else will have to do it. It cannot be done by just anybody, as though one more death could somehow "make up for" innocent deaths beyond numbering. In that way lies the seeking out of scapegoats, the vain effort to heap our collective guilt on another, on the "other." People have been doing that from the foundation of the world. History is filled with scapegoats sacrificed to appease outraged justice.

And the Lord commanded Moses that Aaron should bring the goat before the Lord, "and Aaron shall lay both his hands upon the head of the live goat, and confess over him all the iniquities of the people of Israel, and all their transgressions, and all their sins; and he shall put them upon the head of the goat, and send him away into the wilderness. . . . The goat shall bear all their iniquities upon him to a solitary land." The goat goes off to a distant country. God himself trained ancient Israel in the ritual by which justice was satisfied, but only for a time. It is a training for what was to come, and for what was to surpass it.

Through the myths of millennia, blind and stumbling humanity acts upon the unquenchable intuition that something must be done. From Canaanite altars to Aztec temples, countless thousands have been offered in blood sacrifice. In the cruel twists of mythic imagination, the scapegoat is not expelled but destroyed. In our own enlightened century a nation sought to purify itself and the world by the extermination of the Jews. Even today we witness mobs outside prison walls cheering an execution taking place inside. It is a long, terrible history of bloodlust and vengeance, all in the name of justice, all driven by the insistence—the *correct* insistence—that something must be done.

As much as we are repulsed by it, that long, terrible history bears witness to an intuition that cannot be, and should not be, repressed. Something *must* be done. Otherwise, we live in a world without moral meaning. Otherwise, forgiveness is Bonhoeffer's "cheap grace" that trivializes evil and thereby also trivializes good. Otherwise, the elder brother, the one who resented his young brother's welcome home, was right in protesting that the reconciliation with the father is cheap and easy and dishonest. Forgiveness costs—it *must* cost—or else the trespass does not matter. Is such an intuition primitive? Yes, primitive as in primordial, as in that which constitutes our moral being in the world.

If we cannot set things right, if we cannot even set ourselves, never mind the world, right—who, then, is to do it? It must be someone who is in no way responsible for what has gone wrong. It must be done by an act that is perfectly gratuitous, that is not driven by necessity, by an act that is perfectly free. The act must be by one who embodies *everything*, whose life is not one life among many, but is life itself—a life that is our life and the life of all who have ever lived and ever will live. But where is such a one to be found?

The opening words of the Gospel of John: "In the beginning was the Word, and the Word was with God, and the Word was God. He was in the beginning with God; all things were made through him, and without him was not anything made that was made. In him was life, and the life was the light of men. The light shines in the darkness, and the darkness has not overcome it." The One who is life itself does this because nobody else could do it. He who is light and life plunges headlong into darkness and death and does so in perfect freedom. It is his mission, the reason he came into the world. "No one takes my life from me, but I lay it down of my own accord," he said. "I have power to lay it down, and I have power to take it again; this charge I have received from my Father."

The Father and the Son have colluded in a thing most astonishing, a thing on the far side of our ability to be astonished. Justice cries out to be satisfied; something must be done. From the blood of Abel, to the prison camps of Siberia, to the nine-year-old who this afternoon died of leukemia, justice cries out. These things must not be permitted to have the last word.

Who is at fault? Who is guilty? From the beginning of time, the wise and the good have wrestled with these questions. The wicked all have excuses. The guards at the death camps, the husband cheating on his wife, the executive padding expense accounts, the physician giving a lethal dose of morphine in the nursing home—all have excuses. I was obeying superior orders; I have uncontrollable needs that must be satisfied; everybody does it; we must relieve the world of useless lives. Name the crime and it is fitted out with an excuse. My parents abused me; I was deprived; I was spoiled; my genes made me do it. And we are back to "Adam, where are you?" and his pathetic response, "The woman whom you gave to be with me . . . "

All the Adams and all the Eves join with the brightest and the best of philosophers to declare that this is just the way the world is. And who is responsible for that? And with that question was born what philosophers call the question of "theodicy"—how to justify to humankind the ways of God. And thus was God put on trial. If God is good and God is almighty, how did evil come about? If there is evil, how can an almighty God be good or a good God be almighty? In order to adjudicate these questions, we constituted ourselves the jury and the judge, and we put God in the dock. And soon enough we would constitute ourselves the executioner as well.

From every corner of the earth, from every scene of every crime, from north and south, from east and west, from the rich and from the poor, every mother's son and every father's daughter gathered. The jury deliberated and reached its verdict. The decision was unanimous. With one voice, poor deluded humanity pointed to the prisoner in the dock and declared, "God is guilty!"

The angels were stunned, the stars hid their light, the universe went silent at the audacity of it, the wrongness of it, the outrageousness of it. The Judge of the guilty is himself judged guilty. Here now at last, in all the thick catalogue of human rebellion, is the lie so brazen as to surely bring down upon the heads of the insurrectionists a punishment swift and terrible. But no, the prisoner standing in the dock calmly responds, "For this was I born, and for this I have come into the world, to bear witness to the truth. Every one who is of the truth hears my voice."

In perfect freedom, the Son become the goat become the Lamb of God is condemned by the lie in order to bear witness to the truth. The truth is that we are incapable of setting things right. The truth is that the more we try to set things right, the more we compound our guilt. It is not enough for God to take our part. God must take our place. All the blood of goats and lambs, all the innocent victims from the foundation of the world, all the acts of expiation and reparation, they only make things worse. They all strengthen the grip of the great lie that we can set things right. The grip of that lie is broken by the greatest of lies, "God is guilty!"

God must die. It is a lie so monstrous that to suggest it invites instant annihilation—except that God accepts the verdict. Those who know the awful truth hear his voice. And Jesus said, "Now is my soul troubled. And what shall I say? 'Father, save me from this hour'? No, for this purpose I have come to this hour. Father, glorify thy name."

But how, we must ask, is God glorified by the humiliation and death of God? This great reversal of everything we think we know is too much to bear. Dark is light and light is dark, right is wrong and wrong is right and a lie is recruited to the service of the truth. The order of things is shattered. Precisely so, our disordered order is shattered so that things might be restored to order. And then Jesus said, "Now is the judgment of this world, now shall the ruler of this world be cast out; and I, when I am lifted up from the earth, will draw all men to myself." The ruler of this world—the lord of disorder and of disordered humanity in his thrall—passes judgment on the Judge of all. The judgment is so monstrously false that only by submitting to it can its falseness be exposed. By Christ's submitting to the judgment of the world the world is judged.

Jesus might have been merely a moral teacher pointing out the grotesque error of the judgment. Christianity would then have become a school of thought promoting his moral philosophy. Jesus came, however, to be the Lamb of God, living out and dying out this falsehood that would not die unless taken to its final conclusion. Only in this way would he be lifted up and draw all to himself, not simply as our teacher but as our Savior and our Lord. Only by submitting to our folly could he save us from our folly. The drama had to be played out all the way. St. John writes of the night before he died: "Now before the feast of the Passover, when Jesus knew that his hour had come to depart out of this world to the Father, having loved his own who were in the world, he loved them to the end."

He loved them to the end that they, too, might learn the way that is on the far side of outraged justice. That same night he told them, "This is my commandment, that you love one another as I have loved you. Greater love has no man than this, that he lay down his life for his friends. You are my friends if

you do what I command you." And then he prayed for his
friends, "Father, I desire that they also, whom thou hast given me,
may be with me where I am, to behold my glory which thou hast
given me in thy love for me before the foundation of the world."

From before the foundation of the world. In the beginning
was the Word. Did God—Father, Son and Holy Spirit—know
from the beginning that it would turn out this way? From before
the foundation of the world, from before the time when there
was time, did God hear humanity's fatal verdict: "God is guilty!
Crucify him! Crucify him!"? And did the Son say to the Father,
from the beginning, that he would go in the power of the Spirit
to submit himself to the sentence of death? St. Paul suggests as
much: "But we impart a secret and hidden wisdom of God,
which God decreed before the ages for our glorification. None
of the rulers of this age understood this; for if they had, they
would not have crucified the Lord of glory."

Here we touch on mystery far beyond our ability to
understand; we try to listen in on the conversation that is the
very life of the triune God, the life of God that is the power and
love that enables all to be. Our desire to understand is as
inescapable as our failure to understand. The more we search
and the deeper we go, the more we cry out with Paul: "O the
depth of the riches and wisdom and knowledge of God! How
unsearchable are his judgments and how inscrutable his ways!"
Yet surely the love with which Jesus loved the Father here on
earth is one with the love of the Word that was in the
beginning. The perfect self-surrender of the cross is, from
eternity and to eternity, at the heart of what it means to say that
God is love.

In 1 John it is put this way: "Beloved, let us love one another; for love is of God, and he who loves is born of God and knows God. He who does not love does not know God; for God is love." Yes, from the foundation of the world God heard the rebel verdict, "God is guilty!" And from the beginning he knew what he would do about a humanity he created free to love him, and therefore free to hate him. God subjects himself to the blasphemous lie that he is the guilty one. The rebellion did not take God by surprise. Redemption was not an improvisation, an emergency measure in response to an unexpected setback. From the beginning, "God was in Christ reconciling the world to himself." This is what it means to love; this is what it means to *be* love; this is what it means to say that God *is* love.

Yet it hardly seems possible that injustice could be set right by a still greater injustice, that wrong could be set right by a still greater wrong. That is what St. Paul appears to suggest, however, in the passage in which he speaks of God in Christ reconciling the world to himself: "For our sake he made him to be sin who knew no sin, so that in him we might become the righteousness of God." The language is radical: It was not simply that he bore the consequences of sin, but that he was made to *be* sin. The great reversal reverses all of our preconceptions. God must become what we are in order that we might become what God is. To effectively take our part, he must take our place.

The word "theodicy" means the judgment of God—not God judging us but our judging God. The philosophical problem of theodicy is that of trying to square God's ways with our sense of justice. This assumes that we know what justice is, but the entire story the Bible tells begins with the error of that presumption. It is the original error of our wanting to name good and evil. Right from the start Adam tried to put God in the dock, making God responsible for the fall because, after all, God gave him the woman who tempted him to sin. From the beginning we see the argument building up to humanity's cry, "God is guilty!"— building up to the derelict nailed to the cross.

In the long history of human philosophies, the name of the game has been theodicy. Trying to square the ways of God with our understanding of justice, some have concluded that he is not good, others that he is not almighty and yet others that he is not at all. But the right question is not that of theodicy, but of what we might call "homodicy"—the judgment of humankind. The crisis is not in justifying God's ways to us, but in justifying our ways to God. "God was in Christ reconciling the world to himself." It is the world that needed to be reconciled to God's justice, not God to the world's justice. It does not say, "God was in Christ reconciling himself to the world." After all, he is God and we are not; he is the Creator and we the creatures. It seems only right.

And yet. God reconciling the world to himself is also God reconciling himself to the world. In working out the plan of redemption, the Bible does not say that man became God, but that God became man. Further, he reconciled himself to the world by "not counting their trespasses against them." He forgave us not by ignoring our trespasses but by assuming our trespasses. "For our sake he made him to be sin who knew no sin, so that in him we might become the righteousness of God." God became what by right he was not, so that we might become what by right we are not. This is what Christians through the ages have called "the happy exchange." This exchange, this reversal, is at the very epicenter of the story of our redemption. In the Great Vigil of Easter we sing of the *felix culpa*—the "happy fault": "O happy fault, O necessary sin of Adam, which gained for us so great a Redeemer!"

In Matthew's Gospel this exchange is signaled at the very beginning of Jesus' ministry. John the Baptizer announces that Jesus is the one who "will baptize you with the Holy Spirit and with fire." Jesus, he declares, has come to judge the world. Then we read: "Jesus came from Galilee to the Jordan to John, to be baptized by him. John would have prevented him, saying, 'I need to be baptized by you, and do you come to me?' But Jesus answered him, 'Let it be so now; for thus it is fitting for us to fulfill all righteousness.' Then John consented." God asks our consent when he takes our part by taking our place.

Later, on the night before he was betrayed, Jesus poured water into a basin and began to wash the disciples' feet. He came to Peter and Peter said, "Lord, do you wash my feet?" Jesus answered, "What I am doing you do not know now, but afterward you will understand." Peter declared, "You shall never wash my feet." Jesus said, "If I do not wash you, you have no part in me." He will not serve us against our will.

To those who are accustomed to living in a world turned upside down, setting it right cannot help but appear to be turning it upside down. With our first parents we reached for the power to name good and evil, thinking to assert control, but thereby we lost control. With the prodigal son, we grabbed what we could and ended up impoverished and alone in a distant country. Because God is not the God of the philosophers, because God is the God of Abraham, Isaac and Jacob, because God is love, he sent his Son to the far country to share our lot, to bear the consequences of our folly, to lead us home to the waiting Father.

Such a way of love violates our sense of justice. With John the Baptizer, we protest. But Jesus says, "Let it be so now; for thus it is fitting for us to fulfill all righteousness." Note that he says, "fitting for *us* to fulfill all righteousness." He fulfills all righteousness, he does what must be done to set things right, by assuming the burden of our every human wrong. And we too have a part in fulfilling all righteousness by letting him do for us what we could not do for ourselves. On the one hand, we would not dare ask him to go to the cross. On the other, we joined in humanity's determination to acquit ourselves by condemning him to the cross. It is the necessary outcome of the verdict "God is guilty."

Those who issue a verdict so grotesque deserve to die. Justice would seem to demand it. But God made the long journey into our distant country not to destroy but to give life. John's Gospel puts it this way: "For God sent the Son into the world, not to condemn the world, but that the world might be saved through him"—even if salvation requires that God is the one who is condemned. God cannot agree to a verdict so manifestly unjust, but he does submit to the sentence that the verdict entails.

If we have even the slightest sense of justice, we recoil at the thought. But what else is to be done about all that has gone wrong? Is there any alternative to its being set right by a yet greater wrong? Or can that greater wrong really be wrong if it is the judgment of God that it should be? If we say this way of atonement is wrong, we are back in the garden presuming to name right and wrong, good and evil. Love is the justice of the God who is love. To John the Baptizer and to us Jesus says, "Let it be so now." God asks for our consent. Before such a mystery of unbounded love that is bound even to die for the beloved, we offer not only our consent, but gratitude exultant. *O felix culpa!* "O happy fault! O necessary sin of Adam, which gained for us so great a Redeemer!"

Atonement. At-one-ment. What was separated by an abyss of wrong has been reconciled by the deed of perfect love. What the first Adam destroyed the second Adam has restored. "Father, forgive them, for they know not what they do." We knew not what we did when we reached for the right to name good and evil. We knew not what we did when we grabbed what we could and went off to a distant country. We knew not what we did when, in the madness of excusing ourselves, we declared God guilty. But today we have come to our senses. Today, here at the cross, our eyes are fixed on the dying derelict who is the Lord of life. We look at the One who is everything that we are and everything that we are not, the One who is true man and true God. In him we, God and man, are perfectly one. At-one-ment. Here, through the cross, we have come home, home to the truth about ourselves, home to the truth about what God has done about what we have done. And now we know, or begin to know, why this awful, awe-filled Friday is called good.

2

Judge Not

The Second Word from the cross:

"Truly, I say to you, today you will be with me in paradise."

The first one home is a thief. Jesus is not very fastidious about the company he keeps. A serious question is raised about whether we will be happy with those who are with us in paradise—assuming, for the moment, that *we* will be there. That question comes later.

Recall now the two criminals. Mentioned in all four Gospels, they were called thieves by two of the Gospel writers. Whatever else they had stolen in their lives, the one, commonly called "the good thief," stole at the end a reward he did not deserve. There they were, hoisted on their crosses, one to the left of Jesus, the other to the right. A pious legend has it that the good thief was on the right, much as Matthew 25 depicts the final judgment of humanity with the goats on the left and the sheep on the right. The good thief is a found sheep. More accurately, he is a goat who was made an honorary sheep just before his time ran out.

Both thieves may have heard about Jesus before. If not, they certainly heard about him that day, hanging there on their crosses and surrounded by the mocking crowds. The one thief joined in the mockery with cutting scorn born of his own desperate plight. "Are you not the Christ? Save yourself and us!" Luke tells us that he "railed" against Jesus. Note that there was perhaps a touch of goodness in the man. He did not say, "Save yourself and *me*," but, "Save yourself and *us*." Maybe the other thief was a friend; maybe they were partners in crime. Even in vice there may be a bond not untouched by grace. But whatever grace was there was crushed by the anger and contempt with which he turned against Jesus, the source of grace. In his dying he turned, and it seems he turned definitively, against the light.

Not so with the other one. The other thief rebuked the first, we are told. "Do you not fear God, since you are under the same sentence of condemnation? And we indeed justly; for we are receiving the due reward of our deeds; but this man has done nothing wrong." Painfully twisting his neck, he looked toward Jesus. "Jesus," he said, "remember me when you come into your kingdom." And Jesus said to him, "Truly, I say to you, today you will be with me in paradise." In his dying, the second thief turned toward the light.

Note that this is the only time in any Gospel account that someone addresses Jesus simply by name. Otherwise it is always "Jesus Son of God," "Jesus Son of David" or some other form of particular respect. The first person to be so familiar is a convicted criminal who is the last person to speak to Jesus before he dies. Dying together is a great social leveler. The Greek text suggests that this was a persistent plea, that he "was speaking" to Jesus. But maybe it wasn't really a plea at all. Maybe he was trying to comfort Jesus.

In her play *The Man Born to Be King*, Dorothy Sayers portrays the good thief—Dysmas as legend calls him—as taking pity on Jesus. In answer to the first thief's railings, Dysmas says of Jesus:

> He's loony, that's all. Let 'im think he's Goddamighty, if it
> makes him feel any better. . . . You're all right, mate, ain't you?
> Of course you are. This 'ere's just a bad dream. One o' these
> days you'll come out in a cloud of glory and astonish them all.
> . . . There! he's smiling. He likes being talked to that way. . . .
> (*In a deeply respectful tone, humoring this harmless lunacy*) Sir, you'll
> remember me, won't you, when you come into your kingdom?

According to Sayers, Dysmas turned toward the light, but he did not believe in the light. His "Lord, remember me" was not an act of faith but an act of charity. It is the kind of thing one might say to someone who imagines he is Napoleon. But then, says Sayers, with Jesus' unexpected answer there is a moment of illumination, of insight; it is not unlike an act of faith. Of Dysmas she writes: "He is confused between the crucified man, of whose weakness it would be selfish to demand one added agony, and the eternal Christ, of whose strength he is half-aware, and with whose sufferings he seems to be mysteriously identified, so that in some strange way each is bearing the pain of the other."

Certainly Jesus was bearing the pain of Dysmas, and of the other thief, and of all humanity half aware and unaware. "Today you will be with me in paradise." Jesus does not reject any who turn to him. At times we turn to him with little faith, at times with a mix of faith and doubt when we are more sure of the doubt than of the faith. Jesus is not fastidious about the quality of faith. He takes what he can get, so to speak, and gives immeasurably more than he receives. He takes our faith more seriously than we do and makes of it more than we ever could. His response to our faith is greater than our faith.

Once a father came to Jesus asking him to heal his sick child. "All things are possible to him who believes," Jesus said. The father cried out, "I believe; help my unbelief!" And so cry we all. At another time Jesus said if you have faith no greater than a mustard seed, you can move mountains. Here on Golgotha, the place of death and devastation, Dysmas has faith smaller than a mustard seed, and it blossoms into a tree of eternal life, a tree of paradise. Christ's response to our faith is ever so much greater than our faith. Give him an opening, almost any opening, and he opens life to wonder beyond measure.

It did not look like paradise. On that Friday afternoon two thousand years ago, out on the killing fields by the Jerusalem city dump, it did not look like paradise. And nobody in their right mind would confuse that city or any city in the world in which we live with paradise. There is no shortage of those who say that talk about paradise is a cruel mockery of our hopeless plight, like the mockery of that sign they posted above the head of the crucified Messiah, "This is Jesus, King of the Jews." Some king.

How to put it delicately? The sovereignty of Jesus is a disputed sovereignty. It was then, it is now, and it will be until he returns in glory to establish his kingdom beyond all possible dispute. Christians are those who, like the thief on the cross, have turned to him with faith that is more like a desperate hope and, in listening to his response, have found the faith that moves mountains. When our faith is weak, when we are assailed by contradictions and doubts, we are tempted to look at our faith, to worry about our faith, to try to work up more faith. At such times, however, we must not look to our faith but look to him. Look to him, listen to him, and faith will take care of itself. Keep looking. Keep listening.

In the world and in our hearts, his sovereignty will continue to be disputed. We are the people who say now, who say ahead of time, what one day will be said by all. The Church, the community of faith, is the people ahead of time. One day, St. Paul writes the Philippians, every knee will bow and every tongue confess that Jesus Christ is Lord. What one day will be manifest to all is known now by faith. It is by faith that we follow this disputed sovereign, this crucified king who speaks of paradise when all we see is paradise lost. With arms outstretched in the pain of our yearning we, like desperate Dysmas, catch a glimmer of what had once been, back there in the garden, and what might be again. In Christ is paradise regained. Somehow. We know not quite how. He said it is so. He says it is so. "Lord, I believe; help my unbelief."

For paradise we long. For perfection we were made. We don't know what it would look like or feel like, but we must settle for nothing less. This longing is the source of the hunger and dissatisfaction that mark our lives; it drives our ambition. What we long for is touched in our exaltations; in our devastations it is known by its absence. This longing makes our loves and friendships possible, and so very unsatisfactory. The hunger is for nothing less than paradise, nothing less than perfect communion with the Absolute—with the Good, the True, the Beautiful—communion with the perfectly One in whom all the fragments of our scattered existence come together at last and forever. We must not stifle this longing. It is a holy dissatisfaction. Such dissatisfaction is not a sickness to be healed, but the seed of a promise to be fulfilled.

We know well the statement of St. Augustine: "You have made us for yourself, O Lord, and our hearts are restless until they rest in you." Our restlessness, our holy dissatisfaction bears witness to the One for whom we were made. The only death to fear is the death of settling for something less.

"Today you will be with me in paradise." Indelibly imprinted upon our minds, deeply rooted in our hearts, is the memory of what once was, the innocence of the garden so bright with love. There was no need for hope then, for everything that could be hoped for was there. There was no need for faith then, for truth was transparent and known like the most intimate of friends. Somewhere in the life of each of us there may have been a time that seemed like such a garden. But now we find ourselves in exile from that time and from that place.

For more than a thousand years Christians have sung the plaintive hymn *Salve, Regina, mater misericordiae*, "Hail, Holy Queen, Mother of Mercy." "To you do we cry, poor banished children of Eve. To you do we send up our sighs, mourning and weeping in this valley of tears." Poor banished children of Eve. We remember what was, and what we thought might be. It is all shattered now. We survey the melancholy shards of what was meant to be, the pieces strewn across this valley of tears, this

valley east of Eden. And there is no going back. We read in
Genesis that the Lord placed an angel at the east of Eden. The
angel has a flaming sword and turns every which way, guarding
the path to the tree of life.

There is no returning to that paradise that was. The way to
the tree of life is blocked. Lost is that innocence so bright with
love. Now we need faith, for the truth is not transparent; now
we need hope, for we know we are not what we are meant to be.
The way to paradise is not the way of return; it is the way
restored. It is restored by the one who said, "I am the way, and
the truth, and the life." A new Adam, Jesus Christ. A new Eve,
Mary the mother of the faithful. A new tree of life, the tree of
the cross. All is restored. "Today you will be with me in
paradise."

The tree of death has become the tree of life. In his dying,
Dysmas turned to a fellow sufferer, "Lord, remember me when
you come into your kingdom." Was it an act of charity or an act
of faith? Perhaps both, for charity is but another word for love,
and love bears and gives birth to everything. In the beginning
was love. And in the end is love. This ending was love. Jesus had
said, "Greater love has no man than this, that he lay down his
life for his friends." He laid down his life for his friend Dysmas.

We are his friends, not because we have befriended him, but
because he has befriended us. Jesus had said, "You did not chose
me, but I chose you." Dysmas was chosen, from eternity to
eternity. Before he so painfully turned his head to ask—whether
he asked in charity or in faith—the gift was already given. And
so it is with us. Look at him who is ever looking at you. With
whatever faith you have, however feeble and flickering and

mixed with doubt, look at him. Look at him with whatever faith you have and know that your worry about your lack of faith is itself a sign of faith. Do not look at your faith. Look at him. Keep looking, and faith will take care of itself.

Of course we are glad for Dysmas. But there is something poignant, even pathetic, in this story. Here is the epicenter of the great drama of cosmic salvation. In Jesus the Christ, God has become man; as true man he lives a life in unqualified responsiveness to the Father; on the cross he does what has never been done before—he makes a perfect offering of love without blemish. And what does he have to show for it? The plan was for the salvation of the world, but after all this he returns to his heavenly home with the pathetic prize of one repentant thief.

Jesus had said, "And I, when I am lifted up from the earth, will draw all men to myself." And so he has, men and women beyond numbering of every time and tongue and culture. But the first was Dysmas the thief. Jesus began at the bottom of the human heap. We should not be surprised by this, for he had so often said that the first shall be last and the last shall be first. He began at the bottom to show that none can fall so far that they are beyond the reach of God's love. Perhaps the other thief too, the one who turned from the light, perhaps his turning was not definitive, was not final, was not forever. Perhaps, in the end, knees will bow and tongues confess that did not bow and did not confess in this life. Perhaps, in the end, before the great drama of salvation is complete, every man and woman and child created by God from eternity to eternity will hear Jesus say, "Today you will be with me in paradise."

It is a very old and attractive idea, this idea that, in the end, everyone will be saved. Many theologians routinely dismiss the idea, condemning it as "universalism." But in the early centuries of Christian thought it was not such a settled question. Some Greek fathers had a name for it, *apocatastasis*, by which they meant that in the end, when all is said and done, when the final curtain falls on the cosmic drama of salvation, all free moral creatures—angels, human beings and even devils—will share in the grace of salvation. In the early centuries great Christian thinkers such as Clement of Alexandria and St. Gregory of Nyssa were sympathetic to the idea. Origen embraced it outright and his teaching, or what was thought to be his teaching, was condemned by the Council of Constantinople in the year 553.

Yet some Christians continue to teach that all will be saved, others wonder about it and still others say that we should hope it is true. In his enormously popular book of personal reflections, *Crossing the Threshold of Hope*, Pope John Paul II wrote that, although there is undoubtedly a hell, the Church has never definitively said who, if anyone, is in hell. We do not even know for sure, he says, whether Judas Iscariot is in hell. Traveling in the ragtag company of those on the way to paradise and seeing Dysmas up there in the lead, we sense something in the logic of salvation that should include everybody. If Dysmas, why not everybody? Or for that matter: If *me*, why not everybody?

Objections arise immediately. Yes, the Bible speaks frequently—although not so frequently as some suggest!—about hell and damnation. Yes, Jesus speaks about the separation of the sheep from the goats on the last day. And yes to much else. But I suggest we hold off on the obvious objections for a time, in order to reflect on the entirety of biblical truth. Only then can we bring together apparently disparate parts into a coherent whole. Only then can we think clearly about what we can hope and should hope for all the Dysmases who, in their ignorance and anguish, do not turn to the light, or at least do not turn to the light in any way that we can see their turning.

A relatively recent form of Christian thought, found among both Protestants and Catholics, is strikingly, even shockingly, individualistic. Its sole preoccupation is with individual salvation. Am I saved? Am I going to heaven? Are you saved? Are you going to heaven? Now there surely can be no more important question for me or for you than the question of our eternal destiny. But just as surely, our eternal destiny is not something apart from God's purpose for his creation. The Gospel is sometimes presented as though God is running a desperate rescue mission, saving a few survivors from the shipwreck of what had been his hopes for creation.

First Timothy clearly declares that God "desires all to be saved and to come to the knowledge of the truth." Is it possible that God's purpose will be thwarted? And what might that say about whether God is truly God? Will the sovereignty of God in Christ be forever in dispute?

Admittedly, these are heavy questions. Christians have been debating them for centuries, and we will not here resolve them to everyone's satisfaction, not even to our own. But stay with them for a while, for these questions lead into the mystery of a love that searched out and found such an unlikely soul as Dysmas. It is the same love that found us, and if we don't think that we are equally unlikely candidates for salvation, we have not begun to understand the meaning of grace.

God's plan is not to rescue a religious elite from an otherwise botched creation but to restore all things in Christ. Listen to St. Paul writing to the Ephesians: "In him we have redemption through his blood, the forgiveness of our trespasses, according to the riches of his grace which he lavished upon us. For he has made known to us in all wisdom and insight the mystery of his will, according to his purpose which he set forth in Christ as a plan for the fullness of time, to unite all things in him, things in heaven and things on earth."

Note well: to unite all things in him. The theme is the cosmic Christ and the cosmic promise of salvation. St. Paul once more, this time writing to the Colossians:

> He is the image of the invisible God, the firstborn of all creation; for in him all things were created, in heaven and on earth, visible and invisible, whether thrones or dominions or principalities or authorities—all things were created through him and for him. He is before all things, and in him all things hold together. He is the head of the body, the Church; he is the beginning, the firstborn from the dead, that in everything he might be preeminent. For in him all the fullness of God was pleased to dwell, and through him to reconcile to himself all things, whether on earth or in heaven, making peace by the blood of his cross.

To unite all things in him. To reconcile to himself all things, whether on earth or in heaven. It would seem that you can hardly get more universal than that. Two Swiss theologians, one

Protestant and one Catholic, have in recent years given new currency to the question of whether we can hope, whether we should hope, that in the end all will be saved. Karl Barth, the Protestant, and Hans Urs von Balthasar, the Catholic, came up with significantly different answers, but both have deepened Christian reflection on God's saving purposes. There can be no doubt that we should *desire* that all be saved, for, as we have seen, that is what God desires, and it is axiomatic that we should desire what God desires.

But is there a difference between desire and hope? Thomas Aquinas, among others, says that there is. He writes that "one has to believe of whatever one hopes that it can be attained; this is what hope adds to mere desire. Man can, namely, also have desire for things that he does not believe he can attain; but hope cannot exist in such circumstances." If I am sick, I can hope that I get better. I can *desire* to be a person who has not done all the wrong things I have done in my life, but I cannot *hope* for that, since it is contrary to fact; it is not attainable. I should and do desire that all be saved, as God desires that all be saved, but whether I should hope for that depends upon whether it is attainable. Unlike my desire about my past life, however, the desire for the salvation of all is a desire for something in the future. Our thinking about the future is informed by Jesus' repeated declaration that with God all things are possible. The future is infinitely open, and open to the infinite.

Should I pray that all be saved? Clearly we are commanded to love our neighbor, and Jesus left no doubt that that means loving also our enemies. That includes, it would seem, loving the enemies of God as well. Those whom we love we want to be

saved. Remember Abraham when God was prepared to destroy
the wicked city of Sodom. "Wilt thou indeed destroy the
righteous with the wicked?" asked Abraham. "Suppose there are
fifty righteous within the city; wilt thou then destroy the place
and not spare it for the fifty righteous who are in it?" God said
he would spare the city if there were fifty righteous. And then
Abraham came back again and again—almost, it seems,
bargaining with God. "Oh let not the Lord be angry, and I will
speak again but this once. Suppose ten are found there." And the
Lord answered, "For the sake of ten I will not destroy it."

Let Sodom stand for the world. (Given the current state of
the world, that does not require too much imagination.) Today
there are almost two billion Christians in the world. For the sake
of argument, let us allow that many of them are only nominal
Christians, but still it would seem that the "real" Christians are a
greater percentage of the world's population than were the ten
righteous a percentage of Sodom's population. Will God destroy
the world when it contains so many who are righteous in Christ?
Then we might go back and apply the same consideration to all
the generations past.

But this way of thinking quickly descends into a percentage
game, which hardly does justice to the colloquy between
Abraham and the Lord. Moreover, the proponent of salvation as
a rescue operation might point out that the question then was
whether God would destroy the righteous along with the
wicked. According to today's Christian rescue scenario, the
answer is no. The righteous, the elect, will be plucked to safety
as the overwhelming majority of humankind, the *massa damnata*,
head straight for hell. But note that it apparently did not occur

to Abraham to pray that the righteous—whether fifty or thirty
or ten—be plucked to safety while Sodom is destroyed.
Abraham's prayer was for the city. And God saved Sodom, at
least until the next chapter of Genesis.

The Bible is full of incidents of the prophets and others
interceding for the people, even when God had declared his
intention to destroy them. Especially then. Not to put too fine a
point on it, they prayed against God's declared intention. When,
for instance, Israel bowed down to worship the golden calf, the
Lord said to Moses, "I have seen this people, and behold, it is a
stiff-necked people; now therefore let me alone, that my wrath
may burn hot against them and I may consume them; but of you
I will make a great nation." But Moses would not let the Lord
alone. "Turn from thy fierce wrath," he prayed, "and repent of
this evil against thy people. Remember Abraham, Isaac, and
Israel, thy servants, to whom thou didst swear by thine own
self." And, we are told, "the Lord repented of the evil which he
thought to do to his people."

Yes, the proponents of a well-populated hell might reply, but
that was then and this is now. We are New Testament, not Old
Testament, believers. We do not conceive of God in such
primitive and "anthropomorphic" terms, as though he were a
human being whose mind could be changed by our pleading.
Such an objection, however, sounds suspiciously like Marcion,
the second-century heretic who tried to drive a wedge between
the Hebrew Scriptures and the New Testament. The prayer of
Moses reflects the same understanding of prayer to be found in
the New Testament. Remember the parable of the unjust judge
and the importunate widow, which Jesus told "to the effect that
they ought always to pray and not lose heart."

The judge cared not at all about justice, but he finally gave the widow what she wanted simply to stop her from bothering him. In the same way, Jesus says, "Will not God vindicate his elect who cry to him day and night? . . . I tell you, he will vindicate them speedily." Prayer creates space for possibilities that would not otherwise be possible. The importunate widow pleaded against her adversary. How much more persistently ought we to pray *for* others, especially those who are our adversaries, and God's. The elect are elected not to be against others but *for* others.

In the same way, St. Paul says that Christ is the firstborn not in order to separate himself from humanity but so that all humanity might participate in his triumph. Christ the head and his body the Church are together the total Christ, *totus Christus*. The plan of redemption is "to reconcile to himself all things, whether on earth or in heaven, making peace by the blood of his cross." To be saved is to participate in this plan of universal reconciliation. In this understanding, a Christian is not saved against the rest of humanity, to be separated out from the rest of humanity. Rather, we are saved, as it were, on behalf of all—to be reconcilers, intercessors and mediators for all. In all this, of course, we are simply participating in the continuing work of Christ who is the "one mediator between God and men."

If we pray for the salvation of all, it would seem that we must hope for the salvation of all. How is it possible to pray for what you do not hope for? At the same time, we must take seriously the many statements in the New Testament that some, perhaps many, might be damned. The sheep will be separated from the goats, the wheat from the tares; many take the broad road and few the narrow path to salvation; wicked servants will be cast into prison and never get out until they have paid the last penny, which they can never do; and so forth. Such passages in support of a hell well populated by the *massa damnata* cannot be ignored or belittled.

At the same time, we must inquire into the nature of such passages. Are they predictive, telling us what will certainly happen in the future? Or are they warnings—admonitory and cautionary statements directed to each one of us, alerting us to the consequences of rejecting the truth? If we say they are warnings, while at the same time believing that in the end all will be saved, it would seem that we are watering down these passages, depriving them of their full force. It is as though we are saying that they do not really mean what they clearly appear to mean. There is a great difference, however, between *believing* that all will be saved and *hoping* that all will be saved.

Permit me a slight digression on what we know and don't know. A certain cognitive humility is in order at this point and at all points in our talking about God and his ways. We simply do not know. One day, we are promised, we will see face to face and know even as we are known, but that is not now. Now all our talk about God, including the God-given talk of the Bible, is by analogy. That is to say, the mind of God infinitely surpasses the human mind, the Creator infinitely surpasses the creature. Analogy means that we can draw inferences and make comparisons. We can say, for instance, that God is to the world as the artist is to his or her work. But in saying that we should not think that we thereby understand God or his relationship to the world. The Fourth Lateran Council in 1215 put it very nicely: "No similarity can be found so great but that the dissimilarity is even greater." God is always infinitely "more" and infinitely "other."

Cognitive humility is not the same thing as ignorance. Christians believe that God has in creation, in his dealings with Israel and preeminently in Jesus the Christ, revealed himself within the limits of human understanding. In the very statement from Colossians that we have been considering, Jesus is called "the image of the invisible God, the firstborn of all creation." As Jesus told Philip, "He who has seen me has seen the Father." So cognitive humility is not to be confused with ignorance. What we need to know God has revealed in Jesus Christ, and that revelation we can trust and trust absolutely. But there is more, infinitely more, that we do not know.

Should we, then, believe that in the end all will be saved? Perhaps we should answer that more carefully and say that we believe it is possible that in the end all will be saved. Or we might put the question this way: *If* it is possible that many will be eternally lost and *if* it is possible that all will be saved, which should we hope for? In view of the command to love all people, must we not hope that in the end all will be saved? Can we love others and *not* hope that they will be saved? Again, we recall 1 Timothy and the statement that God "desires all to be saved and come to the knowledge of the truth." In 1 Corinthians, St. Paul asks us to look forward to the time "When all things are subjected to him, then the Son himself will also be subjected to him who put all things under him, that God may be everything to every one." Note: everything to *every* one. Or, as other translations have it, God will "be all in all."

And how about Gestas? That's the traditional name of the

second thief, the one who railed against Jesus. Will he, too, one day hear Jesus say, "Today you will be with me in paradise"? Or is he already there? The Corinthians passage just quoted is immediately followed by St. Paul's mysterious remark about baptism for the dead. "Otherwise, what do people mean by being baptized on behalf of the dead? If the dead are not raised at all, why are people baptized on their behalf?" Why indeed. Mormons baptize for the dead today, but the orthodox Christian tradition has quite lost track of what St. Paul was talking about, although he obviously assumed the Corinthians were familiar with the practice. What is clear is that it was thought that something could be done spiritually for those who had died.

That thought is abhorrent to some Christians. Hebrews 9 is regularly invoked in these discussions, where it says, "it is appointed for men to die once, and after that comes judgment." But it seems doubtful that this is intended as a schedule, stating in a punctiliar way a sequence of events. Not too much weight should be placed on what is, after all, a subordinate clause in a passage making the point that Christ had to die only once for our sins. Cognitive humility is again in order when we try to think about what happens after death, and how. All our thinking is limited by time and space, but God is not so limited. We speak of heaven and hell as "places" because to our limited minds everything has a "hereness" or a "thereness," but it is not so with God.

Again we are reminded that our thinking and talking are *analogical.* This does not mean that we cannot really know for sure. We can. We can because, Christians believe, God has given us true and trustworthy ways of thinking and talking about

what we cannot comprehend. It would seem to be the unanimous experience of Christian thinkers and mystics that, the
farther they travel on the roads of thought and contemplation,
the more they know that they do not know. The most rigorous
thought and the most exalted spiritual adventure bring us, again
and again, to exclaim with St. Paul, "O the depth of the riches
and wisdom and knowledge of God! How unsearchable are his
judgments and how inscrutable his ways!" Therefore it is rightly
said that all theology is finally doxology. That is to say, all
analysis and explanation finally dissolves into wonder and praise.

Jesus told parables, which are a kind of analogy. "The
kingdom of heaven is like . . ." or, "The kingdom of God may be
compared to . . ." So it is with the separation of the sheep and
the goats. Again and again, he calls people to conversion,
alerting them to the moral and spiritual urgency of their lives.
"Enter by the narrow gate; for the gate is wide and the way is
easy that leads to destruction, and those who enter by it are
many. But the gate is narrow and the way is hard that leads to
life, and those who find it are few." Be constantly awake lest you
miss the bridegroom and are excluded from the marriage feast.
Follow the example of the faithful servant, lest with the wicked
servants you are cast into the outer darkness where there will be
weeping and gnashing of teeth. All such warnings and calls to
conversion are entirely in the service of God's desire that all
should be saved.

Those who respond to the call are the vanguard of the
fulfillment of that divine desire. As we have seen, the Church is
the community ahead of time, the people who say now what
will one day be said by all. The Second Vatican Council puts it

this way: "The Church . . . will receive her perfection only in the glory of heaven, when will come the time of the renewal of all things. At that time, together with the human race, the universe itself, which is so closely related to man and which attains its destiny through him, will be perfectly re-established in Christ" (*Lumen Gentium* 48). The New Testament speaks about the "new heavens and new earth." Consider the magnificence of the promise in the book of Revelation: "He will wipe away every tear from their eyes, and death shall be no more, neither shall there be mourning nor crying nor pain any more, for the former things have passed away. . . . Behold, I make all things new."

To be converted is to be alive to this promise, indeed to live by and for this promise. The risen Christ and those who run with the risen Christ are the forerunners. By living in Christ and for Christ we now anticipate by faith the future of all things. Again St. Paul:

> For the creation waits with eager longing for the revealing of the sons of God; . . . because the creation itself will be set free from its bondage to decay and obtain the glorious liberty of the children of God. We know that the whole creation has been groaning in travail together until now; and not only the creation, but we ourselves, who have the first fruits of the Spirit, groan inwardly as we wait for adoption as sons, the redemption of our bodies.

We have the first fruits, but there are Christians who seem to think that the first fruits are the only fruits. Rather, we might think of the Church as the prolepsis, the preview, of the great harvest that is to be. Put differently, the Church, which is the body of the risen Christ, is the future of the world. We cannot maintain, as some theologians do, that there is salvation apart from Christ. St. Peter, preaching in the book of Acts, could hardly have been more explicit: "And there is salvation in no one else, for there is no other name under heaven given among men by which we must be saved." There is no salvation apart from Christ. There cannot be if, as Christians believe, Jesus is the God-man who brought about our at-one-ment with the Father. To suggest otherwise is to suggest that Jesus is not, as he said, the way, the truth and the life, but is only a way, a truth and a life. If, in the mercy and mystery of God, people can be saved who have never even heard of Christ, they are still saved only *because* of Christ, "for there is salvation in no one else."

Many Christians are embarrassed by this claim. They are intimidated by a culture that decrees that all truths are equal. Who are you to claim that you have the truth and others do not? That is indeed an intimidating question, unless we understand that we do not *have* the truth in the sense that it is ours by virtue of our having discovered it; we do not *have* the truth in the sense of its being a possession under our control. The Christian claim is that we have been encountered by the truth revealed by God in Jesus Christ and by his grace we have responded to that encounter by faith. We hope and pray and work for everyone to be so encountered and to so respond.

Christians are often responsible for the common misunderstanding of what is meant when we say, "there is salvation in no one else." We are heard to be saying, "My truth is better than your truth; my religion is better than your religion (or nonreligion)." But Christ is not my truth or your truth; he is *the* truth. He is not one truth among many. He is the truth about everything that is true. He is the universal and cosmic truth. Everything that is true—in religion, philosophy, mathematics or the art of baseball—is true by virtue of participation in the truth who is Christ. The problem is not that non-Christians do not know truth; the problem is that they do not know that the truth they know is the truth of Christ.

When St. Paul was in Athens he came across an altar dedicated to "an unknown god." Speaking in the Areopagus, he did not tell the Athenians that there was no such god; he did not tell them they were worshiping nothing. No, he declared, "What therefore you worship as unknown, this I proclaim to you." And then he told them about God in Jesus Christ. Our world is a vast Areopagus. In one important respect, our task is more difficult than Paul's. That is because many people in our world think they have already heard of Jesus Christ, when in fact they haven't. And they haven't because too often Christians present the truth of Christ as though it is but one truth pitted against other truths—"My truth is better than your truth."

The truth about truth is that every human apprehension of truth, every human aspiration toward truth, is, however partial, an apprehension of Christ and an aspiration toward Christ. John Paul II is fond of saying, "Jesus Christ is the answer to which every human life is the question." Not everything that passes for truth, of course, but everything that *is* truth is one. Christians are those who are, so to speak, "in the know." They have come to understand, by the grace of God, the mystery that has been at work since the foundation of the world. St. Paul once more: "For he has made known to us in all wisdom and insight the mystery of his will, according to his purpose which he set forth in Christ as a plan for the fullness of time, to unite all things in him, things in heaven and things on earth."

The hope that all may be saved, the hope for poor Gestas and all the rest of unknowing humanity living and dead, offends some Christians. It is as though salvation were a zero-sum proposition, as though there is only so much to go around, as though God's grace to others will somehow diminish our portion of grace. Remember the parable of the workers in the vineyard, how those who came early in the day complained that those who came later got the same wages. What does the master say? "Take what belongs to you, and go; I choose to give to this last as I give to you. Am I not allowed to do what I choose with what belongs to me? Or do you begrudge my generosity?" And then Jesus adds, as he does so often, "So the last will be first, and the first last."

But one hears the objection, "What's the point of being a Christian if, in the end, everyone is saved?" People who ask that should listen to themselves. What's the point of being first rather than last in serving the Lord whom you love? What's the point of being found rather than lost? What's the point of knowing the truth rather than living in ignorance? What's the point of being welcomed home by the waiting father rather than languishing by the pig sties? What's the point? The question answers itself.

But, just in case we do not get the point, Jesus makes it very explicit. One day Jesus is calling people to leave all and follow him. Then Peter—wonderful Peter, whom you can count on to say the dumb things we are all prone to say—burst out with, "Lo, we have left everything and followed you." What's the point? he wanted to know. What do we get in return? And Jesus answered, "Truly, I say to you, there is no one who has left house or brothers or sisters or mother or father or children or lands, for my sake and for the gospel, who will not receive a hundredfold now in this time . . . with persecutions, and in the age to come eternal life." And then Jesus adds once again, "But many that are first will be last, and the last first."

The point is that, in this life and in the world to come, those who follow Jesus will receive everything they want, if what they want is to follow Jesus. If, on the other hand, following Jesus is not what they want, then the answer to Peter's question—and the question of so many others—is that there is no point in following Jesus. Living in the way, the truth and the life is—for those who know Christ as the way, the truth and the life—self-evidently preferable to the alternative, which is being lost, ignorant and dead. No offense intended, but people who have to ask why that is the case probably wouldn't understand. Those who presume to think that they and others of like religious doctrine, experience or way of life are the first and will therefore be both the first and the last in line for salvation have not, one fears, understood the generosity of the Lord of the vineyard. Nor do they take as seriously as we all should the sin of presumption.

Is it possible that many, even the great majority, of all the people who have ever lived will be eternally damned? I do not know how we could answer that question definitively in the negative. There is also no way that our minds can reconcile that possibility with what the Bible says about the mercy of God and his redemptive purposes for the whole creation. The prospect of even one person being eternally damned should fill us with immeasurable sorrow. We must hope that it is not so.

Yes, there have been and still are Christians who argue to the contrary. It is said that, if our joy is solely in God's will being done, then we will rejoice also in his condemnation of the *massa damnata*. Some go further and claim that one of the attractions of heaven is the pleasure that the saved will have in watching the torments of the damned. There is a kind of perverse logic in this position—a position associated with proponents of "double predestination"—but it is execrable theology. It changes God's justice into caprice, which is the opposite of justice. It turns upside down the biblical understanding both of God's love and of God's command that we should love our neighbor, an understanding that the Bible invites us to trust. And it shatters any coherence between our language of love and justice— language drawn from revelation!—and the actual ways of God.

We are reminded, once again, that we are dealing with mysteries here. "For my thoughts are not your thoughts, neither are your ways my ways, says the Lord. For as the heavens are higher than the earth, so are my ways higher than your ways and my thoughts than your thoughts." Remember the caution about analogy: "No similarity is so great but that the dissimilarity is even greater." Such statements underscore the *transcendence* of God. Yet there *is* analogy, there *is* similarity. Otherwise there would be no point in God's revelation, no possibility of communicating. There would be nothing we could understand, nothing we could trust.

But the entirety of Christian faith rests on the confidence that God has revealed himself in the history of salvation, and preeminently in Jesus Christ. Although it far transcends our understanding, this revelation càn be understood—and it can be trusted utterly. God's ways are infinitely more than we can understand, but they are not contrary to what he asks us to believe. God is not capricious, he is not playing games with us. He is both transcendent *and* immanent; he is both radically "other" and is present to us in the "thus and so–ness" of his revelation. There is, in other words, a trustworthy analogy between our understanding of love and God's love for all human beings. That understanding would seem to make it nearly impossible for us to love others without hoping that all will be saved.

I say *nearly* impossible because we are cautioned by the memory that there have been thoughtful and orthodox Christians who have said that we should not hope that, in the end, all will be saved. They insist that the entirety of our hope is invested in the prayer that God's will be done, and we cannot presume to know the final will of God. Such Christians are sometimes inclined to accent the paradoxical. Some have suggested, for instance, that there are different levels or qualities of love for God. At one level, we love God because he has promised us salvation. At a second and higher level, we love God without regard to whether he will save us. At the highest level, we love God even though we know that he will eternally condemn us for loving him. In this view, damnation is a matter of indifference or is even welcomed, because it is a consequence of the only thing that matters, our love for God. If our real desire is for God's will to be done, then we want God's will to be done even if it is God's will that we spend eternity in hell.

As strange as it sounds, some saints and mystics have spoken that way. Their intent is to underscore as dramatically as possible what should be the purity, the unalloyed selflessness, of the Christian's love for God. One can sympathize with that intention while wondering whether it does not push a logic to the point of absurdity. It is impressive, even awesome, as a form of spiritual pyrotechnics, but it is psychologically unbelievable. More important, it cannot be squared with the command to love others as we love ourselves, which assumes a due regard for self. Although there is much confusion on the point, God's perfect love—the love that in the Greek is called *agape*—is not "selfless" in the sense of being indifferent to God's nature or desire. On the contrary, the Bible is replete with assertions that God rejoices and takes delight in his creation. Moreover, the entire plan of salvation assumes that God wants company. One may say that God—Father, Son and Spirit—*is* company, and the plan of redemption is that God and we should enjoy one another in a perfect communion that has no end.

In other words, there is a coherence and trustworthiness in what we know of God's way of love. Paradox and pyrotechnics can usefully accent this truth or that, but they should be kept in check lest they eclipse the fundamental truth of the way of love. If we love others, it seems that we must hope that, in the end, they will be saved. We must hope that all will one day hear the words of Christ, "Today you will be with me in paradise." Given the evidence of Scripture and tradition, we cannot deny that hell exists. We can, however, hope that hell is empty. We cannot know that, but we can hope it is the case.

What then is the purpose of everything said about hell and

damnation? It is admonitory, cautionary, a warning and alarm.
Not to put too fine a point on it, we should live in fear of
damnation. "The fear of the Lord is the beginning of wisdom."
There is no contradiction, there is not even a tension, between
hoping that hell is empty and knowing that it is possible we may
spend eternity in hell. The one thing we hope, the other we
know. To hope that hell is empty is, of course, to hope implicitly
for our own salvation, for it would be an astonishing conceit on
my part to think that I might be its first inhabitant. That
presumption regarding the uniqueness of my status as a sinner,
however, has its counterpart in the much more common
presumption that we *know* that we will be saved.

There is a crucial distinction between faith-filled confidence
in salvation and the claim to cognitive certitude that I will be
saved. Only God knows our final destiny. This is not cause for
discouragement or paralyzing insecurity. Quite the opposite; it is
the foundation of the Christian's freedom. St. Paul catches this
great truth in addressing the Corinthians, who had been very
critical of him and his ministry. After explaining himself, he
adds, "But with me it is a very small thing that I should be
judged by you or by any human court. I do not even judge
myself." What a wonderful thing to be able to say, what a
bracing declaration of freedom: "I do not even judge myself."

St. Paul does not claim to know that he will be saved, that
he will be found worthy in the Great Assize. He does not need
to know. It is enough that God knows. He writes: "I am not
aware of anything against myself, but I am not thereby
acquitted. It is the Lord who judges me. Therefore do not
pronounce judgment before the time, before the Lord comes,

who will bring to light the things now hidden in darkness and will disclose the purposes of the heart. Then every man will receive his commendation from God." *Do not judge before the time.* Do not judge yourself, and most certainly do not judge others.

It is both unsurprising and unattractive that theologians who fill hell with a *massa damnata* of sinners are confident of their own salvation. Maybe there is an exception to that rule in the long history of Christian thought, but none comes readily to mind. Also those who say they would love God even though loving God would result in their being damned are claiming a most remarkable quality of devotion. Implicit in such a claim is, I believe, the assumption that it is incomprehensible that God would not reward such devotion. However it is expressed, the sin of presumption, the claim that we *know* we will be saved, puts us in the spiritually parlous place of the Pharisee in the temple: "God, I thank thee that I am not like other men, extortionists, evildoers, adulterers—or even like this tax collector here." To all such St. Paul declares, "Work out your salvation with fear and trembling." But then, lest we be overcome by fear and trembling, he immediately adds, "for God is at work in you, both to will and to work for his good pleasure." And his good pleasure is that you should be saved.

There is a sense in which we can rightly say that we *know* we will be saved. Consider the analogy with a person who has promised to help us if we find ourselves in some kind of trouble. When, then, we do get in trouble, we might say, "I just *know* she will help me." What kind of statement is that? It would seem to be a statement of confidence and trust, of faith-filled hope. Hope is the form that faith takes in relation to the future.

We will come back to this in reflecting on another word from
the cross, but let it be said here that faith can be understood
as a way of knowing. Knowledge and faith need not be pitted
against one another, as is so commonly done by believers
and secularists alike. "I know she will help me." I am certain
of it.

At the same time—as a matter of what philosophers call
epistemology—I recognize that this is a statement about the
future, about a contingent event, and it may turn out that she
will not or will not be able to help me. Put somewhat
paradoxically, the assertion is this: If I did not know that she will
help me, I know she might not help me. This statement about
knowing is not simply saying something about my subjective
state of confidence. It is a statement about what will actually
happen in the future. Whether the statement is true or false will
only be determined by the future.

Of course such a statement of faith as a form of *knowing*
cannot be made about what any human being will do. Human
beings may disappoint us. To place such unqualified trust in
another human being is a form of idolatry. This kind of faith is
properly directed only to God. If we say that we do not *know*
that we will be saved, it is not because God is untrustworthy but
because we do not fully understand God's purposes. *Do not judge
before the time.* Most especially, do not judge others. We are to be
hard on ourselves, working out our salvation in fear and
trembling, while being generous toward others. Our only hope
for salvation is in the mercy of God and therefore, as Jesus
admonishes again and again, we must be merciful to others. The
mercy we give will be the mercy we receive.

St. Paul himself says he does not know how he will fare at the final judgment, and yet there are those who are supremely confident that they are heaven-bound while innumerable others are on their way to hell. That version of salvation—or justification, as it is called—is hard to justify by the biblical testimony. It is God's declared desire that all be saved, and how can we not hope that that desire will be fulfilled? Paul writes, "Beloved, never avenge yourselves, but leave it to the wrath of God; for it is written, 'Vengeance is mine, I will repay, says the Lord.'" If we declare that others will be damned, is that not a kind of anticipated vengeance? There is indeed a "wrath of God," but as we saw in our reflection on the First Word from the cross—"Father, forgive them, for they know not what they do"—that wrath is directed at the entirety of the human race in solidarity with Adam. In view of humankind's rebellious verdict, "God is guilty!" that wrath is deflected to Christ who "was made sin for us."

St. Paul writes, "But the free gift is not like the trespass. For if many died through one man's trespass, much more have the grace of God and the free gift in the grace of that one man Jesus Christ abounded for many." Further, the "many" in that statement can be understood as applying to all. "For God has consigned all men to disobedience, that he may have mercy upon all." The entire discussion of judgment and grace in the Letter to the Romans is to drive home how total is our dependence upon God's grace in Christ. If we draw a distinction between ourselves and others—even if the distinction is that we do and they do not trust God's grace in Christ—we diminish the radicality of our dependence upon grace. We are saying that, at least with respect to our faith, we are different from them; we are somehow not under the same judgment.

The message of sin and grace is not aimed at distinguishing ourselves from others, but is a call for *us* to repent of the presumption that we are in any position to make such distinctions. Paul writes to the Romans:

> Therefore you have no excuse, whoever you are, when you judge another, for in passing judgment upon him you condemn yourself, because you, the judge, are doing the very same things. We know that the judgment of God rightly falls upon those who do such things. Do you suppose that when you judge those who do such things and yet do them yourself, you will escape the judgment of God? Or do you presume upon the riches of his kindness and forbearance and patience? Do you not know that God's kindness is meant to lead you to repentance?

Of course Christians may say they are not guilty of doing any of the things Paul condemns here, in which case such Christians are leading contenders for the role of the Pharisee in the temple.

With a hope that is faith directed to the future, we earnestly hope that someday, by the utterly undeserved grace of God, we will hear the words, "Today you will be with me in paradise." I have heard it said by some evangelical Protestants that Catholics *hope* they will be saved while Bible-believing Protestants *know* they will be saved. That way of putting the matter does not stand up to close examination. In 1997, theologians involved in a project known as "Evangelicals and Catholics Together" produced a common statement entitled "The Gift of Salvation":

We may therefore have assured hope for the eternal life promised to us in Christ. As we have shared in his sufferings, we will share in his final glory. "We shall be like him, for we shall see him as he is" (1 John 3:2). While we dare not presume upon the grace of God, the promise of God in Christ is utterly reliable, and faith in that promise overcomes anxiety about our eternal future. We are bound by faith itself to have firm hope, to encourage one another in that hope, and in such hope we rejoice. For believers "through faith are shielded by God's power until the coming of the salvation to be revealed in the last time" (1 Peter 1:5). Thus it is that as justified sinners we have been saved, we are being saved, and we will be saved. All this is the gift of God.

Our gratitude for a mercy so gratuitous is in no way dependent upon others not receiving the same mercy. Jesus did not say, "You shall be with me, Dysmas, but Gestas shall not." The Bible's words of warning and promise are, as St. Paul says, to lead each one of us to repentance. I am to hear those words addressed to *me*. Curiosity about what will happen to others is an idle distraction. That is God's business. On this score, too, Peter had to be reproached by Jesus. Recall at the end of the Fourth Gospel how Peter wants to know what is going to happen to John. Jesus tells Peter, "If it is my will that he remain until I come, what is that to you? Follow me!" If it is my will that every last child of Adam ever conceived will be with me in paradise, what is that to you? *You* follow me!

I say that I hope that all will be saved. I do not know. Nobody knows. Only God knows. And we must recognize that there are arguments against that hope. Some contend, for instance, that such a hope undercuts the urgency of evangelization, of sharing the gospel with others. I do not think that is the case, and later I will explain why. I recognize also that some of the most venerable of Christian thinkers have denied that we should hope all will be saved. One is given long and careful pause when, for instance, one finds oneself disagreeing with the redoubtable St. Augustine.

Toward the end of his life, Augustine became ever more dour in his conviction that many are predestined to damnation. In the *City of God* he writes about those who hope that all will be saved: "They are in fact moved by a human compassion which is concerned only for human beings; and in particular they are pleading their own cause, promising themselves a delusive impunity for their own disreputable lives by supposing an all-embracing mercy of God towards the human race." No doubt some who hope for the salvation of all do fit Augustine's description. The dying Heinrich Heine is alleged to have said on his deathbed, when asked whether he was sure of his salvation, "God will forgive me. That's his business."

But our hope is not of the sort criticized by Augustine *if* our preeminent prayer is that God's will be done, even when we do not know precisely what that means, and *if* we understand that all the words of warning are aimed at our repentance. In this life *everyone* stands under the judgment of God, and with St. Paul *we each* must confess that we cannot know in advance the outcome of the individual judgment of our lives. We must not presume. We cannot know in advance for ourselves and certainly we cannot know in advance for others. We must not presume, however, promises are made, and promises elicit hope, and hope is the form that faith takes in relation to the future.

It is a relatively recent and unseemly thing in Christian history that people presume to claim cognitive certitude about their own salvation and equal certitude that the *massa damnata* will make for a well-populated hell. The presumption is common in certain strains of Protestant piety, but in these ecumenical times it has also infiltrated much Catholic thought. The idea that Protestants know they are saved whereas Catholics only hope they are saved might imply the high improbability that God has bestowed cognitive superiority along denominational lines. In addition, such a sharp distinction between faith and hope does not hold if we understand that hope is faith directed toward the future. As the Letter to the Hebrews puts it, "Now faith is the assurance of things hoped for, the conviction of things not seen."

"Assurance" means conviction, confidence, trust. Assurance is not cognitive certitude; it is not the certain knowledge that it is impossible that what I am confident will happen will not happen. If we had such certitude, we would not be instructed to work out our salvation with fear and trembling. Faith as hope is confidence in God's faithfulness. We do not presumptuously stride up to the judgment throne confident of being handed the Good Servant Award. Rather, we throw ourselves upon the mercy of God and plead his promises in Christ. It is not like getting a diploma at graduation exercises, the deserved and expected reward for being the good Christians that we are. Least of all is it the expected reward for being the kind of good Christians who are indifferent to the reward.

The last point is pertinent to those Christians who make so much of being saved, or justified, by faith alone. What should one say in response? I can only give my testimony. When I come before the judgment throne, I will plead the promise of God in the shed blood of Jesus Christ. I will not plead any work that I have done, although I will thank God that he has enabled me to do some good. I will plead no merits other than the merits of Christ, knowing that the merits of Mary and the saints are all from him; and for their company, their example, and their prayers throughout my earthly life I will give everlasting thanks. I will not plead that I had faith, for sometimes I was unsure of my faith, and in any event that would be to turn faith into a meritorious work of my own. I will not plead that I held the correct understanding of "justification by faith alone," although I will thank God that he led me to know ever more fully the great truth that much misunderstood formulation was intended to protect. Whatever little growth in holiness I have experienced, whatever strength I have received from the company of the saints, whatever understanding I have attained of God and his ways—these and all other gifts received I will bring gratefully to the throne. But in seeking entry to that heavenly kingdom, I will, with Dysmas, look to Christ and Christ alone.

Then I hope to hear him say, "Today you will be with me in paradise," as I hope with all my being—because, although looking to him alone, I am not alone—he will say to all.

3

A Strange Glory

The Third Word from the cross:

When Jesus saw his mother and the disciple whom he loved standing near, he said to his mother, "Woman, behold, your son!" Then he said to the disciple, "Behold, your mother!" And from that hour the disciple took her to his own home.

In John's Gospel, the way of the cross is the way of glory. It is a strange glory. In chapter 17 we find Jesus in prayer. He has just explained to the disciples what lies ahead. "The hour is coming, indeed it has come, when you will be scattered, every man to his own home, and will leave me alone." The cross casts its long shadow over his prayer, and yet he prays, "Father, the hour has come; glorify thy Son that the Son may glorify thee." It is a very strange glory.

Then the arrest, the mock trial, the cruel jests, the whipping, the crown of thorns, the nailing to the wood and the deed is done. But he is not entirely alone. Not yet. Standing by the cross with his mother are his aunt, Mary the wife of Clopas, and also Mary Magdalene. Numerous stories have been told about Mary Magdalene. She got that name because she came from

Magdala, a Roman city in Galilee that was reputed to be a place
of debauchery. Perhaps that is why Mary has often been
identified as the sinful woman of Luke 7 who anointed the feet
of Jesus with her tears. Thus the word "magdalen" means to this
day a prostitute who has abandoned her trade. But that is the
stuff of legend. What the Gospel writers tell us about her is that
she was the first witness of the empty tomb and the first to
preach that Christ is risen. But that gets us ahead of the story.
We must not rush to Easter. Mary Magdalene is there at the
foot of the cross with Mary, the mother of Jesus, and John, the
disciple whom he loved, all beholding the strange glory of the
crucified Lord of life.

From the beginning, Christian eyes fixed on the mournful
mother and her dying son. *Stabat Mater dolorosa / Iuxta crucem
lacrimosa, / Dum pendebat Filius.* "At the cross her station keeping, /
stood the mournful mother weeping, / close by Jesus to the last."
Now it was all turning out just the way it had been foretold.
Pious Jewish minds remembered now the words of Genesis,
where God put a curse on the serpent that had deceived the first
Eve: "I will put enmity between you and the woman, and
between your seed and her seed; he shall bruise your head and
you shall bruise his heel." Mary, the seed of the first Eve,
acknowledged by Christians as the second Eve, watches as Satan
does his worst to her son. Did she know, as she stood there by
her dying son, that this was the way of the strange glory by
which he would conquer sin and death? We do not know.

But she must have known it would turn out something like
this. Old Simeon was probably long dead by now, but she must
have thought often about that old man who took the baby Jesus
in his arms when she and Joseph had brought him to the temple.

What was it the old man had said to her? "Behold, this child is set for the fall and rising of many in Israel, and for a sign that is spoken against, and a sword will pierce your own soul also, that thoughts out of many hearts may be revealed." Enigmatic words, those. Whatever else they meant, she now knew the piercing sword of grief, cutting her body and soul. That was her body on the cross, for Jesus, virgin born, had no body other than the body he had received from Mary.

For Mary, from the start, it had ever been thus—this strangeness touched by glory. Of the announcement, the annunciation, from which all this sprang, Edwin Muir writes:

> The angel and the girl are met
> > Earth was the only meeting place.
> For the embodied never yet
> > Traveled beyond the shore of space.
> The eternal spirits in freedom go.
> > See, they have come together, see,
> While the destroying minutes flow,
> > Each reflects the other's face
> Till heaven in hers and earth in his
> > Shine steady there. He's come to her
> From far beyond the farthest star,
> > Feathered through time. Immediacy
> Of strangest strangeness is the bliss
> > That from their limbs all movement takes.
> Yet the increasing rapture brings
> > So great a wonder that it makes
> Each feather tremble on his wings.

. . .

But through the endless afternoon
These neither speak nor movement make,
But stare into their deepening trance
As if their gaze would never break.

Of strangest strangeness was the bliss that led, but a little more than thirty years later, to the bleakness of another endless afternoon here on the hill of Golgotha. *Stabat Mater dolorosa.* Maybe she knew back then that it would come to this. She had been thinking so much for so long. When the shepherds came to worship the baby and told her what the angels had told them, it is said with beguiling simplicity, "Mary kept all these things, pondering them in her heart." And now she pondered them in her sword-pierced heart. So much time over the years had been spent in pondering the strangest strangeness of an ever elusive glory.

She had accompanied the glory. She had been with him in the unsurpassable intimacy of the pregnancy and the birth, an intimacy that none other could ever know. We cannot think of Jesus without thinking of Mary, unless we have the misfortune of being Docetists. Docetism was an early Christian heresy that claimed that the humanity and sufferings of the earthly Christ were only apparent, not really real. That way of thinking was picked up by various Gnostics who claimed to have a secret knowledge of what was *really* going on behind the veil of the ordinariness, the everydayness, the thus and so–ness, of Mary and her child. For the Docetists and Gnostics a *real* incarnation, a *real* immersion of the Divine in the flesh and blood and tears of humanity, was not worthy of their lofty conception of God.

Thinking to honor God, they denied the ways of God. Such Christians are still with us today.

But, for us, to think of Jesus is to think of Mary. From her he received his humanity, his Jewish humanity: the color of his eyes, the cut of his nose, that odd way of smiling. She potty-trained him, taught him his first words, encouraged his first steps, kissed his scuffed knee and made it all better, picked him up in the dark of nightmare nights and told him everything will be all right—even as she pondered prophecies about piercing swords and wondered at the meaning of a king from the East who presented as his royal gift myrrh for the birth—or was it the burial—of her lovely child. She accompanied the strange glory to the temple, where the prodigious twelve-year-old dazzled his elders with his learning. She was there for his first miracle, at the wedding of Cana where he turned water into wine.

They could not have been closer, Jesus and Mary, and yet there was a strange distancing. At Cana the wine ran out and she told him, "They have no wine." Jesus responded, "O woman, what have you to do with me? My hour has not yet come." Then Mary said to the servants, "Do whatever he tells you." Those are the last recorded words of Mary in the New Testament: "Do whatever he tells you." Through the centuries Christians have claimed to have received messages from Mary, and when the claims are true it is always the same message: "Do whatever he tells you." But at Cana, Mary is also learning, as all mothers must learn, to let go, to let him go on the way he must go. She knew it had to be, but it must have hurt when he said, "O woman, what have you to do with me?"

The love that lets go is never easy. Such love has to be

learned. In the Great Tradition, both of the East and the West, Mary is hailed as the first of the disciples, and as a disciple she learned. When she and Joseph took the boy Jesus to the temple, they did not find him until "after three days." Some scholars see here an allusion to that other three days when he would be lost, the days from death to resurrection. Be that as it may, when they found him, he said to his mother, "How is it that you sought me? Did you not know that I must be in my Father's house?" How is it that she sought him? What a thing for a twelve-year-old boy to say to his mother!

We are told that he then went back with them to Nazareth "and was obedient to them." And then again Mary pondering: "And his mother kept all these things in her heart." He was back with her, but something was different now, something had happened and it could not be undone. There was a further drawing close to, and a further distancing from, the strange glory. "How is it that you sought me?" Between Jesus and Mary another will was interposed, an infinitely greater will, the will of the heavenly Father. To this will, every other relationship took second place. God came between them, we might think. More accurately, it was becoming clearer that everything between them could be secured only by surrendering it in obedience to the Father.

"Woman, what have you to do with me? My hour has not yet come." He has now no other life than what he calls "my hour," referring to his appointed mission. In relation to Jesus, there is no way to be part, to have part, except to take part in his "hour." There is no independent connection with Jesus, no connection apart from that mission, not even the connection of

a mother with her son. Mary would come to understand this
fully at the foot of the cross, but she was learning it along the
way to that climactic "hour."

All three synoptic Gospels (Matthew, Mark and Luke) tell of
the day when the crowds were pressing Jesus, so much so that
he did not even have time to eat. Maybe Mary was worried
about his health, but, whatever the reason, she and his brethren
came to talk with him. She did not push her way in, but waited
outside, and someone told Jesus that his mother was asking for
him. Jesus responded: "Who are my mother and my brothers?"
Looking at those who sat about him, he said, "Here are my
mother and my brothers! Whoever does the will of God is my
brother, and sister, and mother."

What an unfeeling son, we might think. And we wonder
what Mary thought, and whether she got to see him that day, or
whether, disappointed, she went away to ponder this, too, in her
heart. There was another day when an exuberant woman in the
crowd cried out, "Blessed is the womb that bore you, and the
breasts that you sucked!" A high compliment to Mary indeed.
But Jesus immediately corrects the woman: "Blessed rather are
those who hear the word of God and keep it."

Ah, Mary, you were so close to the child, closer than anyone
else could possibly be, and now it seems you are shut out, put
down, pushed to the margins. It seems he has no more time for
you. Even when it comes to taking care of him, to doing the big
and little things that a mother wants to do—making sure that he
has enough to eat and that his robe is mended—it seems that you
are excluded. In Luke 8 we hear about the holy women who followed him and provided for him, and your name is not on the list.

Mary learned the hard love of letting go, the love that is forged in surrender to a love greater than our own, the love that grows beyond all possessing. Some Christians who have an intense devotion to Mary are embarrassed and offended by these Gospel passages that suggest a distancing between Jesus and his mother. They fail to understand that in this distancing love is a deepening of discipleship, and it is as the first of disciples that Mary is to be honored.

Especially among Catholics, before the Second Vatican Council there was a heaping up of "privileges" and "exemptions" in honor of Mary. The Church had declared that she had been exempted from original sin and bodily corruption, which is the meaning of the dogmas of Immaculate Conception and Assumption. But some took this to mean that Mary was also exempted from the pains of childbirth, from weariness, doubt, temptation, ignorance and even death. All these things, it was said, are the result of sin and, since Mary is sinless, she was above them all.

The inadvertent consequence of such piety was to imply that Mary was somehow above her son, for whose sake alone all generations call her blessed. Jesus was tempted, grew weary, wept and died an unspeakably horrible death. The problem with that earlier way of honoring Mary is not that it was excessive. The more profoundly we understand her place in the drama of salvation, the more we know that Mary cannot be honored enough. The problem with that other way is that it honored Mary for the wrong thing, for a reason almost opposite to the one for which she is to be honored. The disciple is not above the master, Jesus repeatedly said. Mary wants no honor that puts her apart from—God forbid, above!—her child, who is her Lord.

"Do whatever he tells you." Everything about Mary is from Christ and to Christ. In the Second Vatican Council, the teaching about Mary (Mariology) is solidly placed within the teaching about the Church (ecclesiology). Mary is the icon of the disciple-Church. This is no new departure, although it is an accent that had been neglected at times. Protestant Christians have difficulty, to put it gently, with the 1854 definition of Mary's immaculate conception (which does not mean, as the religiously illiterate sometimes think, that she was conceived without her parents' sexual union). The definition, in the 1854 papal decree *Effabilis Deus*, makes clear that her sinlessness is entirely by the grace of God and is entirely dependent upon her sinless son: "The most Blessed Virgin Mary was, from the first moment of her conception, by a singular grace and privilege of almighty God and by virtue of the merits of Jesus Christ, Savior of the human race, preserved immune from all stain of original sin."

Jesus emptied himself. Mary emptied herself. St. Paul writes, "Have this mind among yourselves, which you have in Christ Jesus, who, though he was in the form of God, did not count equality with God a thing to be grasped, but emptied himself, taking the form of a servant, being born in the likeness of men." The Greek word for this self-emptying is *kenosis*; it is the surrender of all that we hold most dear and, for Mary, it was the surrender of her dearest. Long before they looked at one another on Golgotha's place of strangest glory, they had been prepared by many little surrenders for this surrender by which all was restored. I once heard it put well: "Once his public ministry had begun, Jesus had nowhere to rest his head, and Mary had nowhere to rest her heart." And now it had come to this, she pondered in her broken heart, in her heart that by its breaking was made whole. That is the way it is with discipleship. The way of the cross is the way of broken hearts.

In all this, Mary was following her son, step by inexorable step. Her *kenosis* mirrored his *kenosis*, her life's song was entirely attuned to his, a letting go into the vastness of whatever will be, trusting that at the end will be glory. Now his hour had come, and his hour was completely hers. At Cana, with a different idea of his glory in mind, she had tried to rush his hour. No more. Here, here at the cross, this is how it had to be.

Today and, for that matter, at all times, people find this truth off-putting. It is more than off-putting; it is a scandal. "We preach Christ crucified," St. Paul wrote, "a stumbling block to Jews and folly to Gentiles, but to those who are called, both Jews and Greeks, Christ the power of God and the wisdom of God." Some women say that for them Mary can be no model. They want empowerment, fulfillment, control. There is little that is new in this. Men and women—I expect men more than women—have always been scandalized by the cross. The way of the power and wisdom of God is not the way of our power and our wisdom.

Today's sexual politics and disputes over gender are, at least in this connection, but another variation on a long-standing aversion to the way of discipleship. Let it be said that men have much more to answer for than women, for they have been more in charge of contriving alternatives to the way of the cross. But it is time to be completely candid: To say that Mary's way is not our way is to say that Christ's way is not our way, for Mary was in every respect the disciple of her son. In all our promotion of empowerment, fulfillment, self-esteem and self-actualization, we should know what we are doing. We are rejecting the very heart of what it means to be a Christian. "The disciple is not above the master." "The first shall be last, and the last first." "He who would find his life must lose his life." "Take up your cross and follow me." Jesus was relentless; he is relentless. "Do whatever he tells you," Mary said. What she said she also did, and in her loss of her son and her loss of herself she knew "Christ the power of God and the wisdom of God."

Of course this business about losing our lives in order to find our lives goes very much against the grain. On second thought, maybe not. Maybe we have grown so accustomed to living against the grain of our humanity that we have confused ourselves about which way the grain runs. Maybe, if we follow the true grain of our humanity, it leads to our surrendering our all to the Other. Recall again St. Augustine's "You have made us for yourself, O Lord, and our hearts are restless until they rest in you." Recall those old catechisms, both Protestant and Catholic, that asked the question, "Why did God make me?" Answer: "To know and love and serve him in this life, and to enjoy him forever in the next." Why did God make me? If we get the answer to that wrong, we get everything else wrong. Mary, following Christ, got that right.

"When Jesus saw his mother . . ." We will soon reflect on the Fourth Word from the cross, "My God, my God, why have you forsaken me?" That is, of course, the first verse of Psalm 22, and some scholars speculate that, as a devout Jew, Jesus would have recited the entire psalm in the agony of his dying. If so, he also said, "Yet thou art he who took me from the womb, thou didst keep me safe upon my mother's breasts." There before him was the woman who gave him birth. There the mother who once held safely to her breast the one now held by nails to a bloody cross. The drowning, it is said, see their whole lives reprised before their eyes. As he sank under the weight of humanity's crime, perhaps there passed in review before his eyes all the childhood hours in the safety of a mother's love, before his "hour" came.

And Mary, what was she thinking then? They were likely looking at one another face to face. Much later, beginning in the Middle Ages, artists would depict a very tall cross, with Mary and the others far below at its foot. But historians believe that the cross was probably about seven feet tall. They were face to face. The sweat, the blood, the tearing tendons, the twitching, the wrenching, the bulging eyes—she would have seen it all quite clearly, as clearly as she saw him so long ago when she held him safely to her breast. When he was twelve years old they came to Jerusalem, and now she had accompanied him once more, to celebrate his last Passover there outside the walls of Jerusalem. But this time he is the Passover lamb. This time they would not be going home again.

Stabat Mater dolorosa. At the cross her station keeping. There was nothing else to be done, except to be there. The presence of our helplessness is our gift to the helpless. The *Stabat Mater,* some say, was written by St. Bonaventure in the thirteenth century, and it soon became immensely popular. Ten three-line

verses form a prayer that takes us through Mary's sufferings to
the sufferings of Christ, by whose mercy we hope to attain
paradisi gloria. The poem-prayer has been set to music by some of
the greatest composers: Palestrina, Rossini, Verdi, Dvořák and,
in this century, Szymanowski, Poulenc and Pärt. Antonin
Dvořák composed his *Stabat Mater* in 1878, after losing three
children in three years. It is a large and romantic work, both
melodic and painfully intense; it takes the listener into the heart
of darkness, and there, at the heart of darkness, is hope, because
there is Christ. Like the original poem-prayer, it moves through
Mary's suffering to Christ's suffering, there to discover saving
grace.

Ad Jesum per Mariam. "To Jesus through Mary." The Latin
inscription is over the altar of a small parish church in Quebec,
near where I was born. The phrase appears frequently in
Catholic architecture and devotional literature. One might
object that it should be *Ad Mariam per Jesu*. After all, our access to
Mary and all the saints, both living and dead, is "through
Christ." But the two ways of saying it are not in contradiction,
nor even in tension. At least they need not be. We have said
that to think about Jesus is to think about Mary. Even more is it
the case that to think about Mary is to think about Jesus. From
the very beginnings of Christianity, what Christians have said
about Mary is a consequence of what they said about Christ.
Mariology is derived from Christology. More precisely,
Mariology *is* Christology.

In John 16, Jesus promised the disciples, "When the Spirit of
truth comes, he will guide you into all the truth." As history
shows, what we call orthodox Christian teaching did not emerge

full-blown from the New Testament. In fact, it took several centuries to determine even which writings belonged to the content (the "canon") of what we call the New Testament. That Jesus is truly man and truly God, that he is two natures in one person, that he is the Second Person of the Holy Trinity—these and other truths were established after much effort and controversy as the Spirit guided the Church into all truth, just as Jesus promised.

Among the opponents of orthodoxy, we have already met the Docetists and Gnostics, who thought a real incarnation was unworthy of their idea of God. Already in the first century, that bold martyr-theologian St. Ignatius of Antioch saw that defending the truth about Jesus required defending the truth about Mary. He called Mary's virginity, her conception and the Lord's death the "three great mysteries" of Christian faith. "Our God, Jesus the Christ," he declared, "was generated in Mary's womb of David's line, but through the Holy Spirit, according to God's saving plan." Early on, thinkers such as Ignatius were laying the groundwork for formal definitions such as the one by the Council of Chalcedon (451) rejecting the teaching that Christ had only one nature, the divine nature.

The Word really did become flesh, just as the prologue to John's Gospel says, and that great thing happened in a specific place and a specific way, in the womb of the Virgin Mary. Specificity is all in Christian faith—a specific person, a specific place, a specific time. The Gnostics—then and now—are full of "spiritualizing" generalities. But God's plan of salvation—then and now—has everything to do with the thus and so–ness of things. From St. Paul the early Christians had learned to think of

Christ as the "Second Adam," and, as they reflected on that, they began to see how Mary is the "Second Eve." In the incarnation, the whole human story, right from the beginning, is recapitulated and begun all over again. In the second century, Justin Martyr accented the Eve-Mary comparison, and the great Irenaeus saw how Mary's faith is the model of the faithful Church. "But how will men abandon the birth of death," Irenaeus asked, "unless through faith they are regenerated in a new birth, given unlooked-for by God as a sign of salvation, that which took place from the virgin?"

And so it was that the Spirit was leading the Church ever more deeply and more fully into the truth, also the truth about Mary. At every step of the way, Mariology is Christology. For instance, Chalcedon made it definite that Mary is to be acknowledged as "Mother of God" (*Theotokos* is the Greek term). Others said that she is, of course, to be called "Mother of Jesus" and even "Mother of Christ," but "Mother of God" is going too far. No, responded the orthodox party, it's not a question of our going too far but of how far God went in becoming man. She must be called *Theotokos* not in order to honor her, but in order to tell the truth about Christ. Jesus Christ is God and Mary is his mother, and therefore Mary is the Mother of God. Non-Christian historians have had great fun mocking what they view as the early Christian battles over hairsplitting theological distinctions. That is quite understandable, if one is not a Christian. For Christians, however, these are life-and-death matters—matters of eternal life and eternal death. If Jesus Christ is not true God, to worship him is nothing short of idolatry. If he is not true man, our humanity has not been taken into the life of God. Mary is the *nexus*, the meeting point, between the Divine and the human in Jesus Christ. Thus Mary is at the very heart of the mystery of our salvation. In the New Testament, she is there at the defining moments of God's great plan: at the conception and birth, at the cross, and in the midst of the disciples when the Holy Spirit is given at Pentecost. The more the Church reflected on the biblical account of salvation through Christ, the more its richness was unfolded. And the more its richness was unfolded, the more it was seen how Mary is at the heart of it all. It is not too much to say that Mary's consent to the announcement of the angel that she was to be the mother of the Messiah made our salvation possible. To be sure, the death of Jesus Christ on the cross made our salvation possible, but without Mary's consent that would not have happened. Mary's *fiat*—her "Let it be to me according to your word"—inaugurated the central act of salvation history.

What if Mary had said no? We might speculate that, in that event, God would have chosen some other young woman through whom to become a human being. The problem with that, of course, is that the child of any other woman would not have been this specific child, this Jesus of Nazareth, son of Mary. The Word of God, the Second Person of the Holy Trinity, did not become incarnate in humanity-in-general but in this specific human being, Jesus. Specificity is all. Without Jesus, the story of salvation, if there was such a story at all, would be a very different story. And without Mary's consent, there would have been no Jesus. Moreover, her consent had to be freely given, for God does not violate the freedom of his creatures.

Thank God, we need not indulge in impossible speculations

about what if this had happened or what if that had happened. Hilaire Belloc rhymed, "How odd of God / To choose the Jews." That should not be understood as a slur against Jews, but simply an acknowledgment that, by most human standards, there were more impressive candidates for the role of the elect people of God—the Romans, Greeks, or Persians, for example. But God did what he did, and does what he does, and he chose Mary to be the mother of God incarnate. And Mary said yes.

There is a problem, however, with saying that, by her *fiat*, Mary made our salvation possible. And here we meet up with another of those old heresies that still confuse many Christians today. This one is called Pelagianism. It is named after Pelagius, a fourth-century British theologian who taught in Rome. What he taught (or was understood to have taught) is that human beings can take the initial and most important steps toward salvation by their own efforts, quite apart from the grace of God. "God helps those who help themselves," we hear people say. Pelagius said that of salvation as well. Under the guidance of the Spirit, the Church rejected Pelagianism, insisting that salvation is entirely gratuitous, entirely the undeserved gift of God.

But how can salvation be by grace alone if it depended upon the cooperation of Mary? Orthodox Christianity insists that God's action in reconciling the world to himself in the cross of Christ is exclusively his initiative; there is no original or necessary "collaboration" between God and the creature. And yet, as we have seen, there would have been no cross of Christ without the free consent of Mary, and Mary is certainly a creature. We seem to have a contradiction on our hands. Here is

what that eminent Swiss theologian Hans Urs von Balthasar has
to say about this:

> God could not violate his creature's freedom. But where did the
> grace that made this consent of Mary come from if not from
> the work of reconciliation itself, that is, from the cross? And
> the cross, in turn, is made possible only by Mary's consent.
> Here we have a circle—in which the effect is the cause of the
> cause. It has taken centuries to appreciate and formulate this
> truth, resulting in the dogma of the Immaculate Conception of
> Mary and the exact reasoning behind it.

This takes some careful thinking. As it was said of Mary, we
need to ponder it in our hearts. Even those who do not accept
the idea of Mary's immaculate conception can recognize the
logic of the teaching. "The effect is the cause of the cause." The
cross is the effect, and the cross caused the cause that is Mary's
consent. Recall again the exact formulation of the 1854 definition: "The most Blessed Virgin Mary was, from the first moment
of her conception, *by a singular grace and privilege of almighty God and
by virtue of the merits of Jesus Christ, Savior of the human race*, preserved
immune from all stain of original sin" (emphasis added).

Pelagius is wrong. It is grace all the way. It is undeniably true
that Jesus' death on the cross is made possible only through
Mary's consent. It follows that to deny the truth that is
protected by the doctrine of the Immaculate Conception is to
make our salvation dependent upon Mary's saying yes to God by
her own power. In that case, the whole drama of salvation is
made to hinge on a human work. But it is not the case that
salvation is partly by grace and partly by human merit.

Pelagius is wrong. It is grace all the way. And so it is that Mary—the one of whom it is said that she is "full of grace"—is at the heart of the mystery of our salvation.

"Woman, behold your son." "Son, behold your mother." John, the disciple whom Jesus loved, is standing in for all the disciples, all of whom Jesus loves. At the cross, he represents all of us, the entire Church. He represents also the missing disciples, those who forsook him and fled, just as Jesus said they would. To John and to all of us, Jesus says, "Behold, your mother." Therefore Mary is called "Mother of the Church." As we never think of Mary apart from Christ, so we never think of Mary apart from the Church. We have seen that Mariology is really Christology; and so also Mariology cannot be separated from ecclesiology, the doctrine of the Church.

St. Augustine writes: "Holy is Mary, blessed is Mary, but the Church is more important than the Virgin Mary. Why is this so? Because Mary is part of the Church, a holy and excellent member, above all others but, nevertheless, a member of the whole body. And if she is a member of the whole body, doubtlessly the body is more important than a member of the body." It would be a perverse Marian piety that would pit Mary against Christ; so also we cannot pit Mary against the Church, for the Church is the Body of Christ. Her role in the salvation story and her entire being is in devotion to her son. "Do whatever he tells you," says the one who gave Christ his body, and she says it to all those who are, with her, members of his Body, the Church.

In the New Testament writings associated with St. John, the metaphors, symbols and allusions are multiplied. From the cross,

Jesus addresses his mother as "Woman," and we are put in mind of John's report that Jesus said, "A woman in childbirth suffers because her time has come." Is it too much to think that now, in her time of travail at the cross, Mary gives birth to the faithful? In the book of Revelation, we have "A woman, crying out in the pangs of labor." From the Christian beginnings, this was understood to be the Church giving birth to a new humanity, with Mary being the icon of the Church. St. Irenaeus was a disciple of St. Polycarp, who was a disciple of St. John, and he was sure that John was proposing Mary as the new Eve, "the mother of all the living"—the mother of all who have come to life in Christ, the new Adam.

Mary is the model of discipleship in her total availability to the will of God. She had no business of her own. She was always on call. To the angel's announcement, she says, "Let it be as you say." She was dependent on others, on Joseph, for example, and now on John. By saying yes to the angel and agreeing to be the mother of the Messiah, she had created a situation beyond her control. Who was to pick up the pieces? God provides by sending an angel to say, "Joseph, son of David, do not fear to take Mary as your wife." Now at the cross she is once again alone in the world. God provides. "'Son, behold your mother.' And from that hour John took her to his own home." In her total availability to God, Mary is totally independent and totally dependent upon God's providing. True availability to God overcomes the fear of being dependent on others, for God provides. It is our determination to be independent by being in control that makes us unavailable to God. Little wonder that Mary is also called "Our Lady of Poverty" and is a model for those in the consecrated life who have vowed themselves to holy poverty.

Availability is letting God have his way, even when it brings us to the cross. For those who are available, life is at God's disposal, kept in readiness for what he may be up to. All time is God's time, what the Bible calls a "fullness of time," a *kairos*. In each life made truly available, it is as Christopher Fry writes in *A Sleep of Prisoners*:

> Dark and cold we may be, but this is no winter now. The
> frozen misery of centuries breaks, cracks, begins to move.
> The thunder is the thunder of the floes, the thaw, the upstart
> spring. Thank God our time is now, when wrong comes up to
> face us everywhere, never to leave us till we take the longest
> stride of soul men ever took. Affairs are now soul-sized. The
> enterprise is exploration into God.

Exploration into God is exploration into darkness, into the heart of darkness. Yes, to be sure, God is light. He is the light by which all light *is* light. In the words of the Psalm, "In your light we see light." Yet great mystics of the Christian tradition speak of the darkness in which the light is known, a darkness inextricably connected to the cross. At the heart of darkness the hope of the world is dying on a cross, and the longest stride of soul is to see in this a strange glory. In John's Gospel, the cross is the bridge from the first Passover on the way out of Egypt to the new Passover into glory. In his first chapter he writes, "We have beheld his glory, glory as of the only Son from the Father." The cross is not the eclipse of that glory but its shining forth, its epiphany. In John's account, the death of Jesus is placed on the afternoon of the fourteenth day of the month of Nisan, precisely the time when the Passover lambs were offered up in the temple in Jerusalem.

Lest anyone miss the point, John draws the parallel unmistakably. The legs of Jesus are not broken, the soldier pierces his side and John writes, "For these things took place that the scripture might be fulfilled, 'Not a bone of him shall be broken.' And again another scripture says, 'They shall look on him whom they have pierced.'" In the book of Exodus, God commands that no bone of the paschal lamb is to be broken. Then there is this magnificent passage from the prophet Zechariah: "And I will pour out on the house of David and the inhabitants of Jerusalem a spirit of compassion and supplication, so that, when they look on him whom they have pierced, they shall mourn for him, as one mourns for an only child, and weep bitterly over him, as one weeps over a firstborn."

Here on Calvary's hill, all is fulfilled. It is the glory of Jesus' cry, "It is finished." The cross is the moment of passover from the old covenant to the new. Weeping at the cross, Mary is both the mother of sorrows and the mother of hope. The resurrection glory is discerned in the way that Christ dies. Now the reason for the whole drama becomes clear in the Son's unqualified obedience to the Father, even to death, and the Father's promise to glorify the Son. John says nothing about the risen Christ appearing to his mother. The other disciples discovered the resurrection glory at the dawn of the third day. Mary had already discovered the glory in the cross. There she took "the longest stride of soul."

"In the Cross of Christ I Glory," declared the nineteenth-century hymn writer John Bowring. It seems a strange, even bizarre, glory. "We have beheld his glory," St. John wrote, meaning that he was there, with Mary, beholding the final and perfect sacrifice. In the churches of Asia Minor that were founded by John, Easter was celebrated not on Sunday, as with the other churches, but on 14 Nisan, the anniversary of Christ's death. This was his "hour" of glory. The resurrection ratified and reinforced what was already displayed on the cross. When John, therefore, places Mary at the cross, he is placing her at the very center of salvation. She was there, with him, beholding a glory different from, even the opposite of, everything ordinarily meant by glory. It was God's glory, which is love.

This is the light in which we are to understand those exultant passages in 1 John. "That which was from the beginning, which we have heard, which we have seen with our eyes, which we have looked upon and touched with our hands, concerning the word of life—the life was made manifest, and we saw it, and testify to it, and proclaim to you the eternal life which was with the Father and was made manifest to us." (Mary and I, we saw it!) John continues: "By this we know love, that he laid down his life for us; and we ought to lay down our lives for the brethren." "So we know and believe the love God has for us. God is love, and he who abides in love abides in God, and God abides in him."

In the cross we see that of which humanity is capable: self-transcendence in surrender to the Other. All the evidence to the contrary, we are capable of love. The sign of shame and death becomes the sign of cosmic possibility. Here is the *axis mundi*, the moment upon which all reality turns. A third-century paschal homily captures the full reach of the truth:

> This tree of heavenly dimensions rose up from earth to heaven, the foundation of all things, support of the universe, holder of the whole world, cosmic bond keeping unstable human nature united and securing it with the invisible nails of the Spirit so that, firmly gripped to the divinity, it can no longer break away. With its top branches touching the sky and its roots firmly set in the earth, it holds in its infinite embrace the many and intermediate spirits of the air.

It is the cross that binds John to Mary, and binds all disciples to one another in a mutual gift of self. Christ is the gift, and Christ enables us to give the gift, which is finally the gift of Christ. That is what St. Paul is getting at when he declares, "It is no longer I who live, but Christ who lives in me." In his third-century commentary on the Fourth Gospel, Origen reflects on our scene of Mary and John at the cross:

> Whoever is to become a perfect disciple like John must become such, to be chosen, as it were, like the John who is Jesus. There is no other son of Mary besides Jesus and yet Jesus said to his mother, "Behold your son." He did not say, "Behold, this too is your son." What does this mean except that he is saying, "This is Jesus whom you brought forth." In fact, the one who is perfect no longer lives but Christ lives in him. Since Christ lives in John, when he speaks of him to Mary he says, "Behold your son"—meaning, behold Christ.

"The John who is Jesus." What a curious expression that is. Yet Jesus might say the same to Mary about all his disciples. They are all her sons and daughters for he, her son, lives in them. Mary, then, did not lose her son on the cross; she gains sons and daughters beyond number, in all of whom the glory of Christ abides. But this one disciple, this John, was given an extraordinary privilege. We read, "From that hour the disciple took her to his own home." We are invited to believe that Mary spent her last years with John. Perhaps, to use an old-fashioned expression, she kept house for him. We do not know. But we are invited to reflect that John, when he wrote about the Word become flesh, lived under the same roof with the one through whom it happened.

In their life together, in their eating and talking together, Mary knew each day that she had not lost her son. In the Spirit-seared gathering with the disciples at Pentecost, perhaps she heard again the voice from the cross, "Behold, your sons. Behold, your daughters. In them, I am with you." Then, as though for the first time, she really understood what Jesus meant on that long ago day when she had tried to see him and he responded to those who announced that she was there, "Who are my mother and my brothers?" There was no denying that that had hurt. Jesus added, "Whoever does the will of God is my brother, and sister, and mother." But of course! By doing the will of God she first became his mother, and thus did she become the Mother of the Church, the mother of all who do the will of God. Of course her last word had to be and will always be, "Do whatever he tells you." Wherever or however Mary appears, her message can finally be none other than that: "Do whatever he tells you." Her motherhood increases through all who obey her son.

Of strangest strangeness is the glory. It is the wild glory of abandonment. "My God, my God, why have you forsaken me?" She was watching him and he was watching her and they both knew the words of the psalm: "Yet thou art he who took me from the womb; thou didst keep me safe upon my mother's breasts. Upon thee was I cast from my birth, and since my mother bore me thou hast been my God. Be not far from me, for trouble is near and there is none to help."

From our birth, from our mother, we are cast upon God. What was true for us was true for Jesus. There is no danger of accenting too much his humanity. Christians are always getting themselves into a muddle about what it means to say that Jesus is both divine and human, God and man. Some appear to think he was 50 percent one and 50 percent the other, or end up with two persons, one divine and one human. Theologians speak in technical terms about the "communication of attributes" between the Divine and human in the one person. But for the moment I suggest we set aside the conceptual fretting and vain search for precision about what surpasses understanding. Rather, we fix our attention on this mother and this son. We cannot delve too deeply into the human, for it is the fullness of the human that is here redeemed. How is it that from our birth, from our mother, we are cast upon God?

We are cast upon God when we wonder. In wonder is wisdom born. The most elementary and at the same time the most profound of questions is, "Why is there anything at all and not nothing?" Why am I? We must never be embarrassed about asking something so basic, so apparently naive. In our supposed sophistication we may suppress the question, we may become practiced at forgetting it, but we never really get beyond it. The fact that I find myself in a boundless world of innumerable existent beings is astonishing beyond measure. It cannot be explained by any cause derived from the world itself. The expression "I find myself" reflects a measure of self-consciousness, but how did I come to be before I was conscious of my being. Was I "I" then?

At some point, in what appears to be by chance, what I would later call "I" came to be in a fertilized egg inside my mother. It has always struck me as puzzling that some people say that an embryo or a very small fetus does not look like a human being. That is exactly what a human being looks like when it is two weeks or two months old. It is what you looked like and what I looked like. It is what Jesus looked like inside his mother. Of course he was conceived by the Holy Spirit, and we have no medical data on that. But what he would later call "I" developed in the womb, just as you and I did. As with us, a new being came into being. Reflecting upon itself, it could not interpret itself merely as a product of chance. It could not do that because, from the time it began thinking about such things, it had the capacity to view the world as a whole. Finding ourselves in a world of innumerable existent beings like ourselves, we cannot say that we are the product of chance without saying that everything is the product of chance, which is really not to say much of anything. The word "chance" has no meaning unless there are other things that are by necessity.

"Upon thee was I cast from my birth, and since my mother

bore me thou hast been my God." Jesus could have imagined, as we can imagine, that an infinite number of other beings could have taken "our place" in the universe. Why it should have been me, or you or Jesus, we do not know. But so it was. We can add, in the certainty of retrospect, so it was to be. The expression "so it was to be" is uncomfortably, or maybe comfortably, close to "so it had to be." Our recoil from the hint of determinism is mixed with our attraction to the possibility of purpose.

Long before I came to self-consciousness and called myself "I," my mother called me "you." Jesus first heard "you" from Mary. Long before he could understand, I expect she whispered to him what the archangel Gabriel had told her, but she put it in the second-person singular: "You will be great and will be called the Son of the Most High; and the Lord God will give you the throne of your father David, and you will reign over the house of Jacob forever; and of your kingdom there will be no end." Mary did not know what it all meant, and the baby only smiled at the sound of the voice of the woman for whom he was the infinitely treasured "you."

Of course the child does not come into the world asking questions such as, Why is there something rather than nothing? Or, Why am I rather than someone else where I am? Balthasar writes: "And yet the child is aware, in the first opening of its mind's eyes. Its 'I' awakens in the experience of a 'Thou': in its mother's smile through which it learns that it is contained, affirmed, and loved in a relationship which is incomprehensibly encompassing, already actual, sheltering and nourishing." As Martin Buber classically explained, the I-you relationship between persons carries within it the hint of the I-Thou relationship to the mysterious, to the Divine, to the strange glory. Every child who is blessed with a loving mother first discerns in the mother's smile the presence of a Thou by which the child is encompassed and by which his or her being is secured. "Everything is all right," says the mother to the child crying in the night, and in that "Everything is all right" the child intuits a grand metaphysical statement about the nature of reality. In trusting the mother's assurance, the child trusts that the universe is home, that he or she belongs here.

Jesus encountered the Thou in Mary's smile. But here it is different. Mary, pondering in her heart all that happened and whispering to him the words of the archangel, encountered in her baby, however little she understood it, the Thou by which her existence, the world and the stars beyond number are secured. She looked not up but down into the face of her Creator. She is Thou to him and he is both "you" and Thou to her; he is both her baby and the Son of the Most High. As time went by, and as happens with children, she would become "you" to him. As doesn't happen with other children, he would become ever more Thou to her. It would break Mary's heart to lose the one whom she first called "you," as she was led to surrender ever more to the Thou who is the glory of God whom she once held in her arms and who holds all things in being. The mother would come to understand that, from the beginning, she was held by the One whom she held.

Such was the curious bond between Jesus and Mary, in the cradle and on the cross. As a baby he first awoke to the Absolute—to "God"—in the loving presence of a mother who was for him the reassuring field of reality. She was the secure field of all being in which he received unqualified permission to be. The alternative to her was not to be, and that alternative was unimagined and unimaginable because she was. Only later, and with difficulty, does the child learn to distinguish between the love of God and the primordial love of the parent. For most of us the distinction is never absolute, and perhaps is not meant to be.

"Truly, I say to you, unless you turn and become like children, you will never enter the kingdom of heaven," Jesus would later say. That turning is a conversion, and it is in part a turning back. It is a retrieval of that first awakening to a world when all was miracle and all was play, when all was well in the security of a mother's love. (In the deep background, hauntingly, is the return from east of Eden, and the angel has, at least for a time, dropped his fiery sword.) Yet conversion is not regression. For adults, too much has intervened to ever permit return to the home of the mother's breast. Early on, children learn that the mother is not the entirety of the world and that their will and the will of the world are not always at one. Especially in puberty, they discover with alarm the tugs and pulls, both within and outside of themselves, that force them to make a decision about their own identity. Who "I" am is no longer an uncomplicated given but a matter of deciding, and deciding again and again.

For adults to turn and become children, to live again in a world of miracle and play, requires a larger horizon than that provided by the mother. The mother as Thou was but to prepare the way for an encounter with a greater Thou who is able to comprehend the contradictions of one's ever more complex existence. To be a child again, one must be the child of another parent. As an adult, one can only surrender in the way that a child surrenders, if one surrenders to a love that comprehends all. In short, such a surrender means becoming a child of God.

And after three days of looking for the twelve-year-old boy, they found him in the temple. His mother said, "Son, why have you treated us so?" And Jesus said, "How is it that you sought me? Did you not know that I must be in my Father's house?" No, Mary and Joseph did not know. "They did not understand the saying which he spoke to them." Something very fundamental had changed between them. They went back to Nazareth, "and his mother kept all these things in her heart."

Her heart could not keep so much. Her heart would break before she fully understood, with a shudder of fear and wonder, what it was that she had been telling him when she whispered to the baby, "You will be great, and will be called the Son of the Most High. And of your kingdom there will be no end." Perhaps, she was at times tempted to think, it was a mistake to tell him. But she finally had no choice except to follow, step by step, the way of the strange glory to which she had said yes. She was the instrument, she was the mediator, of the secret into which he would grow. And now his "hour" had come, and it had come to this, here at Golgotha.

"Come follow me," Jesus says. The invitation resounds through all the time there is and ever will be, and all who respond in faith—all who exchange their "I" for the "I" of the Christ who lives within them—make their way, one way or another, to the foot of the cross. There they find themselves with John and Mary and a host of bedraggled saints and sinners whose hour has come. And to each of the brothers and sisters in whom he forever lives, to each of us, Jesus says, "Behold, your mother." And to Mary, "Behold, your children. Behold me."

4

Dereliction

The Fourth Word from the cross:

"My God, my God, why have you forsaken me?"

Here is the cry of dereliction, the cry of abandonment, from the derelict, the abandoned one. The cry is reported in both Mark and Matthew. The Greek word used suggests that he *screamed* with a loud cry, "My God, my God, for what reason have you forsaken me?" *Why? Why this?* It is as though something had gone horribly wrong. It was not supposed to be this way.

In Luke's account, the starkness of the horror is tempered. "And having cried out with a loud cry, Jesus said, 'Father, into your hands I place my spirit.' Having said this, he expired." Luke does not tell us what he cried with a loud cry, but we may assume it was the cry of dereliction reported by Matthew and Mark. In John's account, the ending strikes a different note. It is almost tranquil, a going to sleep after accomplishing the great work he had been sent to do. "Jesus said, 'It is finished'; and having bowed his head, he gave over the spirit." As we have already seen, in John's Gospel the glory of resurrection victory is already present in the cross. We must hold all four Gospels together, however, to capture the many dimensions of the death by which the world is born again. John's Gospel does not deny the horror; it anticipates the glory that is on the far side of dereliction.

"*Eli, Eli, lama sabachthani?*" This is the opening line of Psalm 22, "My God, my God, why have you forsaken me." The Hebrew differs slightly between Matthew and Mark. Perhaps Jesus cried out in Aramaic, the language of his everyday world. But, whether in Hebrew, Aramaic or Greek, the English word "dereliction" catches the desperateness of the scene. Like a derelict boat cast up on the shore, like a dog carcass lying by the roadside, here is something no longer of any account; it is forsaken, abandoned, thrown aside. Roadkill.

"Dereliction" is an apt word for the times we call modern. The essence of modernity, we are told, is that we live in a disenchanted world. God and the gods have withdrawn, if ever they were there in the first place. More recently in the cycles of cultural fashion, we have witnessed the advent of "postmodernity," in which we are given permission to speak again about the gods, and maybe even about God. But the children of postmodernity know that they are making it up. Whether it is the ironic liberalism of tenured professors cleverly "deconstructing" reality or whether it is the popular peddling of New Age "spiritualities," it is a matter of telling fairy tales. And no matter how many fairy tales we tell, when we know that they are fairy tales, they cannot re-enchant the world.

Something has been lost, something has been withdrawn, and it cannot be called back. It's been now well over a century since Matthew Arnold sensed it happening in "Dover Beach":

> *The Sea of Faith*
> *Was once, too, at the full, and round earth's shore*
> *Lay like the folds of a bright girdle furled.*
> *But now I only hear*
> *Its melancholy, long, withdrawing roar,*
> *Retreating, to the breath*
> *Of the night-wind, down the vast edges drear*
> *And naked shingles of the world.*

With that loss, with that withdrawal, came dereliction. What is acclaimed as the high culture of our century has been obsessed with the sense of abandonment. People of good taste nurse their refined and regretful unbelief, chattering about the meaning of it all against the easy-listening background music of that "melancholy, long, withdrawing roar." The cultural icons of a time—Picasso, Joyce, Eliot, Stravinsky, Beckett, John Lennon, the Grateful Dead—all take up the themes, whether with ironic lisp or cacophonous rock, of fragmentation, alienation, forsakenness, abandonment.

Finding themselves on Arnold's "darkling plain," some respond with his sentimental, "Ah, love, let us be true to one another!"—there being no truth other than our love. Others embrace the darkness, exult in the darkness, calling it light. The hard-core disciples of Nietzsche claim to have no fear of madness—for by reference to what might we know that we are mad?—while many more indulge what Allan Bloom termed the "debonair nihilism" of stylish flirtation with nothingness that grants a license for anythingness. These and many others are the cultural riffs on the theme of dereliction. But they need not delay us long. They are not the real thing. Were they the real thing, this century now ending would have understood itself as the century of the cross. In that case, it is more than a matter of ignorant armies clashing by night; and instead of beach parties given to diverting talk about the withdrawing sea of faith, the vacated space would be filled with the sustained scream, *Eli, Eli, lama sabachthani?*

Real dereliction is not debonair. I recall being deeply impressed many years ago, when I was still in college, by something the philosopher Bertrand Russell said in his autobiography. He said that anyone who had not been a child before 1914 could never know what human happiness was. Of course, his was a very privileged childhood, but the remark says something important about our cultural sensibility as to where and when things went so terribly wrong. I grew up near a Canadian army camp in northern Ontario, and the streets there had names such as Ypres, Verdun, Somme and Marne. These were the battles of World War I—the "Great War," the "War to End All Wars"—where ignorant armies clashed by night and day, and hundreds of thousands were slaughtered to gain a few yards of muddy terrain. The first poetry by which I was deeply affected was that of Rupert Brooke and other elegists of the innocent dead.

If one is of a certain age, as I am, it is conventionally thought that with the Great War things began to go badly wrong. Until then, smart people, most Christian thinkers included, believed in the inevitability of progress. The world and they in the world were getting better every day in every way. Then came the guns of August 1914, and it was announced that the lights were going out all over the world. It was really one long war, some historians contend, stretching from 1914 to 1945, or even to the collapse of the Soviet Union in 1991, with only a brief and troubled interlude of phony peace from 1918 to 1939. This presumably enlightened century has loosed more rivers of blood and piled up more mountains of corpses than any century in history. The victims of Stalin and Hitler—and of Mao, who killed more than both combined—are calculated to be somewhere around 200 million, give or take 10 or 20 million. We lost count along the way. And, of course, the victors do not usually count at all the firestorms, both atomic and "conventional," of Hamburg and Dresden and Nagasaki and Hiroshima. Yet our nights are not torn by the scream, *Eli, Eli, lama sabachthani?*

For all too many, there was no God against whom to lodge a protest. The melancholy, long, withdrawing roar had been roaring for a very long time and was by now nearly inaudible. Or maybe the roar had become what sound engineers call "white noise," blocking out what we do not want to hear. For other and presumably bolder souls, it was a matter of the titanic decision that God is dead. There was no point in sending a protest to that address, nor was there guilt over what our crimes had done to God. What was to be done about God was that nothing is to be done. God became a nonquestion. Surviving long enough to peep over the edge of the century, Nietzsche in his mad delirium saw more clearly than many others that God could not simply become a nonquestion. A decision must be made.

Nietzsche treated with contempt the pitiable "Last Man" who, accepting the news that God is dead, goes on as though ideas such as truth and falsehood, right and wrong, good and evil still make sense.

Our world is filled with pitiable Last Men and Last Women, as well as debonair nihilists. It is not necessary to call oneself a nihilist or even an atheist. Relatively few, in fact, adopt those labels. The attitude is one of practical atheism and assumed nihilism; it is not so much thought about or even explicitly stated. Of course we live in a meaningless world that came into existence by accident and will go out by accident, and yet, like the Last Man, we insist that our lives have meaning. And they do, we insist, because we say that they do. This is a disposition, a way of being in the world, that is immune to the drama of the cross.

Long before Arnold's sea of faith began its withdrawal and long before Nietzsche, Christians contemplated what it means that God has died. Imagine the worst. The worst that could possibly happen has already happened. Far beyond plague or nuclear annihilation or the withering of the last flower or the death of the last child—it happened a certain Friday afternoon outside the walls of Jerusalem. There we turned on the One who embodied all the light, all the love and all the hope that ever was or ever will be. This is what we did to God. In the unflinching realism of Christian faith, there is nothing to be done about it, there is no undoing of it; there is only the possibility of forgiveness.

In Joseph Conrad's "Heart of Darkness," Kurtz, a slaver who has spent his days trafficking in human misery, cries out as he dies, "The horror! The horror!" We, too, have looked into the heart of darkness and seen the horror. To be sure, at the heart of darkness there is also hope, because the worst word is not the last word. But once again we are tempted to rush to Easter. Stay a while by the cross. True knowledge of ourselves and knowledge of the world leading to the empathy that opens the way to intercessory prayer require that we attend to the scream that goes on and on, *Eli, Eli, lama sabachthani?*

The following story is told by several survivors, and I expect it happened. In a Nazi concentration camp—Dachau, if I remember rightly—there was an escape attempt, and the guards picked out twelve young men to hang as an act of retaliation and a warning to the others. The whole camp was assembled around the gallows to witness the event, and there was a deathly silence until a voice came from somewhere in the crowd, "Where now is your God?" A pause, and then a voice answering, "There, there on the gallows, there is our God." There on the cross is our God.

In the contemporary world, the Holocaust is the only culturally available icon of absolute evil. It is the only thing on which everyone, or almost everyone, agrees. Unlike Stalin or Mao, Hitler has no apologists in respectable circles. So the Holocaust has become the icon of the worst that could happen. As some tell the story, this has been the century of the Holocaust. It is the century of the cross, with the Holocaust representing the cross. But, of course, it is a cross without Christ, which makes all the difference. The cross is not simply the horror and the tragedy and the pity of it all. It is the death of this specific man, who is God and who therefore undergoes in his death every death. *Eli, Eli, lama sabachthani?* Here God cries out to God.

All the while they mocked him. "You who would destroy the temple and build it in three days, save yourself by coming down from the cross!" "He saved others, but he cannot save himself." "Let God deliver him if he cares for him for he said, 'I am the Son of God.'" With slight variation, all four Gospels report a threefold mockery. In this story, things happen in threes. In Gethsemane Jesus prays three times and three times comes back to find the disciples sleeping. Peter denies him three times. The three mockeries at the end of Jesus' life match the three temptations by Satan at the beginning of his ministry. Satan prefaced his temptations with, "If you are the Son of God . . ." And so the echo at the cross: "if you are the Son of God." Satan is there at the cross. Is it possible that he is winning after all?

The past is returning with a vengeance. Mary had whispered to the baby, "You will be great, and will be called the Son of the Most High, and of your kingdom there will be no end." Now in his death struggle the words of Mary and the angel, almost word for word, are thrown back at him, spittle-sprayed with derision. In Matthew's account, the connection between the three temptations and the three mockeries are especially clear. Back then in the wilderness he could have met Satan's challenges. He could have changed the stones into bread; he could have jumped safely from the pinnacle of the temple; he could have held political sway over the world. And so now he could have met the challenge of those who mocked; he could come down from the cross and silence those who are ridiculing his claim to be the Son of God. But had he done so in the wilderness, and if he does so now on Golgotha, he would not be who he claims to be; he would not be the Son living out in perfect obedience the Father's will. Only as he remains on the cross to the death does Jesus prove that he is indeed the Son of God.

It is called the passion narrative, and we are reminded that the word "passion" is from the Latin, meaning "to suffer." In a time when "passion" is associated with heavy-breathing romance and the selling of perfumes, we are caught up short by the reminder that to love is to suffer and the suffering is not always sweet. In real love, the stakes are high; it is risking all. Before the beloved, in the presence of God, Jesus is exposed in the full extremity of his loss. Throughout the story, Psalm 22 keeps intruding. More precisely, Psalm 22 is being played out on Golgotha.

> But I am a worm, and no man;
>   scorned by men, and despised by the people.
> All who see me mock at me,
>   they make mouths at me, they wag their heads;
> "He committed his cause to the Lord; let him deliver him,
>   let him rescue him, for he delights in him."

Where now are all his fine sayings about being one with the Father? Where now that grand tranquillity that comes from knowing that the heavenly Father cares for every sparrow that falls and numbers every hair on our heads? Son of God indeed! Some God. Some Son.

"My God, my God, why have you forsaken me?" Always before Jesus has addressed God as "Father." When speaking to

God or about God, it was with great familiarity. "All things have been given over to me by my Father," Jesus told the disciples. "No one knows the Son except the Father, and no one knows the Father except the Son and any to whom the Son chooses to reveal him." Those to whom he had revealed him he taught to pray, "Our Father in heaven." In Gethsemane he had prayed, "My Father, if it be possible, let this cup pass from me; nevertheless, not as I will, but as you will." Three times he prayed that, and there was no answer, unless this seemingly endless agony on the cross is the answer. Now, having drunk the dregs of the cup, he cries out as mortals beyond number have cried out in their agony—not to a familiar or to a beloved, not to "Father," but to "God" out there somewhere, radically "other," radically indifferent.

But note that even the apparently absent God is still "My God, *my* God." He was mine before—may he not be again? Recall, too, that Psalm 22 does not end on the note of desolation. There is this at verse 24:

> *For he has not despised or abhorred*
> *the affliction of the afflicted;*
> *and he has not hid his face from him,*
> *but has heard, when he cried to him.*

And then the conclusion:

> *Posterity shall serve him;*
> *men shall tell of the Lord to the coming generation,*
> *and proclaim his deliverance to a people yet unborn,*
> *that he has wrought it.*

He has wrought it. God has done it. It will become evident in retrospect that even in the hour of darkness and death he was doing it. But that was not evident at the time. Far from it. Here and elsewhere, the evangelists do not give us a psychological portrait; they do not, in the manner of a modern novelist, tell us what Jesus was thinking and feeling. The Gospel accounts, especially Mark and Matthew, are disciplined, astringent, almost minimalistic. This happened and then that happened and then something else happened. Vast spaces are left to be filled in by our imagination. In a sympathetic and imaginative reading of the passion narrative, we are invited to enter into the sufferings of Christ.

Did Jesus, at the moment he cried out, really think that God had abandoned him? If we answer yes to that question, we would seem to be denying his divinity. In Mark's Gospel, the cry of dereliction is immediately followed by an affirmation: "And when the centurion, who stood facing him, saw that he thus breathed his last, he said, 'Truly this man was the Son of God!'" How could the one who is, also in his dying, true God and true man be abandoned by God? The very idea would seem to split apart the two natures of the one who is Jesus Christ. Such are the questions that tangle our minds as we try to enter into this moment on the cross. These and greater difficulties are to be expected when we reflect on the apparently impossible proposition that on a certain Friday afternoon God died.

In the cry of dereliction it is sometimes said that Jesus despaired. Despair is the grave sin of ceasing to hope for salvation, or for God's help in attaining salvation, or for the forgiveness of sins. The claim that Jesus despaired on the cross flies in the face of the New Testament assertion that he committed no sin. And obviously he could not despair of the forgiveness of sins if he had no sins to be forgiven. One who cries out, "My God, my God"—although he be crying to a God experienced as absent—has not lost hope. The eminent scholar Raymond Brown writes that "Jesus is portrayed as profoundly discouraged at the end of his long battle." The phrase "profoundly discouraged" seems to fall somewhat short of the drama before us. The drama is about dereliction, abandonment, forsakenness. It is about God dying.

It is true, as we have seen, that Psalm 22 ends on a note of triumph. It is also true that Mark, who gives the starkest account of the dying, ends with a pagan acknowledging that this was the Son of God. Luke tempers the starkness of the horror with Jesus' word to the thief, that today he would be in paradise, and with the final prayer, "Father, into your hands I commend my spirit." And in John's Gospel the way of the cross is a veritable victory march of the one who had earlier said, "I am never alone because the Father is with me. . . . In the world you have tribulation; but be of good cheer, I have overcome the world." The final word in John, "It is finished," suggests the glory of completion.

Father Brown writes that, in John's passion narrative, Jesus is "in control" every step of the way, that he "was orchestrating the passion as part of laying down his own life." Surely that is saying too much. There is no hint of playacting here. To be sure, John puts more emphasis on the self-consciousness and serenity of Jesus in the unfolding of this way of strangest glory. True, John does not have Jesus praying in Gethsemane that the cup pass from him. Rather, John has Jesus rebuking Peter, who had drawn the sword of resistance against those who came to arrest him, with the words, "Shall I not drink the cup which the Father has given me?" This is not orchestrating events, however; it is relentless obedience, step by inexorable step, to the Father's will.

The glory was in the obedience. Jesus' awareness that all this had been foreordained does not diminish the horror that attends the glory. To Pilate he declares, "You say that I am a king. For this I was born, and for this I have come into the world, to bear witness to the truth. Every one who is of the truth hears my voice." I submit we should not read this as though Jesus were delivering a homily. There is no hint of bravado here. He has been arrested, humiliated, struck on the face, shuttled around from one hate-filled crowd to another, and now he sees the agony and death looming before him. "For this I was born, and for this I have come into the world . . ." Hear him say it through clenched teeth, perspiring, almost in a whisper.

He does not miss the mockery in Pilate's question, "So you are a king?" He sees arrayed against him all the evidence that proclaims the preposterousness of such a claim. *Nonetheless* "For this I was born, and for this I have come into the world . . ." There is no going back now. The man Jesus is not in charge. The Father is in charge. The four Gospels must be read together. John's accent on the glory lifts up the great "nonetheless" by which the victory is anticipated in the perfect surrender, by which the perfect surrender *is* the victory. It does not preclude the derelict screaming from the cross, "My God, my God, why have you forsaken me?" The surrender is precisely to the unqualified loss of control that is death. That loss is not qualified even by the certainty of knowing what is happening.

Such knowledge may be understood as a kind of control. Jesus knew that he had been obedient, step by inexorable step. And now he had taken the final step. "It is finished."

There are strict limits to our knowing the mind of Jesus on the cross. In *com-passion* we suffer with him in his passion. We know what we think and we feel, and we know what we imagine he thought and he felt, but we have no psychological profile of Jesus. On the questions we moderns call psychological, the Gospel narratives are strikingly reticent. Whether that is intended to discourage or to invite our ventures of imagination, people disagree. I am inclined to side with St. Ignatius of Loyola and other spiritual guides who lead us into the exercise of neglected capacities for empathetic participation in the events of our redemption. But what we can know for sure is limited by the biblical texts, as it is also limited by our ability to really know what others are thinking or experiencing, no matter how close we are to them. The limitations are many times magnified when the person in question is utterly unique, being both God and man.

But the accent on his utter uniqueness can also miscarry, not only and not mainly because it limits our sympathizing with Jesus, but because it limits his sympathizing with us. The Letter to the Hebrews assures us, "For we have not a high priest who is unable to sympathize with our weaknesses, but one who in every respect has been tempted as we are, yet without sinning." Recall again St. Paul's astonishing assertion, "For our sake he made him to be sin who knew no sin, so that in him we might become the righteousness of God." He knew no sin, but he knew the consequence of sin. He died. "Yes, of course he died," many

Christians might respond. But there is no "of course" about it. The bitter, brutal agony of his dying is the wrenching reality at the center of the Christian narrative of salvation.

The passion narrative is not simply a playing out of a script that begins with the catechism statement that "Jesus died for our sins." His dying is not just a necessary preliminary to the good news of the resurrection. The cross is not just what happened to him—it is who he is. "We preach Christ crucified," Paul declares. The God whom we worship is a crucified God. The downplaying of the death of Christ in Christian preaching and piety is a close cousin to the denial of his death. And the denial of his death is a close cousin to the denial of our own death.

Already in the first Christian centuries, the Gnostics and others denied that Christ had really died. It is said with considerable justice that modern-day gnosticism is the natural religion of Americans, including American Christians. Some years ago we began to hear about "New Age" spirituality, but it is hardly anything new. Feel-good religion and spiritual pills to elevate our consciousness and enhance our sense of comfort with our presumably "real" selves—these are American specialties of long-standing. Many years ago the Yale theologian H. Richard Niebuhr, criticizing Protestant preaching and piety, captured the spirit of this optimistic gnosticism: "A God without wrath brought men without sin into a kingdom without judgment through the ministrations of a Christ without a cross."

With hyperbole and a generous dose of contempt for the American ethos, the brilliantly outlandish literary critic Harold Bloom describes gnosticism as "the American religion":

Freedom, in the context of the American Religion, means being alone with God or with Jesus, the American God or the American Christ. In social reality, this translates as solitude, at least in the inmost sense. The soul stands apart, and something deeper than the soul, the Real Me or self or spark, thus is made free to be utterly alone with a God who is also quite separate and solitary, that is, a free God or God of freedom. What makes it possible for the self and God to commune so freely is that the self already is of God; unlike body and even soul, the American self is no part of the Creation. . . . The American self is not the Adam of Genesis but is a more primordial Adam, a Man before there were men or women. . . . Whatever the social and political consequences of this vision, its imaginative strength is extraordinary. . . . The American Religion is pervasive and overwhelming, however it is masked, and even our secularists, indeed even our professed atheists, are more Gnostic than humanist in their ultimate presuppositions. We are a religiously mad culture, furiously searching for the spirit, but each of us is subject and object of the one quest, which must be for the original self, a spark or breath in us that we are convinced goes back to before the Creation.

Bloom, it should be noted, approves, or at least half approves, of the American religion of Gnosticism. He has always been enamored of the Transcendentalist poets, especially Emerson and Whitman, and there is hardly a line more in that tradition than Emerson's assertion that "it is by yourself *without ambassador* that God speaks to you. . . . It is God in you that responds to God without." This lofty sense of being spiritually untouched and untouchable by the grubby stuff of what lesser minds call the real world is evident in Emerson's "Good-bye": "Good-bye, proud world! I'm going home; / Thou art not my friend, and I'm not thine." The gnostic is no part of a world in which crucifixions happen. Certainly the divinity of which gnostics believe they are the eternal emanation cannot be crucified.

Versions of the story in which Jesus was not really killed appeared very early and are remarkably enduring. Raymond Brown observes that people who have never bothered to study the New Testament Gospels "are fascinated by the report of some 'new insight' to the effect he was not crucified or did not die, especially if his subsequent career involved running off with Mary Magdalene to India." According to Irenaeus, already in the first century there was a Gnostic tale in circulation that Simon of Cyrene, the fellow who was compelled to help Jesus carry the cross, was the one who ended up on it. Another Gnostic story was that Jesus had a twin brother who was crucified. Others said Jesus' body was crucified while the real Jesus, being purely spiritual, was untouched. And so the variations on this theme multiplied.

The Qur'an also denies that Jesus was crucified, claiming that it was a double or a counterfeit who died on the cross. Devout Muslims claim that Muhammad received that intelligence directly from God. Various plots and conspiracy theories have been promoted under diverse auspices. In some of them Jesus takes a potion in order to feign death, while in others Jesus connives with Judas Iscariot in what amounts to a grand publicity stunt. Still being read today is H. J. Schonfield's *The Passover Plot*, which, in the name of the "latest scholarship," advances that thesis. (According to Schonfield, the stunt backfired, because Jesus later died of the spear wound received on the cross.)

I do not suggest for a moment that most Christians indulge in these fantastical stories that literally deny the death of Jesus. But there are many ways of denying his death, and ours. The gnostic impulse is still very much with us. We draw back from looking long and hard into the heart of darkness; we recoil from the brute facticity of the horror; we are scandalized by the truth that we worship a crucified God. As well we should be.

The core of the gnostic impulse is the belief that we are not really part of the creation, that we are not really creatures. Put differently, it is the refusal to accept the fact that we are not God. Remember the original temptation in the garden, how it came with the promise, "You will be like God." So what is wrong with that? someone might respond. Isn't that precisely our human calling and destiny, to be like God? After all, the "beatific vision" is perfect communion with God, which is the full restoration of the "image and likeness of God" in which we human beings are created. Yes, but the quintessence of original sin, as it is also reflected in gnosticism, is the desire to be like God *on our own terms*. It is to deny our status as creatures and assume that we can be like God by nature rather than by the gift of divine grace.

God's identification with us in Christ is most dramatically acted out on the cross where a creature dies, as all we creatures will surely die. Note that in everyday language the word "creature" is hardly ever used today except negatively. Horror movies have creatures from the deep, and we speak of bothersome insects as creatures, but most people would not call their pet dog a creature, never mind their best friend. This is a triumph of gnosticism in our popular culture. It is the most elementary fact about what and who we are—creatures. We are not the Creator; we are not God. Balthasar writes:

> This not-being-God of the creature must be maintained as the most fundamental fact of all. That God is God: this is the most immense and absolutely *unsurpassable* thought. It says to me (if it has really struck home to me in the deepest part of my being), with an absolute evidence that can never be gainsaid, that I myself, to the very marrow of my existence, *am not God*.

"God became man." "The Word became flesh." "Incarnation." The words are so familiar to Christians that we become dulled to the astonishing thing they say. The cross shocks and scandalizes and reastonishes, and never more so than in the cry of dereliction, "My God, my God, why have you forsaken me?" Here is opened up the unfathomable distance between creature and Creator. We spoke earlier about the necessity of our speaking about God by analogy. Speaking by analogy, by comparison, can mislead us into thinking there is a smooth correspondence between realities divine and human. But analogy does not mean that there is a neat balance between similarities and dissimilarities, that we can gain an approximate and more or less satisfactory understanding of God by reference to our own experience. No, wherever there is similarity, we discover that the dissimilarity is infinitely greater.

It is necessary to drive this truth home, and to do so again and again, if we are ever to begin to comprehend the astonishment that our salvation is by grace alone. Here is where our own religiosity and so much that today is called "spirituality" can so fatally betray us. Our gnostic consciousness-raising flights, our attunement to "the inner child," our following of our bliss, our pious sensations of at-one-ness with the All—these are soaring escapes from our creatureliness. We are not little sparks of the Divine who have by some cosmic mishap fallen into the mud and matter of creation. We are the very stuff of creation. *We are not God.*

As with the creature on the cross, we cry out to God. In the act of perfect obedience to God is this experienced distance from God. The great mystics of the Christian tradition understood this well, painfully well. The nearer we come to God, the more we become "similar" to him, the more we are astonished by the infinite dissimilarity. The more we know him, the less we know him. Those who toy with the sundry "spiritualities" offered in the religious marketplace know nothing of this. But the authentic mystics who have surrendered themselves to the quest for God tell us that, if the light grows in "arithmetic" progression, at the same time the darkness grows in "geometric" progression. And so we read: "At the sixth hour darkness came over the whole earth until the ninth hour. And at the ninth hour Jesus screamed with a loud cry, *Eli, Eli, lama sabachthani?*"

His hour has come, he has drunk the dregs of the cup that had been given him and the entirety of his mission reaches its crescendo in the cry of dereliction. Far from being in control, he has without remainder surrendered control to the Father. He does not even presume to call him Father. Absolutely

everything, including the judgment of what he has done, is out
of his hands. Everything is in God's hands. Jesus makes no claims
whatever. There is here no contradiction in the Gospel
accounts. It is true that only Mark and Matthew report the cry
of dereliction, but the final words in Luke and John are perfectly
consonant with the radicality of Jesus' surrender. In Luke,
"Father, into your hands I place my spirit." In John, "It is
finished." Reading the Gospel accounts together, it becomes
clear that the secret of the cry of dereliction is that the
abandonment by God is the abandonment to God. Had it not
gone to this extremity, it would not truly have been finished.

It was necessary that it be this way. How else could he have
borne the totality of the world's sin? He had to bear all that the
world did to him, and all the consequences of all the crimes of
all time, of which what we did to him is the chief. John's Gospel,
far from being simply a majestic progression from glory to glory,
right at the beginning introduces us to John the Baptizer, who
declares of Jesus, "Behold, the Lamb of God, who takes away the
sin of the world!" The evangelist has already prepared us for this:
"He was in the world, and the world was made through him, yet
the world knew him not." In the beginning was the way of the
cross.

It had to be this way. How else could it be, as Paul says, that
God "made him to be sin who knew no sin"? Or again, writing
to the Galatians, Paul declares, "Christ redeemed us from the
curse of the law, having become a curse for us—for it is written,
'Cursed be every one who hangs on a tree.'" Not only is Jesus
fully a creature, he is a creature cursed. He is cursed by men,
certainly, and he looks to God to counter their curse, but there

is only silence. There is not at Golgotha—as there was at his baptism, as there was on the mount of transfiguration—a voice from heaven saying, "This is my beloved Son in whom I am well pleased." At Golgotha, heaven is silent. The reports of his dying include the darkness, the rending of the temple veil and the dead rising from their graves. These apocalyptic signs can be read as vindication of him and his cause, or simply as further evidence of a world wrenched out of order by the catastrophe of this day. The important thing, the devastating thing, is that there is no answer from the One to whom he calls out in the darkness. "My God, my God, why have you forsaken me?" *There is no answer.*

I do not think the twelve-year-old boy meant any disrespect, but I confess it took me off guard. This was many years ago when I was teaching a confirmation class at a black parish in Brooklyn where I was for many years the pastor. I was discussing how, in his dying for us, Jesus had lost everything. "I don't say it wasn't real bad," said Michael, "but he did what he wanted to do, didn't he?"

Of course Michael had never read Philip Rieff's brilliant analysis of American culture, *The Therapeutic Society*. But he had, willy-nilly, imbibed its message that in our kind of world everything is reduced to the psychological. Put so bluntly, it sounds blasphemous and, pressed persistently, it is blasphemous, but wasn't Jesus "doing his own thing"? So where is the sacrifice? So where is the abandonment? Is it not rather the case that the Sixth Word from the cross—"It is finished"—is a statement of what in pop psychology is called self-actualization?

Michael was no child prodigy. He simply breathed, as all of

us do, the toxic cultural air of a disenchanted world in which the mark of sophistication is to reduce wonder to banality. Even more, the acids of intellectual urbanity turn sacrifice into delusion, generosity into greed, and love into self-aggrandizement. In academic circles, this is called "the hermeneutics of suspicion," meaning that things are interpreted to reveal that they are not in fact what they appear to be. At least things that seem to suggest the true, the beautiful and the good are not what they appear to be. They must be exposed and debunked if we are to get to "the truth of the matter." The false, the self-serving, the ugly and the evil, on the other hand, are permitted to stand as revealing "the real world."

To see how this works out, one has only to visit an avant-garde art exhibit of smeared feces or depictions of sadomasochistic sex. Art depicting the tenderness of a mother with her child, the heroism of a soldier in battle or the poignancy of an old woman striving to maintain her dignity in her decrepitude—all such are despised as sentimental delusion. Most notorious in recent years was the much celebrated and government-funded exhibition of a crucifix immersed in a bottle of urine. To exhibit a crucifix alone, no matter how art-fully done, would be embarrassingly plebeian. Reverence is vulgar; irreverence is chic. This way of thinking and acting has been around for a very long time in the world we call modern. As someone has observed, everything changes except the avant-garde.

Our subject, however, is not cultural criticism, but self-sacrifice and love untold. The hermeneutics of suspicion, which is suspicious of everything but itself, turns truth into falsehood, good into evil and beauty into the repugnant. It at least has the merit, however perverse, of exploring the extremities, and its accent on what is base can, in reaction, recall us to the elevated. Michael's innocent question, on the other hand, reflects a more insidious mind-set in which everything is flattened out and deprived of moral significance. The psychologized worldview of the therapeutic society does not turn good into evil but eliminates the difference between good and evil. All is reduced to needs, satisfactions and self-fulfillment.

Another word for it is radical subjectivism. One person jumps into the river to save the drowning child, another watches on the bank as the child drowns. One is a gestapo officer killing Jews and gypsies, the other risks his life to save them from death. Each does "his own thing," and who is to judge? The person who pursues the course we call noble receives satisfactions the same as the person who pursues the course we call base. So where is the merit in doing the right thing? Indeed, who is to say what is the right thing? "Follow your bliss," said mythologist Joseph Campbell, holding large audiences in thrall to his supposed wisdom. Many cite Shakespeare: "This above all: to thine own self be true, And it must follow, as the night the day, Thou canst not then be false to any man." But they forget, or never knew, that Shakespeare intended Polonius as the fatuous fool of Hamlet's tragedy.

There is a sense in which we can say that Jesus was being true to himself in going to the cross. We might even say that he was true to himself in the abandonment of self to the experience of being abandoned by God. After all, he did say that it was for this reason he was born and came into the world. But here we are using the word "true" in a quite different way. It is not the truth of psychological disposition or need. Again, unlike a modern novel or biography, the Gospel accounts say almost nothing about what we would call the "psychology" of Jesus. That is to say, there is no analysis of his mental or behavioral characteristics, no attempt to explain why he thought or did this or that. We are told simply that he spoke, he slept, he wept, he felt sympathy, he loved, he died.

Yet we think we know who he was and who he is. Many would claim to know Jesus better, more intimately, than any other person they have ever encountered, although we would not presume to have a "psychological profile" of the man. We know him because we share the truth about him. He was true to himself because he lived out the intention of his life, which is the intention of the life of those who would follow him. The intention of his life, and of ours, is not a subjective thing made up of what we intend. It is the intention that belongs to a life, that forms a life, that gives a life meaning. It is a given; it is objective. All of us can look back upon our lives, trying to "step out" of our lives for a moment, and ask, What does this life intend? That does not mean simply what did I intend at this moment or that, but what the overall intention or direction of my life is.

The word "direction" catches better the objective character of the question. The Greeks spoke of the *telos* of a thing—the *telos* of a life, an action or a story. The *telos* is the ultimate end that gives meaning to the thing in question. Recall Philosophy 101 and the "four causes" of Aristotle: the *final cause*, that is, the "why" or ultimate end of something; the *efficient cause*, that is, the action that brings about the effect; the *material cause*, that is, the thing affected; and the *formal cause*, which gives the whole its particular shape.

How did we get from Michael's question in catechism class to Aristotle on causes? The question was, Didn't Jesus do what he wanted to do? And if that is the case, it follows that he did nothing more noble than anyone else who does what he or she wants to do. The alternative to this way of thinking is hard to grasp—hard for Michael, and hard for all of us who have been deeply influenced by the psychologizing and subjectivizing of human action. The *cause* of my life, the *intention* of my life, the *telos* of my life is not determined by what I want to do. Put differently, who I am is a truth to be discerned, not a choice to be decided. What I want and what I choose may be in conflict with who I am, with who I *really* am.

We are rightly impatient with people who persistently act in a disagreeable way and then say, "But that isn't the real me." We are inclined to tell them to stop fooling themselves, and that is the correct response in many cases. At the same time, however, each of us knows the experience of acting in a way that is not true to who we are. But maybe we are fooling ourselves when we say that what we do is not who we are. Maybe it is the case that what we do *is* who we are. In that case, the person we say we really are is no more than the person we *wish* we were. This is the way of thinking of the psychologically astute, and there is no end of clinical names for such patterns of wishful self-deception.

Yet we have a deep intuitive resistance to the claim that on the cross Jesus did no more than he wanted to do. Were that true, it would make a muddle of what Paul says in Philippians about the *kenosis*—how Christ "emptied himself, taking the form of a slave, being born in the likeness of men." But what if, far from emptying himself, he was full of himself in fulfilling himself? In that event, there is no self-denial, no self-sacrifice, no transcendence of the self. The question is whether the self is an objective truth to be discovered or a subjective choice determined by the self.

St. Paul wrestles with the question in Romans: "For I do not do the good I want, but the evil I do not want is what I do. Now if I do what I do not want, it is no longer I that do it, but sin which dwells within me." Ah, we may think, Paul is taking an easy out. How convenient to excuse oneself by blaming "sin." Isn't this but another version of "the Devil made me do it"? But listen as Paul continues: "For I delight in the law of God, in my inmost self, but I see in my members another law at war with the law of my mind and making me captive to the law of sin which dwells in my members. Wretched man that I am! Who will deliver me from this body of death? Thanks be to God through Jesus Christ our Lord! So then, I of myself serve the law of God with my mind, but with my flesh I serve the law of sin."

This passage from Romans is notoriously dualistic. I say "notoriously," because dualism is today a dirty word in the view of many people. Consult those hundreds of books under the category of "spirituality" in your local bookstore and you will discover the preferred language is all about wholeness, unity, coherence, harmony, synchronicity and the good feelings of being "at one with the All." By way of sharpest contrast, Paul speaks of the Christian life in terms of conflict, tension, antagonism and jarring dissonance. It is the same Paul, however, who declares in Galatians: "I have been crucified with Christ; it is no longer I who live, but Christ who lives in me; and the life I now live in the flesh I live by faith in the Son of God, who loved me and gave himself for me."

Remember the dictum of Alfred North Whitehead: The only simplicity to be trusted is the simplicity on the far side of complexity. So it is that the only definition of the self to be trusted is the self that is on the far side of being crucified. Paul could have found an easier simplicity on the near side of complexity. He could have, as many of us do, simply denied the reality of that in himself which was at war with the good that he would serve. Or he could have said, along with all the gnostics of his time and ours, that the evil he did was no part of him. The *real* Paul, he might have said, is a spark of the divine creation untouched by the countercreation of the demiurges and their unruly passions.

But no, Paul says: "So then, *I* of myself serve the law of God with my mind, but with my flesh *I* serve the law of sin." In both cases, the "I" is not denied. The "I of myself" is no less "I" than the "I of my flesh." Note that the word "flesh" here refers not just to the physical body but to everything that is contrary to his true self. And who is this true self? The "I" of the mind and the "I" of the flesh are both the "I" of Paul. There is no deliverance from the intolerable contradiction of this conflicted "I" unless there is another "I." Which brings us back to Galatians. There is another "I": "It is no longer I who live, but Christ who lives in me."

The complexity on the far side of which such simplicity is

found might be described as the transposition of the ego. In more familiar but no less profound language, it is being "born again." Thus the New Testament depicts the radicality of conversion as dying with Christ in order that a new self might rise with him. Baptism is not just a dipping or a dunking, but a drowning all the way to death. On the far side of the drowning is the self pure and simple. Everything that challenges and contradicts this new self "in Christ" has not disappeared, not yet, although one day it will all be transformed. Nor does the Christ who lives in us destroy the "us" in whom he lives. We do not lose our identities in a great tapioca pudding of homogeneity. There is Paul in Christ, and Carol in Christ, and Jody in Christ and Jayne in Christ, and all together *are* Christ in a literal sense that we are invited to believe is the Body of Christ, the Church.

But we are getting ahead of ourselves. We return to young Michael's innocent question about the crucifixion: "I don't say it wasn't real bad, but he did what he wanted to do, didn't he?" Wasn't he simply doing his own thing? Or, as Polonius would have it, wasn't he being true to himself? In one sense, we must say yes. What he did is who he was, but who he was was not determined by what he did. Who he was, and who he is, was and is determined by what was objectively given. Call it his *telos*, his final cause, his ultimate end, his "hour" or his destiny. His destiny is his very being. He was and is the Son of God. He was the Son of God before he was born of Mary, walked by the Lake of Galilee or set his face toward Jerusalem and the cross. This is what the Son of God does. Precisely as the Son of God, he is abandoned by God.

He is abandoned by God and abandons himself to God. We

are told that he was like us in every respect, except he was without sin. In the sweated prayer of the garden of Gethsemane, and perhaps at other times in his earthly life, he agonized over the will of God. It was not the agony of the conflicted self resisting the will of God, but the agony of the abandoned self seeking to discern the will of God. Because his will and the will of the Father were perfectly at one, young Michael is not alone in thinking that the drama and the merit are somehow diminished. After all, he did what he wanted to do, didn't he? The way of popular religious "spiritualities" is a gnostic escape from the conflicted self; the way of our radically subjectivized art and entertainment culture, whether high or low, is the idolatry of the conflicted self.

At the juvenile level of popular culture, Jesus might be more admired had he defied the will of the Father. One can readily imagine the herd of independent minds cheering his defiant, "I want to be free to be ME!" To the more mature, he might seem to be a greater hero had his final surrender to his destiny been preceded by a titanic struggle against that destiny. Why do so many think the glory of the cross is diminished because Jesus' will and the will of the Father were perfectly one? I expect it is for the same reason that, as we discussed earlier, many people say that the original fall into sin was a fall upward rather than downward. Modern consciousness has no higher interest than itself. In the history of ideas this is sometimes called the "turn to the subject" and is usually associated with Immanuel Kant. The therapeutic society—the reading of reality through the prism of our subjectivity—may be understood as bargain-basement (and deeply distorted) Kantianism.

But we need not be delayed by philosophical history. The evidence of everyday experience—of our conversations, our novels, our movies, our social criticism—is overwhelming. Attention is fixated on interests, motives, ambiguities and hidden designs of the conflicted self. This has everything to do with the driving force behind the hermeneutics of suspicion. The unconflicted self is boring. Jesus is boring. It might be objected that this preoccupation with the conflicted self is nothing new, and there is truth in that. Greek drama, for example, is preoccupied with the interests, ambiguities and conflicts (both tragic and comic) of its characters, all reflecting the same interests, ambiguities and conflicts of the many gods. To note the parallel with our own time is simply to note the degree to which our culture is shaped by pagan rather than biblical sensibilities.

The alternative to the idolatry of the conflicted self presupposes that we human beings are not the most important, nor the most interesting, beings in the universe. And that, of course, presupposes that we are not alone. There is also, quite simply, God. The final truth about a life is the final cause—the *why*—of a life. A life is measured by its *telos*. The question of how a person lived is important, but the *how* is subordinate to *for what* a person lived. "For where your treasure is, there will your heart be also." The great commandment, said Jesus, is this: "Hear, O Israel: The Lord our God, the Lord is one; and you shall love the Lord your God with all your heart, and with all your soul, and with all your mind, and with all your strength."

The repeated statement that he who loses his life will find his life is not a neat psychological formula for finding my true self. Only when I give up on the search for myself in abandonment to another—to the Other—is my "I" reconstituted by the "I" to whom I surrender. The endless rummaging through memories, the poking about in the cluttered attic of self-consciousness, the removing of layer after layer of worn-out "identities"—none of this can produce the authentic self. The truth of the self is in the *telos* of the self.

It may be objected that this does not resolve the problem, because we can never know whether we have truly surrendered ourselves to the *telos*, whether, in fact, we really love the Lord our God as we should. But the very objection indicates that we have missed the point. The objection throws us back on our own self-consciousness, rummaging through our motives to determine whether we have what Kierkegaard called the purity of heart that wills one thing. That is the opposite of the abandonment to the *telos* reflected in Paul's statement to the Corinthians: "But with me it is a very small thing that I should be judged by you or by any human court. I do not even judge myself. . . . It is the Lord who judges me." To abandon myself is to abandon judging myself.

"My God, my God, why have you forsaken me?" Apparently the judgment, the only judgment that matters, has gone against him. He does not, in order to save his self, appeal to another judgment. Obviously, he would not appeal to the judgment of the crowd that declared him a failure and a fake. In view of what appeared to be the adverse judgment of God, he might have substituted his own judgment of his life. He could have made a convincing and self-consoling case for his purity of heart, for his having willed one thing, for his having seen the thing through to its end. But he did not. He left the judgment with God; his abandonment of self was uncompromised even under the ultimate test of being abandoned by the One to whom he appealed.

A psychologized culture sated by suspicion resists the claim, but human beings are capable of this. This is why the Church so persistently holds up the example of the martyrs. The word "martyr," of course, means "witness," and witness, like an arrow, is directed to the Other. The martyrs are frequently depicted as going bravely, defiantly, even insouciantly, to their deaths. But it seems likely that many were gripped by the unspeakable thought that they had made a terrible mistake, that their motives were not pure, that their witness was egoistic grandstanding, that, in Eliot's fine phrase, they had committed the greater treason by doing the right thing for the wrong reason. Worst of all, many may have been shaken by the suspicion that they had been abandoned by the One to whom they abandoned themselves. If there was insouciance, I expect it was often insouciance on the far side of such infinitely complex uncertainty.

Yet human beings are capable of so giving themselves. Some call it fanaticism and some call it faith, but, with Paul, the martyrs deem it "a very small thing" what some call it. They live and die in fidelity to the *telos* by which their lives are defined. The preface in the Mass for Martyrs puts it well: "Your holy martyr followed the example of Christ, and gave his life for the glory of your name. His death reveals your power shining through our human weakness. You choose the weak and make them strong in bearing witness to you, through Jesus Christ our

Lord." It is precisely in the darkness of abandonment that God's power shines through our human weakness.

It is not a matter of doing one's own thing, of doing what one wants to do. It is doing what one must do. Put somewhat paradoxically, it is choosing to do what one has no choice but to do. "You did not choose me, but I chose you," Jesus said. Logically, I am aware that I accept my being chosen. But that awareness is pushed to the sidelines; it is experientially obliterated by the overpowering knowledge that I am chosen. The martyr is living out a truth that is not of his or her own contriving. The 1993 encyclical *Veritatis Splendor* ("The Splendor of Truth") offers a profound reflection on how this works. The call of God is a *"possibility opened up to us exclusively by grace, by the gift of God, by his love."* John Paul II goes on to say that the gift itself generates our free response. He quotes the marvelous prayer of St. Augustine, *Da quod iubes et iube quod vis*—"Give what you command and command what you will."

The martyr cannot betray the gift, even when the gift seems to be a curse. One of the earliest and best-known accounts of Christian martyrdom is that of the elderly Polycarp, bishop of Smyrna, in the second century. After his arrest, the Roman proconsul tells him, "Take the oath to Caesar and I shall release you. Curse Christ." Polycarp answers, "Eighty-six years I have served him, and he never did me any wrong. How can I blaspheme my King who saved me?" Polycarp says he cannot do what he is commanded to do. If he did it, he would no longer be Polycarp. This is not simply a matter of being true to himself. More precisely, he is true to himself only as he is true to the truth by which his self is constituted, namely, his faithfulness to

Christ. Recall St. Paul's "It is no longer I who live, but Christ who lives in me." Polycarp is saying to the proconsul, "You are asking Christ to curse Christ. It is not possible."

In *Veritatis Splendor,* John Paul notes that we cannot always do the good that we would do, but those who live against the horizon of martyrdom can always not do what is evil. To live against the horizon of martyrdom is to have internalized the words of Jesus, "What does it profit a man to gain the whole world and forfeit his own life?" The moral life entails the readiness to suffer martyrdom, even though, happily, most of us are not required to die for our witness. The encyclical cites the examples of many martyrs in the Bible and in Christian history and appeals also to the moral wisdom found in non-Christian traditions. "The words of the Latin poet Juvenal apply to all: 'Consider it the greatest of crimes to prefer survival to honor and out of love of physical life to lose the very reason for living.'"

Jesus' cry of dereliction from the cross, however, goes far beyond a sense of honor or even obedience to a truth that one cannot deny without denying oneself. Jesus understood himself to be in the line of the Old Testament prophets, and his disciples are called to stand in the same line. When you are persecuted, he said, "Rejoice and be glad, for your reward is great in heaven, for so men persecuted the prophets who were before you." And again, "O Jerusalem, Jerusalem, killing the prophets and stoning those who are sent to you! How often would I have gathered your children together as a hen gathers her brood under her wings, and you would not!" Although the cosmic drama of salvation was played out in the history of God's elect people, Israel, the judgment is in no way limited to the Jewish people. Through the Church, the light of Israel is extended to the whole world, and the light encounters the same darkness that killed the prophets, and killed Jesus.

God's chosen ones live out the drama and destiny of God himself. It is a fearful thing to be chosen. It is as though God enters history through his chosen ones. The ultimate incarnation of God in Jesus Christ is anticipated in themes that appear early on in the story of salvation. For instance, in 1 Samuel we read: "And the Lord said to Samuel, 'Hearken to the voice of the people in all that they say to you; for they have not rejected you, but they have rejected me from being king over them. According to all the deeds which they have done to me, from the day I brought them up out of Egypt even to this day, forsaking me and serving other gods, so they are also doing to you.'" What they did to Samuel they were really doing to God. In the drama of history Samuel is God's "stand in." Samuel is encountered by the "Thou" of God who becomes Samuel's "I."

This theme becomes ever more explicit as we move in time up through the prophets of Israel. The chosen are detached from themselves, from their own emotions, desires and hopes, and are called to live out the passions of God's heart—Yahweh's love, wrath, revulsion and yearning for his own. To read the prophets in this light is to recognize intimations of what John's Gospel says about the Word becoming flesh, about the light entering the darkness that rages against it, but cannot put it out. In the prophets, God humbles himself and even humiliates himself. In the prophet Hosea he marries a prostitute. Thus does Hosea experience God's loving of an unfaithful people. But thus also does God, entering history in Hosea, drink the dregs of humiliation, of betrayal, of dereliction.

Throughout these reflections, I have frequently mentioned the gnostic distortions of the Christian Gospel. Perhaps readers may think I am too insistent about the specificity—what scholars call the "historicity"—of the story of salvation. But I am persuaded that everything depends on this. Specificity is all. It is for this reason that I have turned again and again to the *Jewishness* of the Christian story. In the shadow of the Holocaust, it is both morally imperative and good manners to emphasize the linkage between Judaism and Christianity. But much more is involved than a moral imperative, and certainly much more than good manners. It simply is not possible to understand the Christian story apart from its placement in the Jewish story. We have been discussing God's radical identification of his fate with the fate of the Old Testament prophets, and in that identification we have a foretaste, an intimation, of what Christians mean by the mystery of the incarnation. That God became man is not entirely a Christian *novum*; it is not an idea that came out of nowhere.

Michael Wyschogrod is one of the most incisive Jewish theologians of our time. He notes that the crucial disagreement between Christians and Jews is over the Christian claim that Jesus is God. Some Jewish thinkers have said that claim is decisively precluded, because God is pure spirit and cannot be incarnate in space and time. Wyschogrod disagrees, noting that in the Jewish Scriptures there is no doubt that God "dwells" in space and time, for instance, in the elect people of Israel and in the temple of Solomon. "Judaism is therefore incarnational," he writes, "if by this term we mean the notion that God enters the world of humanity, that he appears at certain places and dwells in them which thereby become holy." In both Judaism and Christianity, there is a dialectic, or tension, between transcendence and immanence—between the "otherness" of God and the "here and now–ness" of God's presence. Christianity stresses the radically immanent, so much so that Jesus can say to Philip that "anyone who has seen me has seen the Father."

That possibility, writes Wyschogrod, cannot be dismissed out of hand. "If we can determine a priori that God could not appear in the form of a man or, to put it in more Docetistic terms, that there could not be a being who is both fully God and fully human, then we are substituting a philosophical scheme for the sovereignty of God." Docetism, you will recall, is the early (and enduring!) heresy that Christ's humanity is only apparent, not really real. Like other heresies, it begins by establishing a philosophical idea of God's being (or "ontology," to use the technical term) and then tries to conform the biblical story to that idea. Wyschogrod writes: "No biblically oriented responsible Jewish theology can accept such a substitution of an ontological structure for the God of Abraham, Isaac, and Jacob whose actions humanity cannot predict and whose actions are not subject to an overreaching logical necessity to which they must conform." In short, God is God. He cannot be captured in our philosophical categories.

Wyschogrod is taken with the story, which may or may not be apocryphal, that when Pope John XXIII first saw the pictures of bulldozers pushing Jewish corpses into mass graves at the newly liberated Nazi murder camps, he exclaimed: "There is the

body of Christ!" Here is Wyschogrod's reflection on that insight.
It bears close reading.

> Somehow, in some way which is perhaps still not altogether
> clear, the Church decided that in Jesus there was God, more so
> than in other people who are also created in God's image. This
> man, this Jew, this servant, this despised, crucified Jew, was not
> just human but in him could be detected the presence of God.
> The Church held fast to this belief because it held fast to this
> Jew, to his flesh and not only to his spirit, to his Jewish flesh
> on the cross, to a flesh in which God was present, incarnated,
> penetrating the world of humanity, becoming human. The
> Church found God in this Jewish flesh. Perhaps this was
> possible because God is in all Jewish flesh, because it is the
> flesh of the covenant, the flesh of a people to whom God has
> attached himself, by whose name he is known in the world as
> the God of Israel. Perhaps for some mysterious reason, the
> Church, the gathering of Gentiles drawn to the God of Israel,
> could not see this incarnation in the Jewish people but could
> see it in this one Jew who stood, without the Church realizing
> it, for his people. Perhaps the crucifixion of Jesus can only be
> understood in the context of the crucifixion of the people of
> Israel, whose physical presence challenges those who hate God
> because in this people they see the God they hate. Perhaps the
> bond between Jesus and his people is much closer than has
> been thought.

Wyschogrod concludes:

> God's covenant is with the people and when the Temple is
> destroyed, the rabbis tell us, God goes into exile together with

his people. And now, where a congregation gathers, wherever there are Jews, the *Shekhinah* (Divine Presence) gathers. Is this incarnation in a people? It is a movement in that direction. It is not identical with Christian incarnation. It is a less concentrated incarnation, an incarnation into a people spread out in time and place, with its saints and sinners, its moments of obedience and disobedience. But I do think that he who touches this people touches God, and perhaps not altogether symbolically.

This inescapably Jewish understanding of God's entanglement with real history is evident, as we have seen, in the witness of the Old Testament prophets, who are more than surrogates for God. In their life and witness, God acts and is acted upon. It achieves its complete realization in Jesus the Christ, above all in Jesus the Jewish derelict on the cross. This incarnational entanglement is necessary also to understanding the words of Jesus to Saul of Tarsus on the Damascus road, "Saul, Saul, why do you persecute me?" In touching the disciples of Jesus, Saul touches Jesus, and in touching Jesus he touches God. Similarly, in the final judgment depicted in Matthew, the nations are judged by what they did or did not do to "the least of these my brethren." "Inasmuch as you did it to the least of these, you did it to me."

And so we are brought back to "My God, my God, why have you forsaken me?" God is present in his apparent absence. God's absence is embodied in the body of Israel and in the extension of that body, the New Israel, which is the Church. God is present in the forsaken so that nobody—nobody ever, nobody anywhere at any time under any circumstance—is forsaken.

Not anywhere? Not under any circumstances? Not in hell?
Here we are at the edge of the speculative, but not without
good biblical warrant and not without the reassuring company
of the formidable Hans Urs von Balthasar. On Good Friday, says
Balthasar, Christ descended into the heart of human desolation,
he himself experienced damnation as he entered the uttermost
limits of humanity's alienation from God. Christians must hope
that hell is empty, that the mercy of God reaches also those who
willed damnation for themselves, that God draws them back,
despite themselves, into the heart of love. Balthasar writes:
"Here lies hope for the person who, refusing all love, damns
himself. Will not the person who wishes to be totally alone find
beside him in Sheol the Someone who is lonelier still, the Son
forsaken by the Father, who will prevent him from experiencing
his self-chosen hell to the end?"

It is a question, but it is an inescapable question, that drives
to the hope at the heart of the horror. If, as St. Paul says, Christ
who knew no sin was made sin for us, can there be any sin he
did not bear there on the cross? If the answer is no, as I believe
it must be, then even the utterly forsaken are not bereft of the
company of the utterly forsaken one, the Son of God, and
therefore not bereft of hope. Thus even the will to damnation is
damned and thereby defeated by the One for whom and in
whom damnation is not allowed the last word.

5

Witnesses

The Fifth Word from the cross:

"I thirst."

The Fifth Word is only two words.

Much earlier in John's Gospel we read that the Feast of Booths was at hand and Jesus went up to Jerusalem. The feast commemorated the Israelites' wandering in the wilderness after they had been rescued from Egypt, and in their wanderings they knew what it was to be thirsty. On the last day of the feast, the great day, Jesus stood up and proclaimed, "If any one thirst, let him come to me and drink." Jesus is the fountain, and now, on the cross, the fountain thirsts.

Reflections on this Fifth Word from the cross traditionally refer to the Church's missionary impulse, an impulse driven by Jesus' thirsting for souls. At the entrance of the chapel of Mother Teresa's Missionaries of Charity in the Bronx are the words, "I THIRST, I QUENCH." These are the same words at the entrance of

the community's chapels all over the world. "We want," said
Mother Teresa, "to satiate the thirst of Jesus on the cross for the
love of souls." Our service to others whom we recognize, in the
words of Mother Teresa, as "Jesus in distressed disguise" is a
drink offered to him. In offering that drink, our thirst is
quenched. I thirst, I quench.

In Rome I said Mass for the Missionaries of Charity in their
plain little chapel just outside St. Peter's Square. Six sisters,
including two from India, one from Indonesia and a formidable
Valkyrie, perhaps from Sweden, operate a soup kitchen and
refuge for the street people of Rome. The intensity of the sisters'
devotion and the simplicity of their lives embarrassed me. How
complex and cluttered with plans and projects is my life
compared to theirs. Then it came to me: Their austere
attentiveness was a thirsting for the water of life. It was an
ecstatic thirsting. In the communion their thirst was quenched
and, at the same time, intensified. The reality of this was
palpable; you could feel it. The words of Psalm 42 came rushing
upon me:

> *As a hart longs*
> *for flowing streams,*
> *so longs my soul*
> *for thee, O God.*
> *My soul thirsts for God,*
> *for the living God.*
> *When shall I come and behold*
> *the face of God?*

From the cross, "I thirst." And those who kneel at his cross share his thirst, which is both a thirst for him and for all for whom he thirsts.

The Gospel accounts are riddled with allusions that double back and forth from Golgotha to Old Testament prophecy even as they reach out to the life and mission of the future Church. In John 19: "After this Jesus, knowing that all was now finished, said (to fulfill the scripture), 'I thirst.' A bowl full of vinegar stood there; so they put a sponge full of the vinegar on hyssop and held it to his mouth. When Jesus had received the vinegar, he said 'It is finished'; and he bowed his head and gave up his spirit."

In Matthew and Mark, it is a vinegary wine that Jesus is offered. John apparently thought it more vinegar than wine. The Greek *oxos* likely refers to *posca*, the red peasant wine drunk by Roman soldiers when they were really thirsty. It is far from clear that giving Jesus the drink was intended as a friendly gesture. Remember the crowds have been railing and jeering. Some thought his *"Eli, Eli"* was a call for Elijah to come and rescue him. In Mark's account, the one who gives him a drink says, "Wait, let us see whether Elijah will come to take him down."

Who is this someone and what did he mean by saying that? We do not know for sure. Maybe this someone really does want to help but is intimidated by the bystanders. He is afraid they will think he is a friend of Jesus, because he is offering him a drink. So he pretends to join in the general mockery. Or maybe he is part of the hostile crowd and just wants to revive Jesus with a drink, lest he die too soon and they don't get to see whether Elijah will come. No matter. However ambiguous his

motives, he gave God a drink. As with the sinful woman who
anointed the feet of Jesus with costly perfume, that will be
remembered wherever this story is told, until the end of time.
Whoever that someone was, he did more than he knew.

But what is this about the Scripture being fulfilled? What
Scripture? Some suggest it is Psalm 69:21, "For my thirst they
gave me vinegar to drink." Perhaps that is it. But recall how
Psalm 22 weaves its way, shrieking and whispering, throughout
the goings on at Golgotha. So perhaps "I thirst" is the fulfillment
of this from Psalm 22:

> I am poured out like water,
>   and all my bones are out of joint;
> my heart is like wax,
>   it is melted within my breast;
> my strength is dried up like a potsherd,
>   and my tongue cleaves to my jaws;
>   thou dost lay me in the dust of death.

Here is thirst as dusty as death. Our friend Father Raymond
Brown is uneasy with the suggestion that the reference is to
Psalm 22. It makes it seem that Jesus is too passive, that all this
is just happening to him, whereas, says Father Brown, "John sees
Jesus as the master of his fate." I don't think so. Father Brown
again refers to John 10, where Jesus says he lays down his life
and no one takes it from him. Yes, but as I suggested earlier, that
laying down and taking up again must not be understood as
playacting, as though Jesus is "orchestrating" the drama. Laying
down his life is absolute obedience, abandonment, loss of

control, committing all to the Father. Jesus is eager for this. "I thirst" is essential to his not stopping short of going all the way in the abandonment of self.

In John, Jesus rebukes Peter for drawing his sword to resist those who came to arrest him. "The cup the Father has given me," Jesus says, "am I not to drink it?" He thirsts to drink the cup to its final dregs. It is true that in the Fourth Gospel he trusts that the Father will not finally abandon him. "I am never alone because the Father is with me." But that trust is vindicated only after the cup is emptied. The glory of the cross is precisely in the free abandonment that lets everything go. So I think we make no mistake when we hear Psalm 22 in the words "I thirst."

There is this oddity about the hyssop. The sponge with the vinegary wine is put on hyssop and offered to Jesus. Hyssop is a small bushy plant quite unsuited to bearing the weight of a sponge soaked with wine. Embarrassed by that, some translations have seized upon an eleventh-century manuscript that suggests the sponge was actually put on the end of a javelin or long pole. That is how it is pictured also in some medieval paintings of the crucifixion. But for all the awkwardness, perhaps we should stay with John's hyssop and see in it a deeper meaning. In Exodus 12, hyssop is used to sprinkle the blood of the paschal lamb on the doorposts of the Israelites so that the angel of death will pass over their homes. In the New Testament, Hebrews 9 picks up on this to show how the blood of Jesus seals a new covenant, just as Moses used hyssop to sprinkle the blood of animals in order to seal the earlier covenant.

The connection is between hyssop and the blood of the

lambs. The image of the Lamb of God keeps recurring in John's
Gospel. At the very beginning of the ministry, John the Baptizer
declares, "Behold, the Lamb of God, who takes away the sin of
the world." In John 19, Jesus is judged at noon, the very hour
when the slaughter of the Passover lambs begins in the temple.
Jesus' bones are not broken, just as the bones of the paschal
lambs are not broken. At the cross, the wine is offered in
response to his "I thirst." Thus does "I thirst" complete the work
the Father had given him to do, and thus are the Scriptures
fulfilled. It is fitting that the new covenant should be sealed by
the wine on the hyssop, for the wine is the new covenant in his
blood of the Eucharist. Had Jesus, the ultimate Passover Lamb,
not indicated all this much earlier? There it is in John 6: "Truly,
truly, I say to you, unless you eat the flesh of the Son of man
and drink his blood, you have no life in you; he who eats my
flesh and drinks my blood has eternal life, and I will raise him up
at the last day."

In response to those words, many of his disciples said, "This
is a hard saying; who can listen to it?" And they left him. Jesus
asked the Twelve, "Will you also go away?" Simon Peter
answered, "Lord, to whom shall we go? You have the words of
eternal life; and we have believed, and have come to know, that
you are the Holy One of God." The disciples said they could
drink of the chalice from which he would drink, little knowing
that his "I thirst" would invite the chalice in the form of dregs
borne on the hyssop of a covenant sealed by blood, and
knowing much less that they would be among the lambs
slaughtered in the Church's confirming of that covenant in the
blood of the martyrs. Clearly, they did not know what they were
getting themselves into.

With the mention of the hyssop, a most unlikely instrument for giving someone a drink, all kinds of allusions reel into imaginative play—the hyssop, the sprinkling, the lambs, the blood. In the book of Revelation, Jesus is called "the lamb slain from the foundation of the world." There is nothing impromptu or ad hoc about what is happening here on Golgotha. Everything had been made ready for this since the foundation of the world. The story of Jesus, says Matthew, gives utterance to "what has been hidden since the foundation of the world." In Matthew 25, on the great day of judgment, the king says to the righteous, "Come, O blessed of my Father, inherit the kingdom prepared for you from the foundation of the world." The blood of Jesus, says Luke, makes up for the blood of all the prophets "shed from the foundation of the world." We are ransomed, says 1 Peter, by the blood of Christ, "like that of a lamb without blemish or spot," and all this was "destined before the foundation of the world."

On this Friday called good, everything is at last coming together. All the references to the foundation of the world testify to this event in which the world is refounded. Jesus had earlier prayed, "Father, I desire that they also, whom thou hast given me, may be with me where I am, to behold my glory which thou hast given me in thy love for me before the foundation of the world." And so it is, says St. Paul writing to the Ephesians: "Blessed be the God and Father of our Lord Jesus Christ, who has blessed us in Christ with every spiritual blessing in the heavenly places, even as he chose us in him before the foundation of the world."

From the foundation of the world to the end of the world. As the risen Lord says to the disciples: "Go therefore and make disciples of all nations, baptizing them in the name of the Father and of the Son and of the Holy Spirit, teaching them to observe all that I have commanded you; and lo, I am with you always, to the close of the age."

So it is that the words "I thirst" prompt the offering of the cup—in the form of a sponge on the hyssop of the covenant—that Jesus drinks to the bitter end. Here is intimated the new covenant in his blood, the chalice of wine that becomes his eucharistic blood. It is like and unlike the sprinkled blood of the Passover lambs. Were it not his own blood, were it not the blood of "the lamb slain from the foundation of the world," then, the Letter to Hebrews tells us, "he would have had to suffer repeatedly since the foundation of the world." But this is not the blood of just any lamb; it is the blood of the Lamb of God, and therefore this suffering is definitive; it is enough for now and forever. From the foundation of the world, everything had been pointing to what happened on the cross.

The missionary mandate is to go and make disciples, to incorporate into the eucharistic covenant those who are "chosen in Christ from before the foundation of the world." The mandate is to teach them all that he has commanded us. To teach them how he said on the night before he died, "Do this in memory of me." In the doing of the Eucharist, the hyssop is pressed also to our lips, and we are joined to him on the cross. Our thirst is momentarily assuaged, but the wine also sharpens our anticipation of something still to happen: "I tell you I shall not drink again of this fruit of the vine until that day when I drink it new with you in my Father's kingdom."

Along the way to the kingdom, to share in the cup is to

share in his suffering. St. Paul again: "The cup of blessing which we bless, is it not a participation in the blood of Christ? The bread which we break, is it not a participation in the body of Christ?" To share in the body and blood of the Lamb that was slain is to be with him on the cross. In the vinegary wine on the hyssop there was for him, and there is for us, a foretaste of the new wine of our Father's kingdom, which has no other foundation than crucified love. Of these truths the community of the eucharistic covenant is the witness. This is the connection between mission and martyrdom. "Martyr" is, as mentioned, the Greek word for "witness." Martyrdom should therefore come as no surprise to those to whom the risen Lord said, "And you shall be my witnesses in Jerusalem and in all Judea and Samaria and to the end of the earth." The Church is sent to all the world, hyssop in hand.

When I was a boy, no more than seven years old I think, I attended a "mission festival" in the Canadian hamlet of Petawawa, Ontario. The annual mission festival was a very big event among the people of that time and place. Each parish would take its turn in hosting the mission festival, and since individual churches could not hold the crowds that came from surrounding parishes, the day of preaching, prayer, hymns and picnicking was held outdoors. For such a special occasion, a guest preacher was required, and this year he came all the way from "the States," which meant two hundred miles away in upstate New York. This preacher had a most dramatic flair in making the case for the urgency of world missions. Well into a sermon that lasted an hour or more (which was not unusual for something so auspicious as the annual mission festival), the preacher suddenly stopped. For a full minute there was complete silence as he looked intently at his wristwatch. Then he tossed his head, threw out his arm and, pointing directly at me in the third row, announced, "In the last one minute, thirty-seven thousand lost souls have gone to eternal damnation without a saving knowledge of their Lord and Savior Jesus Christ!"

It was, I believe, the first theological crisis of my life. This seven-year-old boy was electrified. I immediately put my mind to work figuring out how many minutes we had been sitting there while thirty-seven thousand people per minute were going to hell. I looked around and was puzzled to see everybody else taking the news so calmly. Mrs. Appler was straightening the bow in her daughter's hair, and Mr. Radke was actually smiling as he nodded approval at the preacher's words. Hadn't they heard what he said? In my agitated state, I wanted to jump up and shout that we had better get going right now to tell all those hell-bent people about Jesus. The real crisis came later, however. I was excited all day and had spent a restless night contending with dreams about all those people in hell. The next morning I discovered that the visiting preacher and my Dad, who was the pastor of the host church, were taking three days off to go fishing.

Thirty-seven thousand people going to hell every minute and they were going fishing! I knew there was something very wrong here and wrestled with possible explanations. Maybe they didn't care about all those people. It was not only my Dad and the other preacher, but my Mom, my brothers and sisters and the entire parish who seemed to be taking very much in stride yesterday's announcement of cosmic catastrophe. This said something not at all nice about the people who were dearest to me. Slowly, another explanation began to recommend itself: The mission festival preacher didn't really mean what he said. Not really. And everybody understood that, except me. After a time, my initial alarm subsided as I came to think that he and they did not mean it at all, that it was just "church talk" and not to be taken too seriously.

That was a long time ago. Since then, I have come to understand the mission of the Church—and what we call "the missions"—in a very different way, yet in a way not untouched by that electrifying sense of urgency that so gripped me on a Sunday afternoon in Petawawa. "For if I preach the gospel, that gives me no ground for boasting," St. Paul writes to the Corinthians. "For necessity is laid upon me. Woe to me if I do not preach the gospel!" The life of the Church is a perpetual mission festival. The word "apostle" means one who is sent, and all who are called by Christ are also sent by Christ. An apostle is ever so much more trustworthy than a religious genius. A genius may have flashes of insight and come up with a brilliant spiritual scheme, but what he has to say is finally and uniquely his; I cannot enter into it or trust it completely. An apostle's role is much more modest and, therefore, more credible: "I have been told something that I must tell you. Make of it what you will."

The first apostles were also eyewitnesses. The opening passage of 1 John lays out the mandate and the motive of Christian mission:

That which was from the beginning, which we have heard, which we have seen with our eyes, which we have looked upon and touched with our hands, concerning the word of life—the life was made manifest, and we saw it, and testify to it, and proclaim to you the eternal life which was with the Father and was made manifest to us—that which we have seen and heard we proclaim also to you, so that you may have fellowship with us; and our fellowship is with the Father and with his Son Jesus Christ. And we are writing this that our joy may be complete.

Why the urgency about telling others? *So that you may have fellowship with us and our joy may be complete.* If this gospel is true, it is not simply "true for me"—it is true for all or it is not true at all. Here Christians have to bite the bullet and dare to go against the cultural grain. In our culture, the one truth imposed upon almost everybody is that you must never impose your truth on others. Most particularly, you must not impose your religious or moral truth on others. This rule so powerfully imposed by our culture makes many Christians very nervous about the whole idea of mission. Who are we to say that our truth is superior to the truths by which others live? That is an excellent question, if it is a question of "our" truth. But the claim is that the gospel is, quite simply, *the truth.* It is the true story about the world and everybody in the world. That is an insufferably arrogant assertion, unless it is true.

If by "impose" is meant that we try to force people to agree, then we certainly must not impose the gospel. In an encyclical on mission—*Redemptoris Missio* (The Mission of the Redeemer)— John Paul II says, "The Church imposes nothing. She only proposes." But what she proposes she proposes as the truth. This is basic. It is so basic that, if we don't understand this, all talk about mission really is no more than arrogance and presumption. The one who said "I thirst" and received on the hyssop the wine of the new covenant, representing the blood shed and the blood shared by the eucharistic community to which he surrenders his spirit, this one is either Lord of all or he is Lord not at all. I have said that on Good Friday we should not rush to Easter, but on Good Friday we are not playing "let's pretend," as though we don't know what happened the next Sunday morning. What happened in the resurrection vindicates the claim that this One on the cross is, in fact, Lord of all. Only the resurrection could vindicate that claim.

The opening passage of 1 John cited above is all about facts, about things that happened. Specificity is all. When a certain person named Tiberius was emperor at Rome, certain Jews in Palestine took up with a rabbi and prophet called Jesus of Nazareth. They were devastated by his death, which was somehow endured "for their sake," and then they encountered him alive after his execution, and he was alive in a way that precluded his dying again. John writes, "That which we have seen and heard we proclaim also to you."

For devout Jews of that time who shared Israel's messianic hope, the resurrection did not need any theologians to interpret it. It spoke for itself. *If* this happened, the meaning of it was beyond dispute. If the God of Israel raised Jesus from the dead, then Jesus is Lord of all. Given the meaning of being "raised from the dead" in the language and hopes of Israel, no other conclusion was possible.

In what is called the Nicene Creed of the Christian liturgy, the claims follow one another with utter inevitability:

For our sake he was crucified under Pontius Pilate;
  he suffered death and was buried.
On the third day he rose again
  in accordance with the Scriptures;
he ascended into heaven
  and is seated at the right hand of the Father.
He will come again in glory to judge the living and the dead
  and his kingdom will have no end.

What is said after the words "he rose again" are not additional claims about Jesus. To say "he rose again" is also to say everything else that is said. What happened happened to specific people at a specific time in a specific culture. In the context of Israel's faith, everything said after it is said that he rose again necessarily follows. This explains why St. Paul says that "if Christ has not been raised, then our preaching is in vain and your faith is in vain." The appointed signal had been given centuries before through the prophets, and now it had happened. The apostles, those who are sent, are essentially cast in the role of reporters or messengers. Their report is that not only has the story line of Israel's hope been fulfilled but, since the God of Israel is the one God of all, the story of the world is fulfilled in Jesus the Christ—which means Jesus is the appointed Savior of the world.

I have said we should not rush to Easter, yet Easter is the necessary presupposition of our contemplating the derelict on the cross. Apart from Easter, such contemplation would reflect nothing but a morbid, macabre fascination with suffering and death—however "noble" his sacrifice. Because of Easter, the

words from the cross are words of life. The cross is not merely
the bad news before the good news of the resurrection. Come
Easter Sunday, we do not put the suffering and death behind us
as though it were no more than the nightmarish prelude to the
joy of victory. No, the cross remains the path of discipleship for
those who follow the risen Lord. It is not as though there are
two paths, one the way of the cross and the other the way of
resurrection victory. Rather, the resurrection means that the way
of the cross *is* the way of victory.

"Come, follow me," says Jesus. "Take up your cross and
follow me. In the world you will have trouble, but fear not, I
have overcome the world." In the book of Revelation, the white-
robed saints around the throne of the Lamb are those who have
come out of the great tribulation. "I thirst," said Jesus, and so
also those who follow him thirst to drink of the chalice of which
he drank. The way of the Christian life is cruciform. Jesus did
not suffer and die in order that we need not suffer and die, but
in order that our suffering and death might be joined to his in
redemptive victory. As Moses dipped the hyssop in blood and
sprinkled the people of the first covenant, so those who have
tasted of the wine that is now become blood are bound in
covenantal solidarity with the One who is risen never to die
again.

The Christian way is not one of avoidance but of
participation in the suffering of Christ, which encompasses not
only our own suffering, but the suffering of the whole world.
Thus St. Paul can say, "Now I rejoice in my sufferings for your
sake, and in my flesh I complete what is lacking in Christ's
afflictions for the sake of his body, that is, the Church, of which

I became a minister according to the divine office which was given to me for you, to make the word of God fully known, the mystery hidden for ages and generations but now made manifest to his saints." Thus also Dietrich Bonhoeffer, in his classic *The Cost of Discipleship*, wrote, "When Jesus calls a man, he calls him to come and die."

To many this does not sound like good news. Christians also are embarrassed by the cross. A young woman tells me why she left the Church for a New Age empowerment group: "I was sick and tired of all that talk about blood and suffering. I wanted a positive spirituality." Maybe she had been listening to the likes of the California evangelist who declares, "There's nothing downbeat about the cross at New Life Cathedral." It is difficult to imagine an upbeat cross. It is easy to understand why people might want to avoid the cross altogether. Avoiding the cross makes very good sense, if we do not know the One whom we join, the One who joins us, on the cross that is the world's redemption. The victory of Christ is not a way of avoidance but the way of solidarity in suffering. Suffering and death are not "senseless," something to be avoided at all costs. Not if they are understood as "completing what is lacking in Christ's afflictions for the sake of his body, that is, the Church." It is not that Christ did not do enough, but that he invites us to participate with him in the salvation of the world. When Jesus calls us, he calls us to come and die. We will die anyway. The question is whether we will die senselessly or as companions and coworkers of the crucified and risen Lord.

We were taking a train from Grand Central Station, where at any moment one sees thousands, even tens of thousands, of the hurried, harried and worried; it seems the entire human condition on disorderly parade. Musicians regularly perform in the great hall of Grand Central, and today it was a young woman singing "Amazing Grace" with a voice of crystalline purity that echoed through the crowded chamber. "How very sad," observed my Christian friend, "that so many of those people do not know Jesus as their Savior." And of course she is right, it is very sad. Yet I confess that my sensation was very different, looking at this ragtag horde of humanity. How amazing the grace, I thought, that all of them, all of this, all is redeemed.

In the movie *The Third Man*, Orson Welles, who is dealing in lethal drugs in postwar Vienna, explains to his friend as they sit at the top of a Ferris wheel, looking down at the crowds far below. Were the money good enough, Welles asks, would it really matter to his friend, would it really matter to anyone, if one, or two, or three of those anonymous specks down there simply disappeared? The Christian answer, of course, is yes. It matters enormously, it matters infinitely. Each one of those specks is a human life of irreducible complexity and incalculable worth. Each one was seen from the cross, and for each one he died. Each is destined from eternity to eternity and, in the words of Dante's *Paradiso*, each is embraced by "the love that moves the sun and the other stars."

The urgency of the Christian mission is to alert the world to its story, which is the story of the amazing grace by which it is redeemed. A great Protestant evangelist earlier in this century said that he viewed the world as a shipwreck and his mission was to rescue as many survivors as possible. That is one way of thinking about it, and it is a way that has no doubt motivated great missionary endeavors. It is similar to the view of the preacher at the Petawawa mission festival. Another way of thinking about it is that the world has been redeemed. That is the message of certain Jews who took up with a certain rabbi and prophet who encountered them on the far side of death, never to die again. He taught them that the kingdom of God is like a banquet and sent them out to the highways and byways to invite any and all. The banquet fare is his body and blood, which means the life of the crucified and risen Lord who presides at a meal that is the foretaste of the wedding feast of the Lamb, the Lamb who was slain from before the foundation of the world.

The apostles witnessed by their martyrdom, as have innumerable others over the centuries. Many of the noblest were driven by the urgency of rescuing a few from the cosmic catastrophe of sin. In his magnificent *France and England in North America*, Francis Parkman (d. 1893) tells the compelling story of the seventeenth-century Jesuit missionaries to the Indians. It is a story partially familiar to many from the more recent film *Black Robe*. Parkman, a staunch Protestant, had a grudging admiration for a Catholic Church and Jesuit order that, in all their dreadful ambiguity, were driven by the conviction of being God's instrument of salvation in a lost world:

> Holy Mother Church, linked in sordid wedlock to governments and thrones, numbered among her servants a host of the worldly and the proud, whose service of God was but the service of themselves—and many, too, who, in the sophistry of the human heart, thought themselves true soldiers

of Heaven, while earthly pride, interest, and passion were the life-springs of their zeal. This mighty Church of Rome, in her imposing march along the high road of history, heralded as infallible and divine, astounds the gazing world with prodigies of contradiction: now the protector of the oppressed, now the right arm of tyrants; now breathing charity and love, now dark with the passions of Hell; now beaming with celestial truth, now masked in hypocrisy and lies; now a virgin, now a harlot; an imperial queen, and a tinseled actress. Clearly, she is of earth, not of heaven; and her transcendentally dramatic life is a type of the good and ill, the baseness and nobless, the foulness and purity, the love and hate, the pride, passion, truth, falsehood, fierceness, and tenderness, that battle in the restless heart of man.

Isaac Jogues and the other martyrs of the North American mission understood themselves to be the agents of this ambiguous institution that was carrying through time the discovery of certain Jews who had taken up with a certain rabbi and prophet crucified and forever alive. They understood theirs to be a rescue mission, and the rescue was worth the price of their lives. Surreptitiously, they dipped a finger in water and touched the head of a dying Iroquois infant, thus, they believed, rescuing one more soul from the Devil and everlasting hell. Many today dismiss it as magic and superstition, as they similarly dismiss the "decisions for Christ" chalked up by evangelizing Christians of our time, who also believe they are on a rescue mission to save a few from the cosmic catastrophe. They believe they are following their Lord in thirsting for souls, and those who really do thirst and really do follow cannot but elicit our admiration. Parkman once more:

The Jesuits had borne all that the human frame seems capable of bearing. They had escaped as by miracle from torture and death. Did their zeal flag or their courage fail? A fervor intense and unquenchable urged them on to more distant and more deadly ventures. The beings, so near to mortal sympathies, so human, yet so divine, in whom their faith impersonated and dramatized the great principles of Christian truth—virgins, saints, and angels—hovered over them, and held before their raptured sight crowns of glory and garlands of immortal bliss. They burned to do, to suffer, and to die; and now, from out of a living martyrdom, they turned their heroic gaze towards an horizon dark with perils yet more appalling, and saw in hope the day when they should bear the cross into the blood-stained dens of the Iroquois.

Bracing stuff, that. Iroquois country would not do for the little boy at the Petawawa mission festival, since the Iroquois were in reservations close at hand and had long since been "Christianized." But like many boys and girls before and since, he dreamed of going off to some dark continent, probably Africa, and there giving his life in "winning souls for Christ." In missions and revivals beyond number, little Christians have been inspired to such romantic imaginings of heroic self-sacrifice. In the long Christian march through history, countless thousands have lived and died just so. Among American and European Christians, that was certainly the case in the great missionary enterprises of the nineteenth and early twentieth centuries. For many Christians today, however, such dreams are for little boys and girls. Paraphrasing (and betraying?) St. Paul in 1 Corinthians 13, they are among the "childish things" we put away when we grow up.

Despite the flagging of missionary fervor, at the beginning of the third millennium Christianity is poised for unprecedented expansion in world history. Today there are somewhat over 2 billion Christians, about one-third of the world's population, half of them Catholic and the other half Orthodox and Protestants of many varieties. Among Catholics and evangelical Protestants in places such as Africa and Asia, the fervor has not flagged, the good news of the gospel is still news. It is very different in America and, especially, in Europe. Here the gospel is thought to be yesterday's news. As it is said by the jaded who are ever in pursuit of novelty, "Been there. Done that."

In 1991, Pope John Paul II was looking to this third millennium when he wrote the encyclical *Redemptoris Missio* (The Mission of the Redeemer). He was speaking to all Christians then, and his words speak to all Christians now. The very title of the encyclical tells us the most important thing right off: It is *his* mission before it is ours. It is the mission of the One who on the cross cried out, "I thirst!" So we begin by dealing with those anxieties about the cultural impropriety of imposing "our" truth upon others. We deal with them by packing them up and tossing them out. It is not our truth, but the truth of the one who said, "I am the way, and the truth, and the life." He is in mission before we are in mission; the responsibility is his before it is ours. The question for us is whether we will respond to his initiative. Here and everywhere, the question is, as he said, "When the Son of man returns, will he find faith on earth?"

The encyclical on missions cites Paul VI, who years earlier pointed to "the lack of fervor which is all the more serious because it comes from within." The lack of fervor, Paul said, "is manifest in fatigue, disenchantment, compromises, lack of interest, and above all lack of joy and hope." If these are the symptoms, the causes may be uncertainty about the nature of truth, about the imperatives of tolerance in a multicultural world, about how to speak the gospel in our own world that thinks it has heard it all before. John Paul gave voice to the questions asked by many Christians today:

> As a result of the changes which have taken place in modern times and the spread of new theological ideas, some people wonder: Is missionary work among non-Christians still relevant? Has it not been replaced by interreligious dialogue? Is not human development an adequate goal of the Church's mission? Does not respect for conscience and for freedom exclude all efforts at conversion? Is it not possible to attain salvation in any religion? Why then should there be missionary activity?

In sum, wasn't the little boy in Petawawa needlessly excited?

If the excitement of sharing the good news depends on the belief that all who do not know the good news are surely headed for hell, then it is little surprise that the missionary enterprise languishes. Not only Catholics but probably most Christians suspect—some intuitively and some with intellectual clarity—that it cannot be right that the overwhelming majority of people who have ever lived are eternally lost to the love of God. The Second Vatican Council put it plainly in *Gaudium et Spes* (Pastoral Constitution on the Church in the Modern World): "We are obliged to hold that the Holy Spirit offers everyone the possibility of sharing in the paschal mystery in a manner known to God." Note, however, that this does *not* mean that Christianity is simply one way of salvation among others. Christians must hold with the words of St. Peter in Acts: "There is salvation in no one else, for there is no other name under heaven given among men by which we must be saved."

But, we may well ask, doesn't that contradict the claim that God does not deny grace sufficient to salvation to everyone, including those who have never heard the name of Jesus? Not at all. The crucial point is that those who are saved without knowing the name of Jesus the Christ are nonetheless saved *by* Jesus the Christ. *Redemptoris Missio* puts it this way:

> No one, therefore, can enter into communion with God except through Christ, by the working of the Holy Spirit. Christ's one universal mediation is the way established by God himself. Although participated forms of mediation of different kinds and degrees [through other religions] are not excluded, they acquire meaning and value only from Christ's own mediation, and they cannot be understood as parallel or complementary to his.

Other ways may be salvific only because they participate, however unknowingly, in the salvation worked by the One who is the way, the truth and the life.

But we are driven back to the hard question. It is a question closely connected to our earlier reflection on whether we should hope that all will be saved. If we are not persuaded by the motivation proposed by the Petawawa preacher, what is the incitement to urgent, even heroic, commitment to the mission *ad gentes*—the mission to the nations, beginning with our own nation? Perhaps we should just sit back and relax, as some contemporary theologians suggest. They tell us that it was once thought that the "ordinary" means of salvation was through Christ and his Church, while allowance was made for "extraordinary" means in the case of those who never had a chance to hear the gospel. Now, they go on to say, the situation has been reversed. The ordinary has become the extraordinary, and the extraordinary has become the ordinary. Relying on the universal salvation worked by Christ, they suggest, we can leave it up to God as to how people in their own chosen ways avail themselves of that salvation. After all, "we are obliged to hold that the Holy Spirit offers everyone the possibility of sharing in the paschal mystery in a manner known to God." Some go further and say that, if that is true, we actually do people a disservice by confronting them with the gospel. The logic here is that people may be condemned for rejecting a gospel that they have heard, but would not be condemned for not believing a gospel they have not heard. This is a variation on the maxim that ignorance is bliss.

If we live in the truth and for the truth, however, we cannot actively will ignorance for ourselves or for others. Our very humanity is at stake in our bearing witness to the truth. The gospel is the story of the world, and of our lives in the world. In the Old Testament, the prophet Isaiah spoke of this truth as "the light of the nations." Those are the very first words of the Second Vatican Council's document on the Church, *Lumen Gentium* (Dogmatic Constitution on the Church). And of course Jesus speaks of his followers as light of the world and salt of the earth. Possessing the truth and sharing the truth are not two things, but one. As Jesus makes dramatically clear in many parables and sayings, the same is true of forgiveness and love; we do not possess if we do not share, and the more we give away the more we possess. This is the genius of Christian existence, caught in the repeated formula that he who loses his life will find his life. It is, finally, the self-abandonment of the cross.

Here on Golgotha with the derelict crying out "I thirst!" is the great missionary act of all time. It appears as the very opposite of that. It appears as grim defeat, as the end of the road, as the failure of everything hoped for. As in the past, so also today we hear Christians speak of grand missionary strategies for "winning the world for Christ." Such grand strategizing is often derided as "triumphalism," and there is something to that. Or it is caricatured as a grand marketing plan for the gospel, and there is something to that, too. Yet, if the alternative to triumphalism is defeatism, there is something to be said for triumphalism. And concern for effective communication inevitably runs the risk of taking on the appearance of marketing. But mission is not the hawking of a bargain-basement deal. The marketing of bargains is held in check by the cross. What Christians propose to the world is *who* Christians propose to the world—"Jesus Christ and him crucified." We know no Christ other than the crucified Lord, who is Lord precisely in submitting himself to all that defies his lordship. The "upbeat cross" in the cathedral of our California televangelist is another Christ and another gospel.

Why, then, the mission to the nations, beginning with our own? What incites us to missionary urgency? Because it is nothing less than his way, the way he invites us to walk when he says, "Come, follow me." Our missionary charter is the stupendous hymn in Philippians:

> Have this mind among yourselves, which you have in Christ
> Jesus, who, though he was in the form of God, did not count
> equality with God a thing to be grasped, but emptied himself,
> taking the form of a servant, being born in the likeness of men.
> And being found in human form he humbled himself and
> became obedient unto death, even death on a cross. Therefore
> God has highly exalted him and bestowed on him the name
> which is above every name, that at the name of Jesus every
> knee should bow, in heaven and on earth and under the earth,
> and every tongue confess that Jesus Christ is Lord, to the glory
> of God the Father.

Far from imposing our superior religious understanding upon others, the missionary enterprise turns on self-abandonment. St. Paul speaks about having "become all things to all people so that I might save some." The Greek word that speaks of Christ emptying himself is *kenosis*, and authentic missionary work, whether with the neighbor next door or in a distant and exotic culture (recognizing that the world of the neighbor next door may also be a distant and exotic culture), is always kenotic. Our faith in the universal nature of Christ and his redemptive work makes it possible for us to enter into the world of others, confident that we will find there Christ and him crucified. The pre-Christian Roman philosopher Terence declared, "I am a man. Nothing that is human is alien to me." That is the case many times over with the one whom Pontius Pilate, in unknowing wisdom, presented to the world with the announcement, *Ecce homo*—"Behold, the man."

The gospel is the story of the world and of everyone in the world, whether they know it or not. Again, in the words of John Paul II, "Christ is the answer to which every human life is the question." The mission of the Church is to bring the world to itself, as we are told that the prodigal son in that distant country "came to himself." As St. Paul said to the Athenians in the Areopagus, "What therefore you worship as unknown, this I proclaim to you." This kenotic entering into the world of "the other" to reveal the Christ who is to be found there is today commonly called the "inculturation" of the gospel. Like all such terms, "inculturation" has been abused and misunderstood. All too easily it leads to a kind of syncretism, a scissors-and-paste job of patching together religious traditions that end up being, in effect, a new religion quite different from any of the original pieces from which it was assembled. In entering into the experience, culture and religious aspirations of "the other," we know we have not betrayed the missionary mandate when we discover there the one who has been revealed as the Christ, "the same yesterday, today, and forever."

By the *kenosis* of mission the Church today recognizes itself as being in continuity with the Church from the beginning. Again, the Church does not *have* a mission, as though missionary work were one of its programs or projects. The Church *is* the mission of Christ, who continues to seek and to save the lost who do not know their story. Their story is Christ, the way, the truth and the life of all. The Church does have many programs and projects, some of which she shares with other institutions and communities. But the proclamation of God's love in Christ is the most important thing the Church does, because it is what she does uniquely. If the Church did not do this, nobody would.

She does this simply because she is the Church and this is what the Church does. She does this because she lives and breathes and is sustained in being by God's love in Christ, and love is either shared or lost.

What we have we are obliged to share. Others have a right to it, even if they don't know that. *Redemptoris Missio* quotes Paul VI: "The multitudes have the right to know the riches of the mystery of Christ—riches in which we believe that the whole of humanity can find, in unsuspected fullness, everything that it is gropingly searching for concerning God, man and his destiny, life and death, and truth." Others have a right to know, so that they might have an opportunity to believe. Ignorance is not bliss. Ignorance is ignorance. What others have a right to know they also have a need to know, if in fact it is the truth about their lives. To spare other people the chance to accept or reject the most important truth about themselves is not a course of love, but of contempt. It is an act of arrogance, deciding that others will not have an opportunity to decide. Christians impose nothing, they only propose—as a lover proposes to the beloved. Christ, the lover, proposes through us. That is how St. Paul saw the matter: "So we are ambassadors for Christ, God making his appeal through us. We beseech you on behalf of Christ, be reconciled to God."

Ambassadors do not represent themselves but the sovereign power that sends them. Christians are ambassadors of Christ, their sovereign. His is a disputed sovereignty, and it will be that way until he returns in glory. Then, as we learn in Philippians 2, every knee shall bow and every tongue confess that he is Lord. The Church is, quite simply, the community ahead of time, the community that acknowledges now what one day will be acknowledged by all. As ambassadors of a disputed sovereignty, we propose a claim that awaits a future and cosmic vindication. For those who accept that claim, it is already vindicated by faith. For them, the future is now.

A story is told of an old rebbe in a East European shtetl. One day his disciples burst in upon him with the excited announcement that the messiah had come. The old rebbe skeptically raises his eyebrows and shuffles to the window, where he looks out upon the world for a long time. Finally, he turns around and announces decisively, "No, he is has not come. The world is the same." His judgment finds solid support in the faith of Israel. The messianic expectation was that of a cosmic transformation. The resurrection of the dead would be the resurrection of all the righteous in the end time. That attachment to real time, that insistence upon what actually happens in history, was not wrong. The new and surprising thing discovered by the first Christians is that the end time had happened ahead of time. Already now, in Jesus Christ, God's promise had been kept. His death and resurrection is the "prolepsis"—the preview, the down payment, the foretaste— of the cosmic transformation. Those who accept him by faith live now the promise that they will one day be vindicated in the sight of all. St. Paul says, "Therefore, if any one is in Christ, he is a new creation; the old has passed away, behold, the new has come."

The new and surprising thing that has happened is the fulfillment of the old expectation, but in an unexpected way. This is the point of the first Christian sermon, delivered by

Peter after the disciples had received the Holy Spirit on
Pentecost, which, he asserted, was the fulfillment of prophecy:

> Men of Israel, hear these words: Jesus of Nazareth, a man
> attested to you by God with mighty works and wonders and
> signs which God did through him in your midst, as you
> yourselves know—this Jesus, delivered up according to the
> definite plan and foreknowledge of God, you crucified and
> killed by the hands of lawless men. . . . This Jesus God raised
> up, and of that we all are witnesses. Being therefore exalted at
> the right hand of God, and having received from the Father
> the promise of the Holy Spirit, he has poured out this which
> you see and hear.

The missionary imperative does not need the motivation
proposed by our Petawawa preacher. In fact, that motivation,
however well intended, is fundamentally wrongheaded; it
presumes that we know those many thousands are going to hell
every minute and that we are the only ones who can prevent
that terrible calamity. Such a way of thinking can trap us in
astonishing presumption and arrogance. Upon closer
examination, it is also morally incoherent. Although the
prospect is literally inconceivable, we might entertain a thought
experiment: If all the Christians in the world marshaled all the
evangelistic resources imaginable and devoted twenty hours a
day to nothing but relentless proclamation of the gospel, how
many billions of people would still be going to hell? If this is
God's plan of salvation for a world that we are told he so loves,
it would seem to be grievously flawed.

Consider again those crowds coursing through Grand

Central Station. Are they all comprehended, in ways that surpass our understanding, in Christ's redemptive work, or are they, with some happy exceptions, the *massa damnata* headed for certain perdition? If the latter, what are we doing at Grand Central taking a train to hear a lecture at Yale? We should start to work right here. There is enough evangelistic work right here to occupy our entire lives. It is the same question that was raised when my father and the mission preacher went fishing. Underlying both is a nightmarish view of reality that cannot be squared with the Christian's joyful confidence in "the mystery of his will, according to his purpose which he set forth in Christ as a plan for the fullness of time, to unite all things in him, things in heaven and things on earth."

The derelict on the cross crying out, "I thirst!" returned to the Father with one repentant thief. If world evangelization was his goal, what a dismal failure he was. Being both God and man, imagine the resources he could have marshaled, had he stayed on earth and recruited the whole world to his gospel. With his divine powers, imagine the marketing techniques he could have employed. But in that case it would have been a very different gospel. The gospel he proclaimed and lived was that of fidelity to the Father to the very end, to the death. The decision forced upon us is whether this ending was triumph or failure. We will shortly consider the next word from the cross, "It is finished." Does that mean simply that it is over, or that it is completed? Through the ages, the Church has confidently declared that the work of redemption is completed. In the fourteenth-century Julian of Norwich understood that that could not possibly be according to our "sensual" perception, but it is the mystery of

God's love perceived by those who enter by faith into the cross and resurrection. That alone makes it more than wishful thinking when she declares with soaring confidence, "All shall be well, all shall be well, all manner of thing shall be well."

The driving motivation of evangelism is the irrepressible desire to communicate what shall be on the basis of what already is, to which, as Peter said, we are all witnesses. Through such communication, the company of faith is expanded and our joy is made the more complete. Recall again the charter, the rationale, the mainspring of evangelism so movingly set forth in the opening passage of 1 John:

> That which was from the beginning, which we have heard, which we have seen with our eyes, which we have looked upon and touched with our hands, concerning the word of life . . . that which we have seen and heard we proclaim also to you, so that you may have fellowship with us; and our fellowship is with the Father and with his Son Jesus Christ. And we are writing this that our joy may be complete.

In the solidarity of faith, each of us says "we"—*we* have heard, *we* have seen, *we* have looked upon, *we* have touched with our hands. We are baptized into the same Jesus Christ whom John saw on the cross; in the Eucharist we touch and are touched by the same Christ who was in the upper room with the disciples. Yet ours is not precisely the same circumstance as that of John and Peter. We depend upon their testimony that the Christ whom we encounter is the same Christ whom they encountered. From the beginning, the Church has relied upon their assurance that we are not making this up. Guided by the

same Holy Spirit whom they received, the Church has been
led—just as Jesus promised—ever more deeply into the truth to
see Israel's expectation fulfilled in the "suffering servant" of
Isaiah:

> *For he grew up before him like a young plant,*
> *and like a root out of dry ground;*
> *he had no form or comeliness that we should look at him,*
> *and no beauty that we should desire him.*
> *He was despised and rejected by men;*
> *a man of sorrows, and acquainted with grief;*
> *and as one from whom men hide their faces*
> *he was despised, and we esteemed him not.*
>
> *Surely he has borne our griefs and carried our sorrows;*
> *yet we esteemed him stricken, smitten by God, and afflicted.*
> *But he was wounded for our transgressions,*
> *he was bruised for our iniquities;*
> *upon him was the chastisement that made us whole,*
> *and with his stripes we are healed.*

That suffering servant is the same one who hangs on the
cross crying out, "I thirst." And to this we are all witnesses. We
are sent into the world to bear testimony to this. Remembering
that the word "apostle" means someone who is sent, we
recognize that all Christians are sent, for all are, however great
our divisions, part of the one, holy, catholic and *apostolic* Church.
No Christian can feel he or she is not implicated in the words of
Jesus, "As the Father has sent me, even so I send you." But there

are apostles and then there are apostles. There are apostles by implication and apostles by specific assignment. St. Paul again: "And his gifts were that some should be apostles, some prophets, some evangelists, some pastors and teachers, for the equipment of the saints, for the work of ministry, for building up the body of Christ." This is the way he explains it to the Corinthians:

> Now there are varieties of gifts, but the same Spirit; and there are varieties of service, but the same Lord; and there are varieties of working, but it is the same God who inspires them all in every one. To each is given the manifestation of the Spirit for the common good. To one is given through the Spirit the utterance of wisdom, and to another the utterance of knowledge according to the same Spirit, to another faith by the same Spirit.

Everyone is implicated in every gift. No Christian is without wisdom or knowledge or faith. Yet not all are apostles or prophets or evangelists or pastors or teachers. Every Christian participates in the mission of the Church, but, high-voltage mission festival rhetoric notwithstanding, not every Christian has the specific call to be a missionary. St. Paul's calling, his vocation, drove him relentlessly to campaign the then-known world to spread the gospel. It was a life that was anything but peaceable and quiet, yet 1 Timothy urges Christians to "live peaceable and quiet lives in all godliness and holiness." Similarly, in 1 Peter the Christian way of life seems markedly unremarkable: "Maintain good conduct among the Gentiles, so that in case they speak against you as wrongdoers, they may see your good deeds and glorify God on the day of visitation." Do not aim to be provocative, Christians are told, but live lives of such lively hope as will provoke questions, and, with questions, an occasion to bear witness. "Always be prepared to make a defense to any one who calls you to account for the hope that is in you, yet do it with gentleness and reverence."

First Peter was written to Christians who were facing persecution; in that situation nobody had to be reminded that the word "witness" has the original meaning of "martyr." Again today, millions of Christians throughout the world are in that same circumstance. No Christian is in a circumstance, no matter how free and secure, where fidelity to Christ will not exact a price. But the heroic role of the martyr is to be neither shunned nor sought. Until the final Feast of the Lamb, the Church will lift up the martyrs for our admiration and emulation. Echoing that great vision of the book of Revelation, the Mass for Martyrs says: "Your holy martyr (Name) followed the example of Christ, and gave his (her) life for the glory of your name. His (her) death reveals your power shining through our human weakness. You choose the weak and make them strong in bearing witness to you."

It is good that we sing "Faith of Our Fathers," extolling the men and women who "in spite of dungeon, fire, and sword" and "chained in prisons dark, were still in heart and conscience free." "How sweet would be their children's fate," we sing, "If they, like them, could die for thee!" And then the stirring refrain, "Faith of our fathers! holy faith! We will be true to thee till death!" By such dramatics we are taught not to complain and are braced for the everyday tasks of putting up with irritating neighbors and getting the kids ready for school. It is the wisdom of the hymn to tell us as much: "Faith of our fathers! we will love / Both friend and foe in all our strife: / And preach thee, too, as love knows how, / By kindly words and virtuous life." Kindly words and virtuous life are no little thing. The prospect of martyrdom supports us in everyday duties. The readiness to die for the faith sustains us in living the faith.

Long after that Petawawa mission festival, my father died. The text for the sermon at his funeral was from Romans: "None of us lives to himself, and none of us dies to himself. If we live, we live to the Lord, and if we die, we die to the Lord; so then, whether we live or whether we die, we are the Lord's." The preacher at the funeral undoubtedly shared my father's theology of mission, with all those unsaved souls heading for hell, but his pastoral instincts were better than that. Of Clemens Neuhaus he said that, whether he was preparing a sermon or conducting a meeting, whether he was fixing his beloved cars or had gone fishing, he knew he was the Lord's. Exactly right. It is a pity his theology made him, and others, feel guilty about all the time spent in not doing anything very believably related to rescuing those damned souls.

The Christian life is about living to the glory of God. It is not a driven, frenetic, sweated, interminable quest for saving souls. It is doing for his glory what God has given us to do. As with the Olympic runner in the film *Chariots of Fire*, it is giving God pleasure in what we do well. Souls are saved by saved souls who live out their salvation by thinking and living differently, with a martyr's resolve, in a world marked by falsehood, baseness, injustice, impurity, ugliness and mediocrity. "Finally," says Paul, "whatever is true, whatever is honorable, whatever is just, whatever is pure, whatever is lovely, whatever is gracious, if there is any excellence, if there is anything worthy of praise, think about these things."

"I thirst," Jesus cried from the cross. He thirsts for us, and we for him. "As a hart longs for flowing streams, so longs my soul for thee, O God. My soul thirsts for God for the living God. When shall I come and behold the face of God?" This reciprocal thirsting marks the life of all Christians, whatever their calling, whatever their vocation. To paraphrase St. Paul: And his gifts were that some should be engineers, and some mothers, and some brokers, and some professors, and some lawyers, and some nurses, and some plumbers, for the equipment of the saints, for the work of ministry, for building up the body of Christ, until we all attain to the unity of the faith and of the knowledge of the Son of God, to maturity, to the measure of the stature of the fullness of Christ.

We thirst for that attainment, which is not yet within our grasp. We each ask of Christ, "What would you have me do?" And then, to please God, we do what we can best discern we have been given to do. We do it in freedom, with a kind of reckless abandon that is holy insouciance, knowing that the final judgment about whether we have done the right thing is not ours to make. Again it is Paul who sets the example. Remember the part where he is explaining to the Corinthians what he is up to, that he really is an apostle even though he may look like a fool. And then he tells the Corinthians, with perhaps just a touch of exasperation joined to a glorious declaration of liberty: "But with me it is a very small thing that I should be judged by you or by any human court. I do not even judge myself. I am not aware of anything against myself, but I am not thereby acquitted. It is the Lord who judges me. Therefore do not pronounce judgment before the time, before the Lord comes, who will bring to light the things now hidden in darkness and will disclose the purposes of the heart."

There is the perfect liberty of the followers of Christ. I do not even judge myself. Let no one judge before the time. Christ thirsts for those who throw away their lives in the everydayness of duties discerned and duties done. Such lives are a proposal of a different way of being in the world that he has redeemed. Through such lives his mission is advanced, often in ways that elude our sure perception. Every Christian life fully lived presents itself as a proposal to others. In the words of *Redemptoris Missio*, "The Church imposes nothing. She only proposes." But what a proposal. As a lover proposes to the beloved.

A priest friend tells me that when he was still newly ordained he had the opportunity of visiting with the famous Bishop Fulton J. Sheen only days before he died. Sitting by the hospital bed, he told the bishop that he wanted to be like him, a "convert priest" who brings many into the Church.

"I have already," the young priest said, "converted at least fourteen that I know of." What advice did the bishop have?

Bishop Sheen slowly and painfully pushed himself up on his elbows, fixed the young man with his famously penetrating gaze, and said, "The first thing, Father: Stop counting."

From the cross Christ has already counted them all. And he assures us that none of them will be lost. He also sends out those whom we call missionaries, to let them know they have been found. Such missionaries know that they go into no uncharted territories; they can only go where their Lord has already gone before. He has been everywhere; he is everywhere.

They come upon the most forsaken and discover that the most forsaken are already in the company of the Most Forsaken. Missionaries are not bringing Christ where he has not been before; they are meeting him where he has been all along, waiting to be named so that others, too, might live to his glory. For him the whole world thirsts, and Christ thirsts for the thirsty, hungers for the hungry, yearns for the yearning. "And I, when I am lifted up from the earth, will draw all men to myself."

There were seven missionary monks in Algeria during a time of great domestic turmoil. It was the spring of 1996, to be precise, when a group of Islamic terrorists raided their monastery at Titherine, took the monks captive, held them hostage for two months, and then killed them by slitting their throats. Shortly before this happened, Father Christian de Chergé had left with his family in France a last testament "to be opened in the event of my death." Reading it, perhaps through our tears, we may come to know what the Lord meant when he said, "As the Father has sent me, even so I send you."

Last Testament of Christian de Chergé

If it should happen one day—and it could be today—that I become a victim of the terrorism which now seems ready to encompass all the foreigners living in Algeria, I would like my community, my Church, my family, to remember that my life was given to God and to this country. I ask them to accept that the One Master of all life was not a stranger to this brutal departure. I ask them to pray for me: for how could I be found worthy of such an offering? I ask them to be able to associate such a death with the many other deaths that were just as violent, but forgotten through indifference and anonymity.

My life has no more value than any other. Nor any less value. In any case, it has not the innocence of childhood. I have lived long enough to know that I share in the evil which seems, alas, to prevail in the world, even in that which would strike me blindly. I should like, when the time comes, to have a clear space which would allow me to beg forgiveness of God and of all my fellow human beings, and at the same time to forgive with all my heart the one who would strike me down.

I could not desire such a death. It seems to me important to state this. I do not see, in fact, how I could rejoice if this people I love were to be accused indiscriminately of my murder. It would be to pay too dearly for what will, perhaps, be called "the grace of martyrdom," to owe it to an Algerian, whoever he may be, especially if he says he is acting in fidelity to what he believes to be Islam. I know the scorn with which Algerians as a whole can be regarded. I know also the caricature of Islam which a certain kind of Islamism encourages. It is too easy to give oneself a good conscience by identifying this religious way with the fundamentalist ideologies of the extremists. For me, Algeria and Islam are something different; they are a body and a soul. I have proclaimed this often enough I believe, in the sure knowledge of what I have received in Algeria, in the respect of believing Muslims—finding there so often that true strand of the gospel I learned at my mother's knee, my very first Church.

My death, clearly, will appear to justify those who hastily judged me naive or idealistic: "Let him tell us now what he thinks of it!" But these people must realize that my most avid curiosity will then be satisfied. This is what I shall be able to do, if God wills—immerse my gaze in that of the Father, to contemplate with him his children of Islam just as he sees them, all shining with the glory of Christ, the fruit of his Passion, filled with the Gift of the Spirit, whose secret joy will always be to establish communion and to refashion the likeness, delighting in the differences.

For this life given up, totally mine and totally theirs, I thank God who seems to have wished it entirely for the sake of that joy in everything and in spite of everything. In this "thank you," which is said for everything in my life from now on, I certainly include you, friends of yesterday and today, and you my friends of this place, along with my mother and father, my brothers and sisters and their families—the hundredfold granted as was promised!

And you also, the friend of my final moment, who would not be aware of what you were doing. Yes, for you also I wish this "thank you"—and this *adieu*—to commend you to the God whose face I see in yours.

And may we find each other, happy "good thieves," in Paradise, if it pleases God, the Father of us both. Amen.

6

The Sacrifice

The Sixth Word from the cross:

"It is finished."

"It is finished" here should be taken in the sense of *consummatum est*—it is consummated, fulfilled, brought to perfection. This is much more than "It is over." Of a terrible ordeal that has been endured we may say, "That's over with." In that case we mean that it is consigned to the past; now we can get on with life. "It is finished" is quite the opposite. It is a life brought to completion. Pilate said to him, "So you are a king?" Jesus answered, "For this I was born, and for this I have come into the world, to bear witness to the truth." From the cross he declares that he has done just that, borne witness to the truth, to the very end. Some, with Pilate, ask, "What is truth?" That question can be asked honestly, or, as with Pilate, it can be asked to preclude its answer. To those who sincerely ask the question, the answer proposed is this: The truth—the truth about

everything—is Jesus Christ and him crucified. It is not the
answer the world expected then or expects now.

"It is finished." An artist—perhaps a sculptor, painter or
composer—may say that. The artist starts out with an idea,
maybe calling it an inspiration; there are testings and false starts,
but the artist sticks with it, sees it through and at some point
stands back and says, "It is finished. That's it. That's what I had
in mind, or at least it is what came to be of what I had in mind."
So it is with any creative activity, whether it be a painting, the
making of a fine piece of furniture or the opening of a business.
So it is also when something has gone wrong and we set out to
remedy it. The wrong is set to right and there is a deep
satisfaction in having seen it through, in having brought a task
to completion. Perhaps there is something of that in this Sixth
Word from the cross, "It is finished." But the analogy with our
achievements, or with any achievement we can imagine, is
pathetically weak. The dissimilarities are immeasurably greater
than the similarities.

For one thing, it appears that *he* is finished. By any ordinary
measure this is not completion, but poignant failure. It is death.
It is the demolition of all those grand hopes he had aroused. He
started out announcing the coming of the kingdom of God, and
he ends up here. Some kingdom. Some king. The jeering crowds
around the cross are having the last laugh. He talked so
splendidly: "Blessed are the poor in spirit, for theirs is the
kingdom of heaven. Blessed are those who mourn, for they shall
be comforted. Blessed are the meek, for they shall inherit the
earth." What kingdom? What comfort? What inheritance? The
time has come to face the fact: It is finished, it is over.

Standing there with Mary, his mother, is John, the disciple whom Jesus loved, and he saw it all. Seeing it all, he would years later write, "In the beginning was the Word, and the Word was with God, and the Word was God. He was in the beginning with God; all things were made through him, and without him was not anything made that was made." As he wrote, there echoed in his mind the first words of the Hebrew Scriptures, "In the beginning God created the heavens and the earth." And God spoke his Word and said, "Let there be light," and there was light. The Word, says John, is the light. "The light shines in the darkness, and the darkness has not overcome it." And so say people beyond numbering to this very day. It is not over. It is finished.

This is the cross point in the Great Story, from the "In the beginning" of creation to the last words of the Bible, "Amen. Come, Lord Jesus!" At the cross point, everything is retrieved from the past and everything is anticipated from the future, and the cross is the point of entry to the heart of God from whom and for whom, quite simply, everything is. Here the beginning and the end come together, along with everything along the way from the beginning to the end. What is the Word of God but the love of God? In the beginning, God intended love. Why did God create? For love. Not for necessity, for, being God, he needed nothing, but that love might be, and that it might be more and more. Love is necessary, for "God is love."

He created out of nothing—*ex nihilo*—but his love. The Word is both his love and his beloved. "Without him was not anything made that was made." Through him God loved us into being. When he formed Adam from the primordial muck, he breathed into his nostrils the breath of life. He breathes love. Adam inhaled love. Here at the cross point, the new Adam exhales, "It is finished." The first Adam breathes in and the second Adam breathes out, and both breathe love. What began in Genesis is now finished. What began there is that love should give birth to love. So it was that through the Word the first Adam came to be and, because he did not love, the Word became the second Adam, who bore the fault of all the Adams and all the Eves of aborted love. Here at the cross point, that great work is definitively finished. Here is the one person who did and who was what through the centuries and millennia the rest of us had failed to do and be. Quite simply and wondrously, he loved the Father as he was loved by the Father.

It is finished, yet time goes on. It is not over. Through all time, the cross point is the point of entry into his life of love, for that life and that love fill all time. "I am the Alpha and Omega, the first and the last, the beginning and the end." His eternity is not timelessness but the fullness of time, which means time fulfilled. The infinite is not formless but the form of Christ. It is from first to last, and at every point in between, cruciform, the form of the cross. Not any cross, but *this* cross; yet this cross is every cross. At a particular point in time, on a certain Friday afternoon on a dung heap outside the gates of Jerusalem, it is said of all time, "It is finished." Yet it is not over. Now time, reformed because cross-formed, begins anew. The past and the future and this little in-between point we call the present are all in order. What happened at the cross point is what the first Adam was supposed to have done in the beginning. This is the Omega point, the end and the destiny of the love that was to give birth to love. It took the one who is both Alpha and Omega to restore life to love aborted.

It is finished, yet it is not over. It is finished means it is settled, decided, certain, complete and incontestable. *Consummatum est.* Nothing can happen now to undo it. Now there is absolutely nothing to fear. The worst has already happened. On a certain Friday afternoon it could truly be said, "God is dead," and there is no catastrophe beyond the death of God. About the decisive outcome of the contest between light and darkness, love and hate, life and death, we have the answer. Yet time goes on, and we might well wonder why. Perhaps we are still the early Church, with centuries or even millennia to go before every knee shall bow and every tongue confess that Jesus Christ is Lord. The outcome of the human project is incontestable, but it is still contested until all things are subjected to him and God is all in all. The human project cannot fail because God has invested himself in it; the Second Person of the Trinity is truly one of us. God has taken our part by taking our place.

As we may be the early Church, so also we may be in the youth of humanity's life span. Something like that may be suggested by St. Paul's words about our attaining to "the knowledge of the Son of God, to mature manhood, to the measure of the stature of the fullness of Christ." First John says "it does not yet appear what we shall be, but we know that when he appears we shall be like him, for we shall see him as he is." We have science fiction and other imaginative speculations about the future of the human project but, whatever might be in store for us, the end has appeared ahead of time in the Alpha and Omega who perfectly joins the originating intention with the consummating termination. That, too, is what is meant by *consummatum est.* The humanity of Jesus as a Jew, as the son of Mary in first-century Palestine—that is all specific and contingent. As the Word of God incarnate, however, he is universal humanity. Christian thinkers from the beginning have believed that Pontius Pilate said much more than he understood when he declared to the crowd, "Behold, the man." The Latin, which lacks the definite article, catches the meaning. *Ecce homo,* "Behold, man." The thing itself.

If we say that "It is finished" means that the human story is complete, we may be excused for wondering whether everything since then is not anticlimactic. Why wasn't the human drama wrapped up then and there? What is God waiting for? What has he been waiting for these two thousand years? We may wonder why we are here, never mind the human beings who may be here two thousand years from now. In the Letter to the Romans, Paul ponders this with specific reference to the many Jews who rejected the Messiah. He confesses that it is a "mystery," and a mystery is much more than a puzzlement. "Lest you be wise in your own conceits, I want you to understand this mystery: a hardening has come upon part of Israel, until the full number of the Gentiles come in, and so all Israel will be saved." Then speculation turns to wonder: "O the depth of the riches and wisdom and knowledge of God! How unsearchable are his judgments and how inscrutable his ways!" And then wonder turns to praise: "For from him and through him and to him are all things. To him be glory for ever. Amen."

Everything now and forever is to the glory of God. In his

glory is our good. Humanity, said Rabbi Abraham Joshua Heschel, is the cantor and caretaker of the universe. In directing the universe to the praise of God, however, we do not simply put the cross behind us. Quite the opposite is the case. In a cruciform world, the cross is the epicenter of everything. "It is finished" does not mean that suffering and loss and the rivers of tears are things of the past. "It is finished" means that they do not have the last word. It means that love has the last word. Recall Kurtz in Conrad's "Heart of Darkness," who, after a lifetime of slave trafficking in the Congo, dies with the words on his lips, "The horror! The horror!" The cross means that the horror is not the last word; at the heart of the horror is hope, because at the heart of the horror is Christ. In the beginning and in the end and all along the way was and is and ever will be the Word. Jesus told them, "In the world you will have trouble, but fear not, I have overcome the world." He will overcome the world because he has overcome the world. "It is finished."

In the middle of his life the novelist Peter De Vries wrote *The Blood of the Lamb* about his eleven-year-old daughter, Carol, who died of leukemia. At the children's pavilion in the New York hospital the main character, Wanderhope, gets to know other parents going through similar ordeals, including the jaded Stein, who announced, "The future is a thing of the past." The words stick with Wanderhope, even though reassuring doctors talk about new drugs, about remissions that last for years, about promising new research. "Of course!" says a doctor, "They're working on it day and night, and they're bound to get it soon."

On his visits to the hospital, Wanderhope would stop by at the Church of St. Catherine to pull himself together and maybe pray. Stein despised religion and would not go in. De Vries writes of Stein: "In this exile from peace of mind to which his reason doomed him, he was like an insomniac driven to awaken sleepers from dreams illegitimately won by going around shouting, 'Don't you realize it was a placebo!' Thus it seemed to me that what you were up against in Stein was not logic rampant, but frustrated faith. He could not forgive God for not existing."

Visiting parents in the pavilion try to keep the talk light. Aside from Stein and Wanderhope, who "meet and knock their heads together" over the big questions of fairness, theodicy, and what God might be up to, if there is a God, conversation in the children's pavilion goes on "by a kind of conspiracy of grace." It's a matter of pretending that things have a meaning, when you know they don't. The realities encountered in this "slice of hell," Wanderhope concludes, mock any response other than rage and despair. "Rage and despair are indeed carried about in the heart, but privately, to be let out on special occasions, like savage dogs for exercise, occasions in solitude when God is cursed, birds stoned from the trees or the pillow hammered in darkness."

Day after day, week after week, Carol hovers on the edge of life. Wanderhope thinks of the Slaughter of Innocents, and it seems that God and Herod are one. He tries to pray. He does not presume to pray that everything will again be all right; he prays for just one more year with Carol, rehearsing in his mind all they would do together in just one more year. And at last the day comes when the news is good; the marrow report is down to 6 percent, practically normal. Carol is in remission, she can go home tomorrow. The next day he buys a cake and stops by St.

Catherine's to offer a prayer of thanks. Mrs. Morano, the night
nurse, is at her prayers and tells him that an infection is going
through the ward like wildfire.

> I hurried into the hospital. One look at Carol and I knew it
> was time to say good-bye. The invading germ, or germs, had
> not only ravaged her bloodstream by now, but had broken out
> on her body surface in septicemic discolorations. Her foul
> enemy had his will of her well at last. One of the blotches
> covered where they were trying to insert a catheter, and spread
> down along a thigh. By afternoon it had traveled to the knee,
> and by the next, gangrened.

The nurse whispered it was only a matter of hours now, and
all her dreams would be pleasant. "I was thinking of a line of old
poetry. 'Death loves a shining mark.'" Wanderhope saw her on
her bicycle, the sun in her hair, the shining spokes; at the piano
practicing, and the smile of satisfaction when she got it right;
and he knew that none of this would ever be again.

The nurse left and he moved to the side of the bed and
whispered rapidly in their moment alone:

> "The Lord bless thee and keep thee; the Lord make his face
> shine upon thee and be gracious unto thee; the Lord lift up his
> countenance upon thee, and give thee peace." Then I touched
> the stigmata one by one: the prints of the needles, the wound
> in the breast that had for so many months now scarcely ever
> closed. I caressed the perfectly shaped head. I bent to kiss the
> cheeks, the breasts that would now never be fulfilled, that no
> youth would ever touch. "Oh, my lamb."

Later, in the middle of the afternoon, Carol died. Wanting to secure the unfathomable pain of the particulars, Wanderhope looked around for a clock. "I had guessed what the hands would say. Three o'clock. The children were putting their schoolbooks away, and getting ready to go home."

After some legal formalities, Wanderhope went to a bar and had a drink, and then six drinks, and then seven, and then he remembered the cake he had left in the church. On his way out of St. Catherine's he looked up at the crucifix over the central doorway, its arms outspread among the sooted stones and strutting doves.

> I took the cake out of the box and balanced it a moment on the palm of my hand. Disturbed by something in the motion, the birds started from their covert and flapped away across the street. Then my arm drew back and let fly with all the strength within me. Before the mind snaps, or the heart breaks, it gathers itself like a clock about to strike. It might even be said one pulls himself together to disintegrate. . . . It was miracle enough that the pastry should reach its target at all, at that height from the sidewalk. The more so that it should land squarely, just beneath the crown of thorns. Then through scalded eyes I seemed to see the hands free themselves of the nails and move slowly toward the soiled face. Very slowly, very deliberately, with infinite patience, the icing was wiped from the eyes and flung away: I could see it fall in clumps to the porch steps. Then the cheeks were wiped down with the same sense of grave and gentle ritual, with all the kind sobriety of one whose voice could be heard saying, "Suffer the little children to come unto me, for of such is the kingdom of heaven."

Then everything dissolved, and Wanderhope, no longer able to stand, sat down on the worn steps of the church. "Thus Wanderhope was found at that place which for the diabolists of his literary youth, and for those with more modest spiritual histories too, was said to be the only alternative to the muzzle of a pistol: the foot of the Cross."

De Vries does not say whether the hands on the cross, having wiped away the cake, were then extended once more, whether the crucified one repositioned himself to be hit again and again. But I think that is what happened. By the bedside of his dead Carol, Wanderhope cries, "Oh, my lamb." His cry is taken up in the sacrifice of the Mass, joined to the desolation of pilgrims beyond number: "*Agnus Dei, qui tollis peccata mundi, miserere nobis . . . dona nobis pacem.* Lamb of God, who takes away the sins of the world, have mercy on us . . . give us peace." It is, writes De Vries, "the recognition of how long, how long is the mourners' bench upon which we sit, arms linked in undeluded friendship—all of us, brief links, ourselves, in the eternal pity." The eternal pity is concentrated here when, we are told, it was about the ninth hour, which is three o'clock in the afternoon, and he cried out, "It is finished."

At the foot of the cross we join Gerard Manley Hopkins in the eternal pity and cry with him as in "Carrion Comfort," "*I can no more.*" But then, "I can; / Can something, hope, wish day come, not choose not to be." Hopkins looks back:

> *That night, that year*
> *Of now done darkness I wretch lay wrestling with (my God!)*
> *my God.*

In the pitch darkness of that night we wrestle with abandonment, to discover we are wrestling with the Abandoned One. In the experience of abandonment by God we are most securely embraced in the love of God. This love of God is the very life of God—Father, Son and Holy Spirit. It is the love of the Father that incorporates the godforsakenness of the Son by the power of the Spirit. What is definitively "finished" is the power of division to divide, of separation to separate.

From now on, in the abandonment of Christ the alone are never alone. That is because, as paradoxical as it may sound, aloneness is no longer alone, but has been brought into the good company of God. We may go further and speak of the good company who *is* God, although the usual word is not company but "communion." "God is what happens between Jesus and his Father in their Spirit," writes theologian Robert Jenson. That is another way of saying that "God is love," for what happens in the life of God is love. The human suffering and death of Jesus is an event in the triune life of God, and because Christ is also the Word by whom and through whom everything exists and is sustained in being, all innocent suffering and death has been enclosed in the life of God. Every heartbroken cry of "Oh, my lamb" is taken up and finally overtaken in *Agnus Dei, qui tollis peccata mundi,* in whom is our peace.

In the Catholic Church, the Good Friday liturgy includes the veneration of the cross. Beginning at the back of the church and moving slowly toward the front, the deacon holds up the crucifix, which he gradually unveils as he sings three times, "This is the wood of the cross, on which hung the Savior of the world." The people respond, "Come, let us worship," and then, one by one, they come forward and kneel to kiss the feet of the dead Christ. This is one of the more poignant moments in the Church's liturgy, but it is not loved by all. Some years ago, a friend attended the Good Friday liturgy, but refused to participate in this part of the service. "To kneel and kiss the crucifix," she said, "is morbid. Moreover, isn't it idolatry to worship an image?" At first I didn't know what to say in response.

My parents have both died, and I keep a picture of them near my desk. Sometimes it happens, quite spontaneously, that I will kiss the picture as a sign of affection and of the hope that I will see them again. I suppose that most people engage in similar gestures of devotion toward pictures or other objects associated with loved ones. There is no confusion of image and reality, although, at least in our own consciousness, each participates in the other. Between the sign and the reality signified, there is an interpenetration that we might call the sacramentality of everyday life. We likely would think it very odd, however, if people were invited to venerate pictures of their ancestors and they responded, "Come, let us worship." That would be idolatry, not because it is idolatry to venerate a picture, but because it is idolatry to worship one's ancestors. Such a thing might be done in the Shinto rituals of Japan, but is entirely alien to Christianity.

In Shusako Endo's powerful novel *Silence*, the seventeenth-century Jesuits of Nagasaki and their converts can avoid crucifixion by stepping on the crucifix. "It is such a little thing to require," their tormentors say enticingly, and so apostates came to agree. But those who became the martyrs knew that the little thing was everything. It was the absolute antithesis of Good

Friday's veneration of the cross. The contempt or the veneration is absolute, because the reality signified by the cross is, in the words of the creed, "God from God, Light from Light, true God from true God." Yet, as with Wanderhope's cake splattered in his face, the crucified One accepts the rejection driven by fear or rage. This act, too, was anticipated in his "It is finished." Our rejection is impotent against a loss that is total. Having accepted extinction, the light of this love cannot be extinguished. "The light shines in the darkness, and the darkness has not overcome it." No darkness can overcome it, for it is the light on the far side of darkness, the life on the far side of death, the everything on the far side of nothing.

Good Friday's veneration of the cross, then, is the very opposite of idolatry. Idolatry is the effort to capture the Divine and employ it to our purposes. In the words of Psalm 115:

> *Their idols are silver and gold,*
>   *the work of men's hands.*
> *They have mouths, but do not speak;*
>   *eyes, but do not see.*
> *They have ears, but do not hear;*
>   *noses, but do not smell.*
> *They have hands, but do not feel;*
>   *feet, but do not walk;*
>   *and they do not make a sound in their throat.*
> *Those who make them are like them;*
>   *so are all who trust in them.*

We venerate the crucified One, who no longer speaks nor sees nor hears nor smells nor feels nor walks nor makes a sound in his throat. Unlike the idols, all these things he once did, but now no more. Precisely in his inability to serve our purposes, in his helplessness, we pledge allegiance with a kiss. We do well to hesitate, remembering the one to whom he said in the garden, "Would you betray the Son of man with a kiss?" By false veneration he is betrayed again and again. For those who have accepted his invitation, however, it is following him all the way. "Come, follow me," he said, and now it has come to this. We kneel under the weight of doubt and fear and say, yes, we are prepared to surrender all. It is a rite of rehearsal, preparing us for the times when much, maybe all, will be required. "Oh, my lamb." *Agnus Dei, qui tollis peccata mundi* . . .

Here he is on Good Friday, taking away the sins of the world by bearing the sins of the world, bearing also the consequences of the sins of the world. The innocent Lamb of God bears the pain of all the innocent lambs, and the sorrow of Wanderhopes beyond numbering in the loss of the innocents. At the foot of the cross we recognize that we are not merely victims of a senseless fate; we are implicated in the mystery of sin and redemption. We are participants in this drama, although exactly how we do not know. We have not seen the entire script; our lines are given us one at a time. Through our tears and through our rage at all that has gone wrong, we kneel and kiss the feet of the crucified One in whose death we acknowledge our part. At the veneration, as the people come forward one by one, the choir sings the Reproaches.

> O, my people, what have I done to you?
> How have I offended you? Answer me!
> I led you out of Egypt, from slavery to freedom,

but you led your Savior to the cross.
My people, answer me!

For forty years I led you safely through the desert.
I fed you with manna from heaven
and brought you to a land of plenty;
but you led your Savior to the cross.

The entire story of salvation and our sorry response is rehearsed:

I gave you saving water from the rock,
but you gave me gall and vinegar to drink.

I gave you a royal scepter,
but you gave me a crown of thorns.

I raised you to the height of majesty,
but you have raised me high on a cross.

After each reproach is the acclamation. It is called the Trisagion, the "thrice holy," and has played a prominent part in Eastern Orthodox liturgy since the fifth century. It was received into the Latin Rite only in the eleventh century, and then only for the veneration of the cross on Good Friday, precisely for the occasion when it might seem most inappropriate.

Holy is God!
Holy and mighty!
Holy immortal One, have mercy on us!

Do not try to sort it out in a systematic fashion—what sin caused what consequence and why, and who precisely is responsible for what and how. At the foot of the cross it may seem everything is a muddle. Clear laws of cause and effect are thrown into consternation. In the veneration of the cross, three truths cut searingly through the muddle. First, we are implicated, deeply implicated. During Holy Week's readings of the passion story, the entire congregation joins us in crying out, "Crucify him! Crucify him!" It is not what "they" did; it is what we did, and what we do. Second, and despite all, God is holy, God is strong, God is immortal. If we lose our hold on that truth, everything is lost. Third—and this is the paradox at the heart of the muddle—God's loss of everything on the cross, his taking our place, is our only hope that all is not lost. Holy is the God-man! Holy vulnerable and faithful! Holy immortal One, dying and dead, have mercy on us! *Agnus Dei, miserere nobis.*

Here we lay down our burdens; here we collapse under our burdens. In the Good Friday liturgy, the priests and deacons lie prostrate, collapsed, before the cross. St. Patrick's Cathedral in New York is directly across from Rockefeller Center, and at the entrance to Rockefeller Center is the great sculpture of Atlas holding up the world. On Good Friday, the doors of the cathedral are opened, and you can see the great cross from the street. Turn in one direction and there is the mythical Atlas holding up the world; turn in the other, and there is the One broken by the world. Which image speaks the truth? Is the world upheld by our godlike strength or by the crucified love of God? Upon that decision everything, simply everything, turns.

"Come, follow me," Jesus said, and now it has come to this.

In the good days, when all was bright with promise, we said yes to the invitation to follow. And should we pull back now? Can we? Much earlier, at the first intimations of trouble ahead, long before it came to this, Jesus asked the Twelve whether they, too, would leave him. Peter answered, "Lord, to whom shall we go? You have the words of eternal life." Whatever other leader we might follow, he would, in time, also die. With anyone else it would come to this as well. And yet not really to *this*, for the death of any other would be simply loss and deprivation. Of the death of another it would be said that it was inevitable; of this death it is said, "It is finished." And how would we explain to some other lord or how would we explain to ourselves, why we left Jesus now? His word was, "Greater love has no man than this, that he lay down his life for his friends." And we should stop being his friends because he kept his word?

In the seventeenth century George Herbert in "Affliction" considered the alternatives:

> *Yet, though thou troublest me, I must be meek;*
> *In weakness must be stout.*
> *Some other master out.*
> *Ah, my dear God! though I am clean forgot,*
> *Let me not love thee, if I love thee not.*

What should we make of that? If I do not love you now, did I love you ever? If that—which was beyond measure in its beauty—was not love that I had for you, let me not love? No, this is better: Let me not love you if I do not love you in your loving me to the end. For me it is simply to be meek, to accept what I did not want, what I did not ask for, what I could not imagine, although you tried to prepare us for this. You said that later we would come to understand. "Then he poured water into a basin, and began to wash the disciples' feet, and to wipe them with the towel with which he was girded. He came to Simon Peter; and Peter said to him, 'Lord, do you wash my feet?' Jesus answered him, 'What I am doing you do not know now, but afterward you will understand.'"

It is afterward now, and we begin to understand. Embracing the work of a slave he died the death of a slave, so that we may no longer be slaves to the fear of slavery and death. Kneel now, here at the veneration of the cross; embrace and kiss the lowest of the low, the poorest of the poor, the deadest of the dead. Do not be afraid; it is not morbid, nor is it a rite of self-denigration. It is not about the self at all. It is far beyond the self. The psychologizing, the sickeningly complex consciousness of our own consciousness—all that is left far behind. Enter into the heart of darkness, love following love, to the end. "Let me not love thee, if I love thee not."

"It is finished." But it is not over. It will not be over until every knee shall bow and every tongue confess that Jesus Christ is Lord. That triumphant note does not mean the simple displacement of suffering with victory. The innocent lambs still go to the slaughter, and we have not finished with "It is finished" until we understand the connection between their suffering and his, between his suffering and ours. Paul writes, "Now I rejoice in my sufferings for your sake, and in my flesh I complete what is lacking in Christ's afflictions for the sake of his body, that is, the Church." Does this mean that Christ's sufferings on the cross are not complete, that it is not finished after all? No, it means that at the cross point of history everything past is retrieved and everything future is anticipated, and here is suffered all the suffering of all time.

Those who enter into the heart of darkness with love following love to the very end are participants in the cross point of all time. On the night before the end that began the world anew, he gave his followers the Eucharist as the rite of their continuing companionship with him. In the Eucharist as sacrifice, the sufferings of all time are gathered to his suffering. It is not Christ's sacrifice repeated, but his once-for-all sacrifice reaching out to embrace, complete and make whole every human moment of the horror. All those on the long mourners' bench of the eternal pity, all who have this day received the dread news of cancer, all victims of genocides beyond number, all the old and forgotten hovering in the dark corners of shabby nursing homes—for all, their suffering need not be "senseless," but is caught up by faith in the once-for-all-time sacrifice of which it is said, "It is finished."

In what we think of as the piety of a simpler time, Christians undergoing trial or affliction were urged to "offer it up." I recall being deeply impressed as a young man by the death of Pope John XXIII. It was slow in coming, and over the days there were regular news bulletins reporting that he was offering up one day's suffering for those with cancer, another day's suffering for homeless refugees, another for mothers with difficult pregnancies and so forth. He seemed to be going about his dying with such purpose, with almost workmanlike efficiency, wasting none of it. And I began to understand what St. Paul

meant by rejoicing in his sufferings for our sake, completing
what is lacking in the afflictions of Christ.

It is a great understatement to say that this way of thinking
and believing is deeply offensive, indeed repugnant, to many
today. The idea of self-sacrifice has probably never been terribly
popular. When I was fiercely ill and near to death, I tried
"offering it up" and discovered I was not very good at it. Mainly,
I just wanted it to be over with one way or another. That is
likely the case with most Christians of all times. But in our
culture the idea of redemptive suffering runs into a fusillade of
intellectual and even religious attack. It is, we are told, more
than morbid; it is pathological, destructive of self-esteem,
conducive to masochism and generally a Very Bad Thing. For
the healthy-minded, the key terms are empowerment, control,
achievement and pleasure. In the view of many, there is nothing
worse than the loss of control, with its attendant suffering and
pain. Life itself is valued less than freedom from suffering, as
witness the attraction of mercy killing in its various forms. Little
wonder that we are tempted to get Good Friday quickly over
with and rush on to the joy of Easter.

"It is finished" refers to a life and work complete and perfect.
The life and work of Jesus was about many things, but, most
important to the story of salvation, it was about offering the
complete and perfect sacrifice. Earlier we touched on the ways
in which Christians have tried to think about the atonement, the
reconciliation of God and humanity that results in at-one-ment.
If we are to think with the Bible about these matters, there is no
going around the fact that at the heart of atonement is sacrifice.
Consider just a few of the pertinent texts. We will then have

time to examine how these texts have been used and abused in preaching, teaching and popular devotion, all with a view toward entering more deeply into the darkness, in hope of the light on the far side.

That sacrifice is central to the biblical story there can be no doubt. The persistence of the theme is striking. The Letter to the Hebrews speaks of the earlier ritual sacrifices of animals and says, "How much more shall the blood of Christ, who through the eternal Spirit offered himself without blemish to God, purify your conscience from dead works to serve the living God." Then it speaks of how Christ "offered for all time a single sacrifice for sins . . . [by which] he has perfected for all time those who are sanctified." Paul writes in Romans that redemption is in Christ Jesus "whom God put forward as an expiation by his blood, to be received by faith." In Ephesians, Christ "gave himself up for us, a fragrant offering and sacrifice to God." First John declares that Jesus is "the expiation for our sins, and not for ours only but also for the sins of the whole world." First Peter tells us we have been saved "by the precious blood of Christ, like that of a lamb without blemish or spot." Repeatedly in the book of Revelation the saints and angels are in festive gathering around the Lamb who was slain from before the foundation of the world, whose blood redeemed those of "every tribe and tongue and people and nation."

Ah, yes, it is objected by some, but that elaborate sacrificial theology was added by Paul and the early Church; it is not to be found in the simple Gospel accounts of Jesus. On the contrary, in both Mark and Matthew, to cite but two instances, Jesus says that the Son of man came "to give his life as a ransom for many."

In all three of the synoptic Gospels, Jesus institutes the Eucharist by explaining that his body is to be broken and his blood to be poured out as the ratification of the new covenant. The covenant is sealed by blood, just as Exodus 24 tells us the old covenant under Moses was sealed by pouring out the blood of goats and oxen.

As for John's Gospel, it opens with the declaration of John the Baptizer that Jesus is "the Lamb of God who takes away the sin of the world." Six chapters later, Jesus shocks his hearers with, "I am the living bread which came down from heaven; if any one eats of this bread, he will live forever; and the bread which I shall give for the life of the world is my flesh." We have already seen how, in his telling of the passion story, John depicts the crucifixion as the fulfillment of the offering of the Passover lamb. Throughout the story, Jesus is acting in obedience to the Father. In John 10 we read: "No one takes [my life] from me, but I lay it down of my own accord. I have power to lay it down, and I have power to take it again; this charge I have received from my Father." In the synoptic accounts of the anguish in the garden of Gethsemane, Jesus cries out, "Not my will but thine be done!" The next day's cry from the cross, "It is finished," signifies that God's will has been done, the perfect sacrifice has been made.

Yet the idea of sacrifice, of expiation, of making satisfaction is alien to many today. A woman, well educated and very successful in business, tells me:

I think I am almost ready to be a Christian. I have no doubts about God, and I completely agree with the Church's moral teachings. I'm not sure I understand them, but the idea of the sacraments—communion, forgiveness, the meaning of marriage, and all that—makes sense to me. I am a little embarrassed to say it, but my problem is with the cross. Why Jesus had to die, this whole business about sacrifice and blood, I just don't get it. Since the cross is the main symbol of Christianity, and the Church keeps saying it's the key to everything, I suppose that's a pretty big problem, right?

Right. It is also a problem shared by many who do not hesitate to call themselves Christians, despite their "not getting" this business about sacrifice and blood.

Why deny it? Talk about sacrifice conjures up images of primitive tribal rites in which blood-splattered priests offer up slaughtered beasts or virgins to appease the wrath of the angry gods. Such images are not too far from the way some Christians preach the cross. Theories of "substitutionary atonement" frequently depict a wrathful God who must, in unrelenting justice, punish everyone who has sinned, unless a substitute is found who will, as it were, take the rap in their stead. That substitute, of course, is Jesus. This way of thinking about atonement can be very dramatically presented and has the additional merit of being closely connected with an idea of sacrifice that is grounded both in the Bible and in our human intuitions about what justice requires. It is also fraught with problems.

Here in New York an elderly man lived next door with his son, who took care of him. They were very close. One day we met on the street and, quite out of the blue, he announced:

I want to tell you something. I would go to church, but I can't.
I could never worship a God who tortured and killed his son.
It's as simple as that. If he was really God, he could have found
some other way to fix whatever was wrong with the world. I
couldn't respect a man who did that to his son, no matter what
the reason, and I won't worship a God who did it. I just wanted
you to know that.

I was quite taken aback by the vehemence of his announcement.
I tried to explain, but I don't think it did much good. The man
and his son moved away a couple of years ago, and I lost track
of them.

Some theologians who are attuned to contemporary
sensibilities have decided that, in order to get rid of the
suggestion of divine vindictiveness, punishment and cruelty, it is
better to jettison the notion of sacrifice altogether. Actually, this
has been going on for more than a century in the tradition
known as liberal theology. The result is a different, and by no
means unattractive, theory of atonement. In this theory, the
point of the crucifixion is to show God's unconditional love. The
cross evokes from believers a deep sense of gratitude and shows
us the virtues we are to imitate.

Although it has attractive elements, there are major problems
in this way of thinking about the atonement. For one thing, it
ignores most of what the Bible says and the Church has taught
about the meaning of the cross. And my old next-door neighbor
might continue to wonder how the death of Jesus shows God's
unconditional love. Then too, since we are only human, most of
us might have severe doubts about our ability to do what Jesus
did. This "exemplification theory" of the atonement—the

crucified Jesus as the supreme example—is strong on challenge but weak on comfort. It has little to say about what the crucifixion actually did, what it actually accomplished, in terms of reconciling God and humankind. That we are alienated from God and need to be reconciled is the premise of the entire biblical story, without which it simply makes no sense. In this liberal theory, it is hard to know what is meant by "It is finished." Perhaps that Jesus lived to its conclusion an extremely good, even uniquely good, life. That might elicit our admiration and our efforts at emulation, but it doesn't say much about our inability to be what we strive to be. It doesn't say much about the ways in which we are what we hate. In short, it doesn't say much about our salvation. Christianity is about salvation.

Theologians who are influenced by existentialist philosophy propose a somewhat different understanding of atonement. Whatever happened in the death of the historical person called Jesus, they say, the experience of the "Christ event" produced an Easter gospel (called the kerygma) that has redemptive power. There is no denying the fact, they point out, that from the early apostolic community to the present, the lives of people responding in faith to this gospel have been brought to "authentic existence." In that sense, the gospel of God's unqualified and victorious love in Jesus is demonstrably redemptive. "You are accepted," declared the noted existentialist theologian Paul Tillich. "Accept your acceptance!"

Tillich's favorite text from St. Paul was the statement, "Therefore, if any one is in Christ, he is a new creation; the old has passed away, behold, the new has come." This is a very bracing message. If one believes it, it may certainly have a very real effect on one's life—an existential effect, if you will. But Tillich and others leave unexplained the "therefore" in Paul's statement. In Paul, something *happened* that creates a new circumstance in which everything really is new. As he says in the same passage, "God was in Christ reconciling the world to himself, not counting their trespasses against them." The *message* of the cross and resurrection, as powerful as it is, cannot be separated from what God *did* in the cross and resurrection. The message cannot be separated from what some dismiss as the myth of atoning sacrifice.

"It is finished" refers to something done, and the something is done by God. Without that, the message of acceptance may indeed change people but, for all the profundity of someone like Paul Tillich, it is finally another form of positive thinking. It cannot bear the weight of the question "Is it true?" Except, of course, for those who are satisfied with the response, "Well, it's true *for me*." I do not wish to be unfair, for sophisticated thinkers hold to this theory of atonement, but I cannot help but think that it is, when pressed, a rhetorically inflated equivalent of the yellow smile button or the exhortation "Have a nice life!" Those seated on the long mourners' bench of the eternal pity will not likely be impressed.

There is yet another theory of atonement, this one favored by those who are called liberation theologians, which includes some contemporary feminist thinkers. It, too, has definite attractions, depicting Jesus as the champion of the poor and oppressed in their struggle against the rich and powerful. Here the crucifixion of Jesus is seen as the consequence of his preaching a message of social justice in an unjust world. The cross is both protest and promise. It is a protest against injustice and a promise that God is on the side of those who suffer, and especially those who suffer for others. The liberationist view tends to be highly political and ideological, but, quite apart from politics and ideology, most of what it says about the crucifixion needs to be said. Jesus did challenge the religious authorities of his day, and he also challenged the political authorities by preaching a sovereignty higher than theirs. Remember that on the cross was pinned the political statement "King of the Jews." And there is no question that those who killed him acted unjustly. Moreover, he certainly had a most particular devotion for the poor, oppressed and marginal, and he calls his disciples to join him in that devotion. All this is true.

But the liberationist view does not say enough. It does not say nearly enough. And some of what it says is misleading at best, and disastrous at worst. It does not say what we earlier noted the New Testament says about the crucifixion as a sacrificial offering that decisively and once and for all brought about a changed relationship between God and his human creatures. In addition, the claim that Jesus was a champion of social justice who advanced a cause of revolutionary social, economic and political change can appeal to a few texts in the Gospel accounts, but, as we know from both the Gospels and the rest of the New Testament, it is certainly not what the apostolic community proclaimed to be the significance of his death and resurrection. Potentially devastating is the liberationists' relentless focus on transforming the world here and now. The kingdom of God that Jesus proclaimed is, in this way of thinking, either a human project that is achievable here and now or is dismissed as pie in the sky. The effort to establish the kingdom of God here on earth invites fanatical delusion and when it fails, as it inevitably must fail, it invites hopeless despair.

Neither the liberals nor the existentialists nor the liberationists do justice to "It is finished." Here on the cross something has been completed that makes it true that Jesus is, in the words of 1 John, "the expiation for our sins, and not for ours only but also for the sins of the whole world." An expiation is an act of atonement, and the atonement is effected, says 1 Peter, "with the precious blood of Christ, like that of a lamb without blemish or spot." It seems that, despite our repugnance for primitive images of blood-spattered priests, despite my neighbor's abhorrence of a father killing his son and despite the well-educated businesswoman's simple puzzlement about the big deal made of the cross, Christianity is stuck with the idea of sacrifice.

The repugnance, abhorrence and puzzlement are understandable. Is it possible that they reflect a profound misunderstanding of what the Church means by the crucifixion as sacrifice? I am convinced the answer is yes. At the same time, we should not be surprised by such misunderstanding. It has always been the case. "We preach Christ crucified," Paul wrote, "a stumbling block to the Jews and foolishness to the Greeks." A stumbling block and foolishness to the Americans and everyone else as well, we might add. Nor should we think that the acceptance of this apparently foolish truth is merely an intellectual matter of clearing up a few misunderstandings. It is a matter of venturing into the mystery at the veneration of the cross. It is a matter of crying out with Wanderhope, "Oh, my lamb!" and hearing the echo of *Agnus Dei, qui tollis peccata mundi*. It is a matter of understanding, or beginning to understand, what he meant by "It is finished." And knowing that it is not over.

At the same time, it is also a matter of clearing up misunderstandings. The distinguished Catholic theologian Avery Dulles says that the Church means by sacrifice "an external act that symbolically expresses the interior homage of the creature to God." It is an act dramatizing the most elementary truth that, as we discussed earlier, we are creatures. We are not the Creator; we are not God. Sacrifice is an act of homage, of worship. It is also an act that intends to change a relationship by way of reparation or making amends. In Christian preaching and on billboards along highways all over America, we encounter the bald assertion, "Jesus died for your sins." In Pope Paul VI's "Credo of the People of God," it is put this way: "We believe that our Lord Jesus Christ by the sacrifice of the cross redeemed us from original sin and from all the personal sins committed by each one of us." Similar statements are found in the classic texts of all Christian bodies. Remove the idea of sacrifice, the reality of sacrifice, from Christianity and it becomes something other than Christianity.

The concept of expiation, of making amends by sacrifice, is indeed primitive. It is primitive in the sense that it is deeply rooted in human nature and variously expressed in all cultures that we know about. Once again, to say something is primitive does not mean that it is naive and should be outgrown. That which is most deeply rooted in human nature and culture—whether it be attitudes toward sexual relations, property and theft or the love of children—reflects a wisdom that we ignore at our peril. About such matters, there is an unreflective naïveté, a childish naïveté, that most of us do outgrow. As we learn to reflect critically on our elementary intuitions, we dissect them and take them apart, with the result that they are exposed or debunked. This is the course of the modern mind-set we call critical consciousness. Nothing escapes its relentless interrogation; everything is, in the fashionable language of the academy, "deconstructed." Under the reign of critical consciousness, everything that seemed self-evident, given, obvious and beyond question turns out to appear arbitrary, contingent and, as it is said, "culturally constructed." Everything, we come to think, could be other than it is.

The final outcome of critical consciousness, however, need not be that we are sure of nothing. It can lead to our being graced with a "second naïveté." We are indebted to the philosopher Paul Ricoeur for that happy phrase. The second naïveté is an understanding reached on the far side of critical analysis and debunking. Having come to recognize that things could theoretically be other than they are, we are brought to the perception that they are as we thought them to be; but on the far side of all our questioning, we *know* that in a way we did not know it before. This is the destination of the path that theology describes as "faith in search of understanding." It is surely part of what Jesus meant when he insisted that we must be born again, becoming not again childish but, for the first time, childlike. Eliot puts it nicely in *Little Gidding*:

> *We shall not cease from exploration*
> *And the end of all our exploring*

Will be to arrive where we started
And know the place for the first time.

So it is with sacrifice, and so it is with beginning to understand the cross. Remember our much earlier discussion of the broken cookie jar on the kitchen floor. The child knows that something has gone terribly wrong with the world and something must be done about it if the world is to make moral sense. We can try to cover it up, pretend it did not happen or deny that it has anything to do with us, but only at the price of bearing the guilty knowledge that we are living a lie. Thus is the first offense of stealing the cookie compounded by our lie, until step by step in a life dishonestly lived the broken cookie jar represents a universe in which all moral meaning is shattered. Admittedly, that is making an awful lot out of the case of the broken cookie jar, but the world rests—better to say that it teeters—on intuitions so elementary as to be almost embarrassing. When we find such intuitions to be inconvenient, and they often are, we try to dismiss them as primitive. But they keep coming back.

The most deep-seated wisdom can be expressed in ways that are bizarre and morally odious. The truth that something must be done about a wrong committed—that it must be punished or amends be made—can lead to vengeful and sadistic acts. Lives are made miserable by demands for expiation that cannot be satisfied. Many people twist their whole lives into a futile effort to make up for some great wrong they did. Such efforts can have a constructive purpose but a destructive effect. Making up for wrong is not just an individual problem, nor does it typically result in constructive activity. Whole peoples go to war, slaughtering one another in order to "settle the score" of collective guilt through collective retribution. Crowds gather outside prisons to cheer when the lights dim, indicating that a prisoner has been electrocuted. So terrible and twisted is the history of sacrifice and punishment that we can understand why many decent people have turned their backs on the idea altogether, dismissing it as a primitive vestige that civilization should transcend.

Christian morality, it is said, has tempered and tamed the idea of punishment, and that is true. There is in the biblical view no room for collective guilt; already in the prophets of Israel it is emphasized that each person is held responsible for his or her own acts. Moreover, Jesus tells us followers, "Be merciful as your heavenly Father is merciful," and he gave us many parables illustrating such mercy in action. St. Paul quotes Deuteronomy in his admonition to the Romans, "Beloved, never avenge yourselves, but leave it to the wrath of God; for it is written, 'Vengeance is mine, I will repay, says the Lord.'" These and other teachings temper and humanize the idea of punishment and satisfaction, but they do not abolish it. Abolition, which may at first seem so very humane, would leave us in a morally senseless and infinitely cruel world in which wrong, even the greatest wrong, finally makes no difference. How, then, is the endless round of bloody retribution to be brought to an end? By a perfect act of reparation. By a sacrifice to end all sacrifices. By the cry from the cross, "It is finished."

As we have seen, Christians have been pondering for a very long time exactly how this was brought about. Among such ponderings of the atonement, few have had so much influence as the eleventh-century reflection of St. Anselm of Canterbury, *Cur Deus Homo* (Why God Became Man). It is a profound work we cannot examine in detail here, but among Anselm's insights is that there are only two things that can be done to remedy the wrong against God that we call sin. If we live in a universe that makes moral sense, sin must either be punished or satisfaction for the offense must be made. In Jesus, satisfaction takes the place of punishment. We have said that Jesus takes our part by taking our place. That may sound like "substitutionary atonement," but "substitution" is not the right word. That would mean that somebody else is taking the punishment for us, which, though surely loving if freely done, hardly seems just. Even worse, it is sometimes suggested that God vented his wrath by inflicting a terrible punishment on his perfectly innocent Son, which, as the elderly man next door rightly protested, would be outrageously unjust.

We do well to get rid completely of the notion that the atonement is about what God *did to* Jesus. This requires returning to the truth that the God who brought about our atonement is the Holy Trinity—Father, Son and Holy Spirit. Atonement is from beginning to end the work of the three divine Persons of the triune God. In collusion with the Father, the Son, in the power of the Spirit, freely takes our part by becoming our *representative*. A representative is different from a substitute. The atonement is not a quantitative matter. It is not as though there is a certain amount of wrong for which a certain amount of punishment is due, and so somebody must be found to take the punishment. That way of thinking produced the ritual of the scapegoat, a ritual reenacted in many different ways throughout history. Christ's atoning sacrifice is not about quantities of sin and punishment but is intensely personal. It is the mending of a personal relationship between God and humanity that had been broken.

Justice requires that satisfaction be made; we were and we are in no position to make such satisfaction. Jesus Christ actively intervenes on our behalf; he freely takes our part in healing the breach between God and humanity by the sacrifice of the cross. To speak of a collusion between the Persons of the triune God suggests the word "conspiracy." It is a helpful word when we remember that conspire means, quite literally, "to breathe together." In the beginning, God breathes life into Adam; Jesus breathes upon the disciples and says, "Receive the Holy Spirit." The triune God conspires for our salvation. The entire plan is love from beginning to end, and the fullness of God—Father, Son and Holy Spirit—is engaged every step of the way. It is not an angry Father punishing an innocent Son, with the Spirit on the sidelines helplessly watching. No, it is the Father, Son and Spirit conspiring together to save us from ourselves. At the Father's command, the Son freely goes forth in the power of the Spirit to become one of us. On our behalf, as Representative Humanity, he lives the life of perfect obedience that Adam—and all of us "in Adam"—failed to live. And he completes that life by dying the perfect death.

This is what the Church means when she speaks of Christ as the Second Adam. In Christ, the old order of sin gives way to the new order of grace. St. Paul writes, "For those whom [God] foreknew he also predestined to be conformed to the image of his Son, in order that he might be the firstborn among many brethren." Or, as he tells the Colossians, "He is the head of the body, the Church; he is the beginning, the firstborn from the dead, that in everything he might be preeminent." In Christ—and it is impossible to overemphasize how crucial are those two words "in Christ"—there is nothing less than a new humanity. It begins with the Church, but the Church is the sign of promise reaching out to all. That is what it means when we say that the Church does not just *have* sacraments, but *is* the cosmic sacrament to the world. She is the means by which people enter into the new order of grace established by the One who represents us to the Father.

Of course, no matter how loving his intentions, Jesus could not be Representative Humanity unless he really was God incarnate, God-become-man. Otherwise, whatever his intentions, he would be only one good person, even if the best person who ever lived. That is why John begins his Gospel with the assertion that he is the Word of God, the Second Person of the Trinity, who was in the beginning and through whom all came to be. Only the One through whom we came to be in the beginning could make a new beginning. Atonement, then, is not simply a transaction, the paying of a debt or the exacting of a punishment; it is Father, Son and Spirit actively at work to remedy our great wrong. This is what God wanted to do and, in some sense, what it was necessary for God to do. *If* it was to be done, it was necessary for God to do it, for we could not do it for ourselves. But maybe God could have left it undone, could have left us permanently alienated from himself?

It sounds odd to say that anything is really necessary for

God. The philosophers tell us that the very idea of deity implies self-sufficiency; God has no needs and knows no necessities. Yet we have seen how, already in the Old Testament, God binds himself to his people Israel, how the Creator makes himself vulnerable, as it were, to his own creatures. Why should he do such a thing? Why should the Word of God, who *is* God, be the Lamb that was slain "from before the foundation of the world"? The only answer is love. God does not want to be without us. We may go so far as to say that our turning against him was a wound, a disorder, in the very life of God. It was necessary that this wound be healed. The risen Christ asks the disciples on the way to Emmaus, "Was it not necessary that the Christ should suffer these things and enter into his glory?" Did God need to save us from sin and its consequences? If we think of God as pure self-sufficient Being, the answer is surely no. But the being of God is inseparable from the love of God. Which is another way of saying with 1 John, "God is love."

God is what God does. Atonement means that, at the command of the Father and in the power of the Spirit, the Son did the perfect deed of love that is the life of God. It was utterly gratuitous, driven by no necessity other than love. The new order of the Second Adam is immeasurably better than the original order of the first Adam. In the original order, Adam was God's beloved creature; in Christ, the Second Person of the Holy Trinity, our humanity is taken into the very life of God. In the cross, then, God was not punishing sin in order to restore humanity to where we began. Punishment, as an act of justice, must be strictly proportioned to the offense—just so much punishment for just so much sin. But satisfaction, as a work of love, is superabundant. Thomas Aquinas says that Christ "offered to God more than was required to compensate for the sin of all humanity." It is not the case that the angry Father demanded justice and the loving Son then satisfied the demand by his dying on the cross. Justice had to be done, but "justice" here means not a legal relationship of crime and punishment, but a personal relationship of reciprocal love between God and his creatures. From God's side, so to speak, it was love all the way; the failure was on our side. In Jesus Christ and through Jesus Christ, who is the Son of God, we reciprocated God's love and did so superabundantly. That's the way it is with love: Love is superabundant.

Moreover, our new situation is radically different from and radically better than the original human situation in yet another way. Now humanity can never again be alienated from God, the bond between God and humanity can never be broken, for in the God-man Jesus our humanity participates in the eternal life of God. Humanity, *our* humanity, is eternally one with the Second Person of the Holy Trinity. God has invested his very being in the human project, and therefore it cannot finally fail. Because Jesus Christ is true God and true man, the human destiny "in Christ" is to share in the perfect unity of Father, Son and Holy Spirit. He is the firstborn of the new creation; his victory is ours; where he has gone we will follow. The first Adam need not have sinned, but his sin was necessary for the establishment of the new and immeasurably better order in the Second Adam. Thus the *felix culpa* of the exultation in the Easter Vigil: "O happy fault! O necessary sin of Adam, which gained for us so great a Redeemer!"

"It is finished." But it is not over. From now until it reaches
its final consummation in the coming of the kingdom of God,
the human story, including all its suffering and tears, is gathered
up and redeemed in the cross of Christ. There is absolutely
nobody in any need whose circumstance has not been embraced
by the cross. The Letter to the Hebrews tells us: "For we have
not a high priest who is unable to sympathize with our
weaknesses, but one who in every respect has been tempted as
we are, yet without sinning. Let us then with confidence draw
near to the throne of grace, that we may receive mercy and find
grace to help in time of need."

Is it really true that absolutely nobody is beyond the loving
reach of the cross? Has the way home been cleared for
absolutely every prodigal son and daughter? Is there not even
one lost sheep who is not found by the Good Shepherd? No,
not one. Some decline to take the way home; some persist in
getting lost again and again. But the high priest who offers
himself as the perfect sacrifice has been tempted in every respect
as we are. That means there is nobody in any circumstance
where he has not been as well. Not only *has* he been there but
he *is* there, for all time is caught up in the eternity of love
crucified and triumphant.

Yet we may ask, how about the circumstance of those
abandoned by God and without hope? Has Jesus been there,
too? Is he with such people now? Our old friend Hans Urs von
Balthasar insists that Jesus underwent the experience of
godforsakenness, of knowing what it is to be hopelessly
separated from God. He adds, somewhat paradoxically, that
undergoing the experience of separation from the Father

becomes "the supreme proof of definitive unity." Here perhaps the great Balthasar risks moving beyond what our minds can conceive or our words express. As we have seen, even in the moment of godforsakenness, Jesus cries out, "My God, my God." The horror was such that he was tempted to think he had been forsaken, but the One who seemed to forsake him was still "my God," and therefore he was not forsaken. He was tempted, but he did not sin the sin of despair.

From beginning to end and every step along the way, the work of atonement is the work of Father, Son and Holy Spirit. Even as he penetrates to the heart of darkness, Jesus is not abandoned by the light. He was always on a mission, from the Father to the Father. And his penetrating to the heart of darkness means that nobody, absolutely nobody, is alone in the heart of darkness. Christ has been there; Christ is there. From the cross point of history the word goes out that those who think they are abandoned by God are in fact not abandoned. We can despair of God, but he never despairs of us. We can turn our back upon God, but he never turns his back upon us. Never! There is absolutely nobody seated on the long mourners' bench of the eternal pity who is in a place where Jesus has not been before, where he is not now. This is what it means to find ourselves at the foot of the cross, which is the alternative to the muzzle of the gun and every other act of despair.

Repeatedly Jesus says we are to take up our cross and follow him. However hesitatingly, we can dare to do so because his cross is our cross, our suffering is his suffering, his victory is our victory. We take up our cross and discover that he is already there, bearing it with us, bearing it for us. From before the foundation of the world to the end of time. Again, Julian of Norwich understood that when she said, "All shall be well, all shall be well, all manner of thing shall be well." In the sacrifice of the cross, all is endured and all is redeemed. For all that ever was wrong, is wrong, and will be wrong, the price has been paid. Beyond our capacity to understand or explain, justice has been done, and justice was done by love, because the justice of God is love, and that is because God is love. At the foot of the cross, faith discerns, through our tears, that nothing is left unattended, nothing unknown, nothing unloved, nothing unredeemed.

Atonement. The Great Thing, the thing that had to be done or else nothing could be done, has been done. On a certain Friday afternoon at about three o'clock, when the children were going home from school, when the Lamb of God cried, "It is finished." Let me not love thee, if I love thee not now. Let me not trust thee, if I trust thee not in this. Atlas, foolish and failed, kneels to venerate the wood of the cross, on which hangs our every hope, by which all that we must and cannot do has been done. Let me not love thee, if I love thee not now. Let me not trust thee, if I trust thee not in this. How strange that in this end should be our beginning. *Agnus Dei, qui tollis peccata mundi, miserere nobis.*

7

The Scars of God

The Seventh Word from the cross:

"Father, into your hands I commend my spirit."

Luke alone gives us this Seventh Word from the cross. Mark says that "Jesus uttered a loud cry, and breathed his last." Similarly, Matthew reports, "And Jesus cried again with a loud voice and yielded up his spirit." According to John's Gospel, "When Jesus had received the vinegar, he said, 'It is finished'; and he bowed his head and gave up his spirit." So Mark, Matthew and Luke say there was yet another word, indeed a loud cry, but only Luke tells us what it was. Note that in this last word God is once again "Father."

When I go to bed at night, the last thing I do is sign myself with the cross by which I was signed in baptism and say, *In manus tuus commendo spiritum meum,* "Into your hands I commend my spirit." I once mentioned that in conversation with a friend who thought it very depressing to make one's last words each night the words of death on a cross. I thought it better not to mention that, before those last words, I also say the little prayer that Christian children have been praying at least since the twelfth century:

> *Now I lay me down to sleep.*
> *I pray thee Lord my soul to keep;*
> *If I should die before I wake,*
> *I pray thee Lord my soul to take.*

I recently saw in a prayer book for children that somebody has thought to improve on that by adding a new line at the end, "If I should live another day / I pray thee Lord to guide my way." It is not, I think, an improvement. Tomorrow will take care of itself. Every going to sleep is a letting go, an act of closure, a little death. "Into your hands" is a statement of trust, of *en*trusting, of trusting in another. The "other" for Jesus was always "the Father," except for that once, just once, when it was "My God, my God."

The Aramaic *Abba* captures the intimacy of the relationship. Even in the anguish of the garden the night before he was to die, especially then, it was "Abba, Father." "Abba, Father, all things are possible to you; remove this cup from me; yet not what I will, but what you will." The early Christians understood that, in Christ and through Christ, they could approach God in the same way. St. Paul writes, "But when the time had fully come, God sent forth his Son, born of woman, born under the law, to redeem those who were under the law, so that we might receive adoption as sons. And because you are sons, God has sent the Spirit of his Son into our hearts, crying, 'Abba, Father!'"

Apart from that adoption, we could not presume to address God so. Only because we are brothers and sisters of the Son dare we say "Father." Some Christians have problems with addressing God as "Father." In some cases it is because they are averse to the masculine connotation. "If God is male," declares one feminist writer, "then male is God." But of course God is not male. The source and end of all that is transcends all that is, including maleness and femaleness. God's relationship to us is personal, however, and we only know persons as male and female. Moreover, the one in whom he revealed himself, Jesus the Christ, addressed him as "Father," and we cannot address him at all except through and with Jesus. In truth, calling God "Father" is probably more of a problem for men, for sons typically have a more problematic, even conflicted, relationship with their fathers than do daughters.

It is often said that in the intimacy of personal prayer one may address God in many different ways, depending on one's sensibilities and experiences. Perhaps so. The range of the religious imagination should not be unduly shackled, so long as it is not forgotten that the only God we know is the God of Abraham, Isaac and Jacob whom Jesus called "Father." Once again, specificity is all—*this* man, *this* life, *this* death—apart from whom we cannot address God at all. Of course there are many different ideas of God, to which we can apply names that make us, as it is said, "comfortable." But we do not worship an idea of God; we do not pray to an idea of God. As adopted brothers and sisters of Jesus, we pray to his Father who is now our Father.

There is the objection that such prayer is infantilizing, a regression to the dependencies of childhood. Grown-ups, it is said, do not need the crutch of a "parent figure" to lean on.

Good for them. I once asked an old priest, a famous spiritual director, what he had learned from hearing thousands of confessions. He had a ready answer: "There are no grown-ups." There are grown-ups who pretend, and then there are those who have grown up to know the "second naïveté" of our utter dependence. The Child who was utterly faithful in his utter dependence was given not a crutch to lean on, but a cross to die on. To those whom he calls his brothers and sisters he says, "Take up your cross and follow me." Pretending to be grown-up is easier. One might be well advised to keep it up, were it not for the truth that the darkness we feared as a child is real; the darkness we feared is but a slight premonition of the darkness from which he cried, and we with him, "Father, into your hands I commend my spirit."

This Seventh Word is typically depicted as tranquil resignation at the end of the storm and the horror. I am not sure that is the right reading. We are told that it was uttered as a loud cry, which is not the mark of tranquillity. I expect this cry is closer than we might think to "My God, my God, why have you forsaken me?" That was the cry of desolation, and this Seventh Word is a cry of trust, hurled almost defiantly, into the absence of the One of whom Jesus spoke when he said, "Yet I am not alone, for the Father is with me." Prayer can be an expression of childlike faith, and it can be trust defiantly hurled. Parents change their mind about a promise made, and the child, teetering on the edge between disillusionment and faith, exclaims, "But you said so! You promised!" There is, I suspect, something of that in this Seventh Word.

Certainly there is something of that in our praying. When

we pray that way—holding God to his word, as it were—it is
not a prayer that is alien to Christ, our high priest who, without
sin, was tempted in all respects as we are. Temptation is not sin.
Sin is to conclude, definitively, that God has broken his word or
that he had never given it in the first place. Faith can be holding
fast to the promise even as we are haunted by the thought,
"Maybe I just imagined it." This is not blind faith but faith with
eyes wide open to all the evidence to the contrary. The Seventh
Word is adamant prayer, like that of Abraham, whom in the
Roman canon we call "our father in faith." Of Abraham, St. Paul
writes, "In hope he believed against hope, that he should become the father of many nations; as he had been told"—even
though he was a hundred years old and as good as dead. But
you said so! Hope against hope; hope amid the wreckage of
shattered hope; hope that there is hope beyond hope. Faith
and hope are finally one. Hope is faith disposed toward the
future; it is faith holding on; it is faith holding out; it is faith
defiantly, trustingly, hurled into the present absence; it is hand-
ing over our hopelessness. "Father, into your hands I commend
my spirit."

Prayer is persistent, and sometimes it is despite everything.
Jesus had told the story of the widow who persisted until an
indifferent judge finally vindicated her cause. "And will not God
vindicate his elect," Jesus asked, "who cry to him day and night?
I tell you he will vindicate them speedily." Then he added,
"Nevertheless, when the Son of man comes, will he find faith on
earth?" Here on the cross, and wherever there are those who
take up the cross and follow him, there is faith on earth. It is
faith disposed toward the future in the form of hope. Abraham

was elect, and God vindicated him. Jesus is the elect one in whom all his adopted brothers and sisters are elected; God vindicated him and will vindicate them. They surrender themselves into the hands of a Father who, unlike the judge in Jesus' story, is by no means indifferent.

In manus tuus—the prayer is said in unison with Jesus on the cross. This is most intensely what is meant by "the imitation of Christ." In the book of Acts, Stephen, deacon and first martyr, bore faithful witness to the hope that was in him. "And as they were stoning Stephen, he prayed, 'Lord Jesus, receive my spirit.' And he knelt down and cried with a loud voice. 'Lord, do not hold this sin against them.' And when he had said this, he fell asleep. And Saul was consenting to his death." There Saul, soon and most improbably to be the Apostle Paul, began to learn what it means to hope against hope. Stephen commends himself to Jesus who, on the cross, commended himself to the Father. Now the disciples understood what Jesus had meant when he said, "I and the Father are one." Between Father and Son is the unity of the mutual abandonment that is love. In our lives we may be blessed, once or twice, now or then, with a glimmer of an intimation of the love that the New Testament calls by the Greek word *agape*—a love pure and unalloyed by self-interest or fear of rejection. A glimmer, and then it is gone. But it is enough to alert us to more.

Thomas Becket, in Eliot's *Murder in the Cathedral,* says:

> *I have had a tremor of bliss, a wink of heaven, a whisper,*
> *And I would no longer be denied; all things*
> *Proceed to a joyful consummation.*

Between Father, Son and Holy Spirit, the joyful consummation is forever. Their love, which was from before the foundation of the world, is now magnified by the homecoming of all the prodigal children adopted into their love. Stumbling our way toward home, we worry to ourselves about the unworthiness of our love, only to discover that it has already been attended to. It was taken care of in that representative moment, that vicarious moment, in which he cried out, "Father, into your hands I commend my spirit," and so saying he handed over to the Father all that he had assumed in the womb of Mary. There on the cross the life of every mother's child who ever lived or ever will live was handed over to the Father. Every hair has been numbered, every fallen sparrow taken into account. Once on Golgotha and re-presented in the Eucharist until the end of the world, all has been offered up, all has been redeemed, nothing is lost.

To fret about the quality of our love is to miss the point. Yes, we examine ourselves, confess our failings and pray for grace to offer the best. But it will never be good enough, unless with all its flaws it is handed over and taken up into his love for the Father. Foolishly we rummage through what Yeats called the "rag and bone shop" of our hearts to find a love that is pure, untouched by self-interest or pretense. It is an endless and futile search, compounded by complexity the more rigorously it is pursued. Among the things we give up, among the things we hand over, is that futile search. In Luke's Gospel, the parable of the judge and the persistent widow is immediately followed by that of the Pharisee and the tax collector who went up to the temple to pray. This Pharisee recommended himself to God by virtue of his good behavior. A more scrupulous Pharisee, of a kind too often found among Christians, might have recommended himself for his thorough understanding of his unworthiness. The tax collector made neither claim, saying simply and starkly, "God, be merciful to me a sinner!" Unrecommended, he commended himself to God and thus was embraced in the cry from the cross, "Father, into your hands I commend this tax collector."

To let ourselves be commended to the Father by the Son, that is the secret. In the words of the third eucharistic prayer: "May he make us an everlasting gift to you and enable us to share in the inheritance of your saints, with Mary, the virgin mother of God; with the apostles, the martyrs, and all your saints, on whose constant intercession we rely for help." He does the commending, and all the saints, living and dead, pray on our behalf that we may let him do it, that we may let ourselves be commended. This is enacted in every Eucharist, for, as St. Paul tells the Corinthians, "as often as you eat this bread and drink this cup, you proclaim the Lord's death until he comes." It is proclaimed in the very doing of this, just as he told us to do the night before he died. At the altar the cross is raised, the perfect sacrifice of the Son is displayed to the world and presented to the Father. Once and for all, and therefore forever, he commends himself, and us with him.

Here, as the Letter to the Hebrews says, "we are surrounded by so great a cloud of witnesses." Here "you have come to Mount Zion and to the city of the living God, the heavenly Jerusalem, and to innumerable angels in festal gathering and to the assembly of the firstborn who are enrolled in heaven, and to a judge who is God of all, and to the spirits of the just made perfect, and to Jesus, the mediator of a new covenant, and to the sprinkled blood that speaks more graciously than the blood of Abel." As we proclaim his death he lays claim to his own and commends them to the Father, who acknowledges the claim, for the Son who went out to seek and save the lost is now inseparably one with those whom he found.

It is as St. Paul says, "I have been crucified with Christ; it is no longer I who live, but Christ who lives in me; and the life I now live in the flesh I live by faith in the Son of God, who loved me and gave himself for me." Who I most truly am—my ego, my "I"—is exchanged. It is Christ who lives in me and I, there on the cross, am commended to the Father. All this is dramatically re-presented in the eucharistic liturgy, where we proclaim the Lord's death until he comes. God acts in our reenactment, and therefore it is so; it is enacted, once and for all, and therefore forever as long as there are those who act on his command, "Do this in memory of me." And in every doing of this, even if we see only two or three people present, the congregation includes so great a cloud of witnesses.

There on the cross everything is offered up, nothing is lost, nothing forgotten. Not a hair, not one fallen sparrow. Not one tear of one mother's child on the long mourners' bench of time. The Psalmist cries:

> *You have kept count of my tossings;*
> *put my tears in your bottle!*
> *Are they not in your book?*

Yes, now we know that they are. Into the hands of the Father everything, simply everything, is commended. Nothing is unknown or unnoticed, nothing is dispensable.

> *O Lord, you have searched me and known me!*
> *You know when I sit down and when I rise up;*
>   *you discern my thoughts from afar.*
> *You search out my path and my lying down,*
>   *and are acquainted with all my ways.*

The very little children beyond numbering who, while still in the womb, were thought to be dispensable. Not one was dispensable, not one is. They, too, are here.

> *For you did form my inward parts,*
>   *you did knit me together in my mother's womb . . .*
> *Your eyes beheld my unformed substance;*
>   *in your book were written, every one of them,*
> *the days that were formed for me,*
>   *when as yet there was none of them.*

The days that God made for them, the days that we denied them, are lived at last in the eternal feast of the Lamb who was slain from before the long slaying of the lambs began. Nothing will be lost. There we will be encountered by much that we had forgotten, so much that we wanted to forget. There is nothing that cannot find its way to the Father through the commendation of the cross. What we feared will no longer be fearful. The wounds will be healed, but they will bear the scars, as the risen Christ bore and bears the scars from the nails. From now on, God bears the scars of his love, the surest sign that all is redeemed. Trace now the story of humankind in the scars of God.

In the hymn "Lo, He Comes with Clouds Descending," Charles Wesley anticipates the tracing of the scars when Christ returns in glory:

> *Those dear tokens of his Passion*
> *Still his dazzling body bears,*
> *Cause of endless exultation*
> *To his ransomed worshipers.*
> *With what rapture,*
> *With what rapture*
> *Gaze we on those glorious scars!*

The scars of God, the Second Person of the Holy Trinity. On the cross the wounded Word is returning from his mission, bringing with him the totality of all that love assumed; in the lead a thief who believed and half believed, followed by a ragtag band of tax collectors and sinners and the victims of history beyond numbering, victims who only now know the sacrifice of which their sacrifice was part. Choirs of angels, cherubim and seraphim come out to meet him, to welcome home the Son of God. They stand aghast at the battered, tattered company he is bringing with him. "They are all mine," he says. "They are my brothers and sisters; they are the ones whom I went to seek and to save. I am taking them to the Father. I am taking them home."

Back at Golgotha: "Father, into your hands I commend my

spirit." Into the hands of the Father he commended a mission that seems to have ended in a shambles of betrayal and death. Of those he had chosen, we are told that they forsook him and fled. His enemies surrounded him, mocking him in his defeat. The one thief turns to him in pity, and Jesus says, "Yes, come with me to the Father. Despite all, I believe I am going to the Father. Come with me." This is a statement of faith. Do we have problems with saying that Jesus had faith? Faith, after all, is a grace that we mere humans need. Jesus, who is God incarnate, knows everything; he knows how this will turn out. Yes, that is a perfectly orthodox way of putting the matter, but it is not without its dangers. It can reduce the cross to playacting; it can compromise the great truth that we have in Jesus a high priest who was tempted in every way as we are. Moreover, it assumes a clear line dividing faith and knowledge, forgetting that faith is also a way of knowing. We recognize ourselves in his last cry from the cross when we recognize it as a cry of faith.

One scholar has reckoned that in the Bible and the subsequent Christian tradition there are more than twenty distinct variations on the meaning of the word "faith." We do not need to consider so many. Faith is, in one variation, rocklike conviction. On the far side of the cross, St. Paul is able to declare, "I am persuaded that neither death, nor life, nor angels, nor principalities, nor things present, nor things to come, nor powers, nor height, nor depth, nor anything else in all creation, will be able to separate us from the love of God in Christ Jesus our Lord." That is faith with all stops pulled: faith militant, faith defiant, faith audacious.

Faith is also assent; it is saying yes to a truth proposed or a course of action proposed. Here, preeminently, is the Marian form of faith, her *fiat*—"Let it be to me according to your word"—in response to the angel's strange announcement. Mary's entire being is, as we have seen, one sustained act of faith. The mother's "Let it be" and her son's "Into your hands" flow into one another. Standing by the cross, she heard that final cry, and we can imagine that in her heart and through her tears and tremulously whispered on her lips were the words, "Let it be. Let it be." From Bethlehem to Golgotha this persistent refrain: "Let it be as the angel said. Let it be as my son said. God of Abraham, Isaac, Jacob and Jesus, let it be that you keep your promise. I believe you will. I *know* you will!"

And faith is trust, without which we are left, quite literally, with nothing. We trust our senses, we trust that there is reality external to ourselves—although both can be doubted and have been doubted by thinkers beyond numbering. We *entrust* ourselves to the truth of things that can be doubted. When we say that some things are beyond "reasonable" doubt, the adjective "reasonable" simply indicates where we draw the line of trust. Such things are not proven beyond *possible* doubt— doubt that the relentlessly skeptical think is reasonable. We entrust ourselves to others, without which life would be intolerable. Again we are returned to the child in the arms of the mother whose "I" constitutes the child's "Thou," which primordial experience is the window opening to the world of the other, and finally to the Other, who is God. Surely this is the continuum of faith as trust, from the arms of Mary to the arms of the cross, "I commend myself."

We speak of a "leap of faith," and we all know that experi-

ence in ways both great and small. Sometimes we are mulling
over a decision; we don't know whether to go this way or that,
and finally we know that we simply have to decide one way or
the other; so we decide and hope we made the right decision.
There is an element of faith there, but it is more like a gamble, a
throwing of the dice. It is not so much entrusting ourselves to
another as hoping in "luck" or "fate." Moving from a gamble to
faith is trusting that another person will do what he or she
promised to do. Here is something almost all of us experienced
as little children. We're standing on the stairs and someone—our
father, an older brother or sister—said, "Jump. Don't be afraid.
I'll catch you." But we were afraid and needed to be assured
several times that the person really would catch us, that he or
she wouldn't pull away at the last moment and let us fall to the
floor. We were assured, we jumped, we were caught and faith
was vindicated. We entrusted ourselves, we commended
ourselves and we were saved.

Faith as trust does much greater things than that, however.
The child on the stairs and the adult at the foot of the stairs
have a plan, and the child trusts that the other will do his or her
part. It is a much greater thing to entrust myself to another
when the plan is by no means clear, when the circumstance
appears to contradict the promise. This is faith, we might almost
say, contrary to fact. It is faith like Abraham's when he trusted
God's promise, even though he was a hundred years old and as
good as dead. As when Jesus' ministry of proclaiming the
coming kingdom ends up with him on the ground in the garden
of Gethsemane, contemplating his death and the catastrophic
end of the hopes he had aroused. We are told that the sweat

flowed from his brow like great drops of blood as he prayed, "Father, if it is possible, let this cup pass from me." Please, please, take it away; let it not be. Then: "Nevertheless, not my will but yours be done."

"Nevertheless." The cry in the garden and the cry the next afternoon on the cross catch up, and offer up, everything that happens in between. This is faith as will: nevertheless, despite everything, to *will* that God's will be done. When the disciples asked him to teach them to pray, he taught them to say, "Your will be done on earth as it is in heaven." Christian children are taught from early on always to say, "Not my will but yours be done." It is something we add to our prayers, much like a lawyer's codicil to an agreement. We pray for what we *really* want to be done, but then remind ourselves that God knows best, and so add the appendix, "Your will be done." What we mean is, "If I can't have my way, then you have your way, Lord." The suggestion is that God's way is second best. We humbly resign ourselves to it.

That is not the prayer of Jesus. The entire burden, drive and urgency of his prayer is that the Father's will be done. He had said again and again during his ministry that the entirety of his existence was "to do the will of him who sent me." All that would be negated if, here at the end, the man Jesus were to prefer his own will to the will of the Father. His prayer is this: "Your will be done because, if your will is not done, if your will is not done in me and by me, if I do not *will your will*, then the whole thing has been a lie. Everything from the beginning depended on my doing your will. If now at the end, with the horror before me fully displayed, I stop doing your will and start

doing my own will, then it is better that my life and my mission
had never been." Then it would have been said of Jesus as he
said of Judas, that it would have been better had he never been
born.

Everything is at stake here. At stake is whether Jesus truly
was (and is!) true God and true man. We may be tempted to
impatience with what some think are the arcane theological
controversies of centuries past, but they have an immediate
bearing on how we believe and what we believe today. In the
early centuries, there were those, called Monophysites, who said
that Jesus had only one nature, not two. Christians were bitterly
divided over this question in the ancient world. The early
councils of the Catholic Church determined that Jesus Christ is
one person with two natures, human and divine. Later, and
directly pertinent to the cry in the garden and the final cry from
the cross, a heresy arose called Monothelitism, claiming that
Christ had only one will. In the year 681 the Council of
Constantinople determined that the orthodox faith is that there
are two wills in Christ, divine and human.

So what difference does it make? Think about it. If Jesus had
no will distinct from the will of the Father, the drama of his
obedient suffering and death was no more than playacting. "Not
my will but your will be done" would no longer be agony but a
pretense aimed at inspiring his followers. Moreover, it would be
a cruel pretense, for the fact is that we human beings do have a
will that is not only distinct from God's, but is in our fallen
circumstance bent against the will of God. His calling us to
follow him in obeying the Father would ring hollow, for if he
had only a divine will, he had no possibility of *not* obeying the

Father. In short, he would not be God incarnate, he would not *really* have become a human being, he would not be one of us. And, if he was not one of us, there is an end to the entire promise of Christianity that we can, through the God-man Jesus Christ, be adopted as his brothers and sisters into the very life of God—Father, Son and Holy Spirit. As if that were not enough, if Jesus had no human will distinct from the will of the Father, then his sacrifice was not freely offered and satisfaction has not been made for our sins, for a gift that is not freely offered is no gift at all.

Then it would not be true that "It is finished." The old order would still be in place. All that would have happened on the cross is that a wrathful God was punishing a human being who was not truly even a human being, for he had no will of his own. This, as we saw earlier, is a grotesque and ugly distortion of what Christianity means by the sacrifice of the cross. Jesus would not have been the Universal Representative freely joining us to take our part; he would have been little more than a stand-in, a puppet, in a morality play that finally changes nothing.

"Not my will but yours be done." "Father, into your hands I commend my spirit." It could have been otherwise. Had he chosen his own will in the garden, had he on the cross denied God, then he would have turned out not to be the one he claimed to be. Because his will was perfectly responsive to the will of the Father, because he perfectly surrendered himself to the Father, he turned out to be the one he claimed to be. And because he turned out to be who he claimed to be, it turns out that it could not have been otherwise. He really is the Word of God *incarnate*, which means one of us. It follows that the story of

Jesus is not about the exploits of a Superman whom we call true God and true man; it is the story about us. This human stuff of which we are made is capable of living in perfect responsiveness to God. We know that because it was done in the life, death and resurrection of a human being named Jesus, and we are his brothers and sisters.

Theologians have a lovely phrase, *Finitum capax infinitum*—"the finite is capable of holding the infinite." The whole of incarnational and sacramental living is caught up in that phrase. Time and eternity, the finite and the infinite, the physical and the spiritual, the immanent and the transcendent, the earthly and the heavenly—all these distinctions are no longer divisions; they are no longer pitted against one another. In the incarnation Jesus assumed the fullness of our humanity, and on the cross he commended it to the Father. As improbable as it seems in view of our tragic imperfections, our prayer in the Eucharist has been answered: We have been made a perfect gift to the Father.

The more we put our minds to it, the more those old formulations that we might otherwise dismiss as dry-as-dust doctrine come excitingly alive. For instance, this from the Council of Chalcedon in the year 451:

> Following the holy Fathers, we unanimously teach and confess one and the same Son, our Lord Jesus Christ: the same perfect in divinity and perfect in humanity, the same truly God and truly man, composed of rational soul and body; consubstantial with the Father as to his divinity and consubstantial with us as to his humanity; "like us in all things but sin." He was begotten from the Father before all ages as to his divinity and in these

last days, for us and for our salvation, was born as to his
humanity of the virgin Mary, the Mother of God.

That should not be stuck away in a theological textbook.
You want to set it to music and sing it, walk around the house
and around the world belting it out—which, of course, is just
what the Church has been doing all these centuries. As Mary is
the Mother of God, so we are the brothers and sisters of God.
The human destiny, which is to say salvation, is nothing less
than adoption into the life and love of God. With Christ and
because of Christ, we can will what God wills. "Not my will but
your will be done" is no longer a resignation to accepting second
best to what we really want. What we really want is that God's
will be done. "Into your hands I commend my spirit" is finally a
cry of triumph, and it is more believably that because it does not
simply come after but catches up and comprehends the earlier
cry, which is also the cry of broken humanity, "My God, my
God, why have you forsaken me?"

The cross is not the dark side of which the resurrection is
the bright side. In John's Gospel, Jesus speaks repeatedly of
being glorified in his death. The glory is in having kept faith, in
having seen it through to the end, in having surrendered himself
in unqualified love to the Father. This is now, because of him
and through him, a human possibility. The only dark side, for
him and for us, would be to turn against the light by setting our
will against the will of God. At the cross point of history, at the
moment of catastrophe beyond all catastrophes, the entirety of
the human project was definitively turned toward the light.
"Father, into your hands I commend my spirit." From now on,

the eternally important decision in every human life is whether, with him and through him, we say the same.

There are difficulties in speaking of the cross as glory. At the beginning of these reflections we were cautioned against rushing to Easter. In some church buildings, the cross over the altar is not a crucifix that depicts Christ in his agony, but one from which he reigns regaled in splendor as *Christus Rex* (Christ the King). Of course the latter is perfectly true; one might even argue that it is the fuller truth, since it comprehends both the suffering and the resurrection triumph. In a culture such as ours, however, which is prone to the denial of suffering and death and is addicted to the psychologized spirituality of "positive thinking," there is much to be said for the clear sign that we, with St. Paul, "preach Christ and him crucified." Of course the Christus Rex does assert that he rules from a cross, which ought to be a scandal, but it is that only for those who know the cross as an instrument of cruel and bloody execution and not just an article of religious decoration.

Yet there is no denying that the cross is surrounded by glory. It is, at the same time, the sign of utter defeat and indomitable hope. The defeat and the hope must be ever held together; the hope is not finally hopeful unless it has taken into account everything that contradicts hope. Especially in John's Gospel, however, Jesus is "lifted up" to glory. "As Moses lifted up the serpent in the wilderness," Jesus said, "so must the Son of man be lifted up, that whoever believes in him may have eternal life." "When you have lifted up the Son of man, then you will know that I am he, and that I do nothing on my own authority but speak thus as the Father taught me." Or again, "And I, when I am lifted up from the earth, will draw all men to myself."

The meeting on the cross of catastrophe and glory is reflected in an early Christian belief that Jesus spiritually ascended to the Father from the cross. There is a hint of this in Peter's great sermon on Pentecost where, speaking of Jesus, he quotes Psalm 16: "You will not abandon my soul to Hades, nor let your Holy One see corruption." Yet there is also the suggestion that between the cross and Easter, Jesus went to preach to the spirits in hell. In the Gospel accounts, and between them and the book of Acts, the timing of events between Good Friday and Pentecost appears to be jumbled. For instance, Luke in his Gospel appears to have Jesus ascending to heaven on the evening of Easter Sunday, while in the first chapter of Acts he ascends forty days later. The suffering, death, resurrection and ascension of Jesus are all aspects of his glorification. Taken together, they complete his mission and vindicate his claims about who he was and who he is. Like us, the disciples were locked into the strict frame of time past, present and future. From God's perspective, so to speak, all time is present; there was one event of the glorification of the Son. For those who remained in history, however, aspects of what was happening flashed forth in a way that jumbled the neat sequence of time. Moreover, the Gospel writers perceived Golgotha in retrospect, refracted through their knowledge of the resurrection, and it is not surprising that, in retrospect, they saw in what was happening then glimpses of what was to be. Throughout, they are not merely reporting; they are proclaiming the crucified and risen Messiah.

We, too, know how the story turns out, yet we neither rush to Easter nor, when we come to Easter, do we put Good Friday behind us as though it were a nightmare past. The risen Christ, and indeed Christ returning in glory to judge the living and the dead, is always the crucified Christ who bears the scars. It is finished but it is not over. The reality of salvation is definitively settled, but history continues to be cruciform, a way of the cross for pilgrims headed home. Salvation is "now" and "not yet"; it is a matter of certitude and a matter of seeing in a mirror dimly; it is a present possession and a hope to be worked out with fear and trembling.

As one might expect from a story centered in the cross point, Christian faith is a crosscutting dynamic that cannot be contained within familiar time frames, conceptual cages or psychological definitions of reality. It is eccentric in the precise sense of the Greek *ex-kentron*, "out of the center" and "off center." We think we have grasped the matter and pinned it down, and then we have to start out all over again, always becoming as little children in our understanding. The truth is elusive not in order to tease us, but to keep us ever relying not upon our own understanding but upon the One who is the truth. The strangeness of the story testifies to its truth, for, whatever else we know about reality, we know it is surpassingly strange. If the story was simple, logical and step-by-step coherent, we would have good reason to doubt its truth. That it embraces every strangeness is testimony to its truth.

These Seven Last Words do not address directly all the strange things going on that awe-filled afternoon: the darkness, the torn veil of the temple, dead people rising from their graves and much else. From the early centuries on, Christians have pondered and speculated about these strange doings. Of the death itself, Luke and Mark say that Jesus "breathed his last."

Matthew says he "yielded up his spirit," while John is best translated as "he gave over the spirit." The last has often been interpreted to mean that Jesus gave his spirit, which is the Holy Spirit, to those standing near the cross. Much earlier Jesus had declared that out of the heart of those who believe in him will flow rivers of living water. John adds the explanation, "Now this he said about the Spirit, which those who believed in him were to receive; for as yet the Spirit had not been given, because Jesus was not yet glorified."

But now, on the cross, Jesus has been glorified, according to John, and perhaps we have a kind of Pentecost long before the usual dating of Pentecost. The Spirit is given first to those who had not deserted him at the end. Perhaps. The crosscutting dynamic of these mysteries leaves time frames wobbly, as we would expect. If John's "he gave over the spirit" refers to the Holy Spirit, it seems improbable that the Son would have given over the Spirit to the Father. He had promised the Spirit to his followers, and perhaps here on the cross we already have Jesus living on in, being resurrected into, the life of the Church.

Other elements of this scene have over the centuries been given a churchly, or ecclesial, interpretation. For instance, a soldier pierces his side with a spear, "and at once there came out blood and water." This has been understood sacramentally, especially in light of 1 John where we read, "This is he who came by water and blood, Jesus Christ, not with the water only, but with the water and the blood. And the Spirit is the witness, because the Spirit is the truth." Christian thought on the triad of Baptism, Eucharist and Spirit has been richly elaborated by reflection on the wound in the side. It is said that the water and blood flowed from his pierced heart, and this gave rise to the devotion to the Sacred Heart of Jesus, which has been enormously popular since the eighteenth century, but goes back to mystical writings centuries before that. The pierced heart is now empty, open for all to enter. It is both the final *kenosis*, or emptying, that Paul speaks of in Philippians 2 and the invitation to all humanity to enter into the Body of Christ, which is the Church.

Then the body of Christ was on the cross, and now the Body of Christ, the Church, is on the cross, and with it the whole of humanity. There in the Sacred Heart of Jesus every heart is broken, and every heart is healed. A distinguished psychiatrist, Irvin D. Yalom, tells about Carlos, a terminally ill cancer patient, who discovered that "everyone has a heart." In a group meeting at the hospital, people were speaking about their loneliness, their lost friends, their failed hopes. Carlos speaks:

> I don't know why, but suddenly I saw them in a different way. They were like me! They were having the same problems of living that I was. At that moment I had a vision of their naked hearts. Their chest wall vanished, just melted away, leaving a square blue-red cavity with rib-bar walls and, in the center, a liver-colored, glistening heart thumping away. All week long I've been seeing everyone's heart beating, and I've been saying to myself, "Everybody's got a heart, everybody has got a heart." I've been seeing the heart in everyone—a misshapen hunchback who works in reception, an old lady who does the floors, even the men I work with.

Dr. Yalom describes a therapeutic exercise he has conducted many times. He brings together in a room a large number of people who are strangers to one another. They are told to pair up and ask their partner one single question, "What do you want?" and to ask it over and over again.

Could anything be simpler? One innocent question and its answer. And yet, time after time, I have seen this group exercise evoke unexpectedly powerful feelings. Often, within minutes, the room rocks with emotion. Men and women—and these are by no means desperate or needy, but successful, well-functioning, well-dressed people who glitter as they walk—are stirred to their depths. They call out to those who are forever lost—dead or absent parents, spouses, children, friends: "I want to see you again." "I want your love." "I want to know you are proud of me." "I want you to know I love you and how sorry I am I never told you." "I want you back—I am so lonely." "I want the childhood I never had." So much wanting. So much longing. And so much pain, so close to the surface, only minutes deep. Destiny pain. Existence pain. Pain that is always there, whirring continuously just beneath the membrane of life.

On the cross the membrane is exposed to reveal the Sacred Heart of Jesus, and every heart. Here one enters also into the heart of darkness. There is the curious business of the darkness that Matthew, Mark and Luke say covered the whole earth from the sixth to the ninth hour, which is from noon to three o'clock. (Remember Wanderhope's child dying as the children were getting ready to come home from school.) The darkness is redolent with Old Testament prophecy. When the sequence of day and night is broken, said Jeremiah, it will be a sign that God is breaking his covenant. The prophet Joel predicts, "The sun will be turned to darkness . . . at the coming of the great and terrible day of the Lord." Also the prophet Amos: "On that day, says the Lord God, the sun shall set at midday, and the light shall be darkened on earth in the daytime. . . . I will make them mourn as for an only son and bring their day to a bitter end."

As the membrane is torn open to reveal the very heart of God, so our three Gospels tell us that the veil of the temple sanctuary was torn in two from top to bottom. One early Christian interpretation has it that this was God's angry response to the high priest's tearing of his clothes before the Sanhedrin as he demanded the death of Jesus. After all, did not Jesus at that very moment in his trial tell the high priest that he and his fellow judges would see the Son of man coming in judgment? Now the judgment has begun against all those of all time who cruelly afflict the innocent.

The New Testament sees also another significance in the tearing of the temple veil. The book of Hebrews says that Jesus is our intercessor, a "priest forever after the order of Melchizedek," who has entered into the inner shrine behind the veil. Where Jesus goes his adopted brothers and sisters can also go. "Therefore, since we have confidence to enter the sanctuary by the blood of Jesus, by the new and living way which he opened for us through the veil, that is, through his flesh, . . . let us draw near with a true heart in full assurance of faith, with our hearts sprinkled clean from an evil conscience and our bodies washed with pure water." In the Jerusalem temple, once a year the high priest went through the veil that separated the Holy Place from the inner Holy of Holies; there he incensed the Ark of the Covenant and sprinkled it with the blood of a bull or goat. So now, according to Hebrews, Christ the high priest has passed through the veil, which is his flesh, to the real Holy of Holies, which is the throne of God. He takes with him his own blood in order to consummate the sacrifice begun on the cross, and thus has he opened the way for his brothers and sisters to enter the presence of the living God. In this way we can understand St. Paul's statement, "You who were once far off have drawn near by the blood of Christ."

There is a cosmic back and forth here, a movement to-and-fro, from earth to heaven and back again. In Christian worship, the body of Christ on the cross is perpetually lifted up by the Body of Christ, the Church, which is itself conducted through the veil to the Holy of Holies, and then returned to earth, renewed in its redemptive mission. This maddeningly wondrous movement is caught in the imagery of the Roman canon of the Mass: "Almighty God, we pray that your angel may take this sacrifice to your altar in heaven. Then, as we receive from this altar the sacred body and blood of your Son, let us be filled with every grace and blessing." What is happening on earth is happening in heaven, and vice versa. What is binding on earth is binding in heaven. It is maddeningly wondrous, surpassing our understanding, but no more than one might expect if the greater wonder is true, that heaven and earth are joined in God become man. Of the forgiveness of sins he said, "Truly, I say to you, whatever you bind on earth shall be bound in heaven, and whatever you loose on earth shall be loosed in heaven." The veil between heaven and earth has been torn from top to bottom.

The blood of bulls and goats has been replaced by the blood of the Lamb; the cry of innocent Abel's blood has been answered. Jerusalem's temple—the symbol of human longing for the righting of wrong, for the world that was meant to be—has given way to the New Jerusalem. Such is the vision of Revelation 21: "And I saw no temple in the city, for its temple is the Lord God the Almighty and the Lamb. And the city has no need of sun or moon to shine upon it, for the glory of God is its light, and its lamp is the Lamb. By its light shall the nations walk; and the kings of the earth shall bring their glory into it, and its gates shall never be shut by day, and there shall be no night." There shall be no night. Never again.

It is finished, but it is not over. The veil between earth and heaven is torn, and faith, following the path that Christ has taken, sees through. But the faith that sees is in a world still covered by darkness. The only way to the light is the way he took, the way through the heart of darkness, the way of the cross. That is where he is to be found; that is where he finds those whom he takes to the Father. This has always been, and is today, the great offense of Christianity: the cross. "We preach Christ crucified, a stumbling block to Jews and folly to Gentiles."

A century after Paul, Justin Martyr wrote about how the Christians were mocked for worshiping as divine a crucified man: "They say that our madness consists in the fact that we put a crucified man in second place after the unchangeable and eternal God, the Creator of the world." A second-century preacher, Melito of Sardis, put it nicely:

> He who hung the earth in its place hangs there, he who fixed the heavens is fixed there, he who made all things fast is made fast upon the tree, the Master has been insulted, God has been

murdered, the King of Israel has been slain by an Israelite
hand. O strange murder, strange crime! The Master has been
treated in unseemly fashion, his body naked; not even deemed
worthy of a covering that his nakedness might not be seen.
Therefore the lights of heaven turned away, and the day darkened, that it might hide him who was stripped upon the cross.

Little wonder that the world mocked. Little wonder that
some early Christians, those whom we call the Gnostics, wanted
to remove the scandal by claiming that the *real* Christ, the
spiritual Christ, did not die. According to one Gnostic text,
Christ remained above it all, untouched by what was happening;
he was actually in the heavens laughing at those who thought
they were putting him to death. But he was there all right,
battered and bloodied and dead. Just what God knew he would
get if he became man. Just what we needed God to bear for us,
and need him to bear with us. The God who is love is identified
by his scars.

We must not turn away from what we have done to God,
lest we be found to have turned away from what he has done for
us. It is not easy to look, to really look and see. John Donne,
that great spiritual master knew it well. "Good Friday, 1613:
Riding Westward" bears close and careful reading:

> Yet dare I almost be glad I do not see
> That spectacle, of too much weight for me.
> Who sees God's face, that is self life, must die;
> What a death were it then to see God die?
> It made his own lieutenant nature, shrink;
> It made his footstool crack, and the sun wink.

Could I behold those hands which span the poles,
And tune all spheres at once, pierced with those holes?
Could I behold that endless height which is
Zenith to us, and our Antipodes,
Humbled below us? Or that blood which is
The seat of all our souls, if not of His,
Make dirt of dust, or that flesh which was worn
By God, for his apparel, ragged and torn?
If on these things I durst not look, durst I
Upon his miserable mother cast my eye,
Who was God's partner here, and furnished thus
Half of that sacrifice which ransomed us?

The half furnished by Mary was his humanity. Through Mary he received his humanity, and in receiving his humanity received humanity itself. Which is to say, through Mary he received us. In response to the angel's strange announcement, Mary said yes. But only God knew that it would end up here at Golgotha, that it had to end up here. For here, in darkness and in death, were to be found the prodigal children who had said no, the prodigal children whom Jesus came to take home to the Father.

The liturgy of Good Friday is coming to an end now. A final prayer replaces the usual benediction:

Lord,
send down your abundant blessing
upon your people who have devoutly recalled
the death of your Son

in the sure hope of the resurrection.
Grant them pardon, bring them comfort.
May their faith grow stronger
and their eternal salvation be assured.
We ask this through Christ our Lord.

Let all the people say Amen. The church is dark now. The altar is stripped and bare. Some are getting up and leaving in silence. Others remain kneeling, looking into the darkness. Holy Saturday is ahead, the most quiet day of the year. The silence of that silent night, holy night, the night when God was born was broken by the sounds of a baby, a mother's words of comfort and angels in concert. Holy Saturday, by contrast, is the sound of perfect silence. Yesterday's mockery, the good thief's prayer, the cry of dereliction—all that is past now. Mary has dried her tears, and the whole creation is still, waiting for what will happen next.

Some say that on Holy Saturday Jesus went to hell in triumph, to free the souls long imprisoned there. Others say he descended into a death deeper than death, to embrace in his love even the damned. We do not know. Scripture, tradition and pious writings provide hints and speculations, but about this most silent day it is perhaps best to observe the silence. One day I expect he will tell us all about it. When we are able to understand what we cannot now even understand why we cannot understand. Meanwhile, if we keep very still, there steals upon the silence a song of Easter that was always there. On the long mourners' bench of the eternal pity, we raise our heads, blink away our tears and exchange looks that dare to question,

"Could it be?" But of course. That is what it was about. That is what it is all about. *O felix culpa!*

O happy fault, O necessary sin of Adam,
which gained for us so great a Redeemer!

To prodigal children lost in a distant land, to disciples who forsook him and fled, to a thief who believed or maybe took pity and pretended to believe, to those who did not know that what they did they did to God, to the whole bedraggled company of humankind he had abandoned heaven to join, he says: "Come. Everything is ready now. In your fears and your laughter, in your friendships and farewells, in your loves and losses, in what you have been able to do and in what you know you will never get done, come, follow me. We are going home to the waiting Father."

Biblical References

7 "Come to me": Matthew 11:28.

8 "God was in Christ": 2 Corinthians 5:19.

9 "God is love": 1 John 4:16.

11 "Unless you become": Matthew 18:3.

12 loving the Lord our God: Matthew 22:37; Mark 12:30; Luke 10:27.

13 "they glory": Philippians 3:19.

13 "Therefore a man": Genesis 2:24–25.

14 "Where are you": Genesis 3:8–11.

16 "the chief of sinners": 1 Timothy 1:15.

17 "foolishness": 1 Corinthians 1:23.

18 "It was the woman": Genesis 3:12–13.

19 "He who looks": Matthew 5:28.

21 "Who can discern": Psalm 19:12.

22 "A voice was heard": Matthew 2:18.

23 "I can will": Romans 7:18–19, 24.

23 "and Aaron shall": Leviticus 16:21–22.

25 "In the beginning": John 1:1–5.

25 "No one takes": John 10:18.

27 "For this was I born": John 18:37.

27 "Now is my soul": John 12:27–28.

28 "Now is the judgment": John 12:31–32.

28 "Now before the feast": John 13:1.

28 "This is my commandment": John 15:12–13.

29 "Father, I desire": John 17:24.

29 "But we impart": 1 Corinthians 2:7–8.

29 "O the depth": Romans 11:33.

30 "Beloved, let us love": 1 John 4:7–8.

30 "For our sake": 2 Corinthians 5:21.

32 "will baptize you with the Holy Spirit": Matthew 3:11, 13–14.

32 "Lord, do you wash my feet": John 13:6–8.

33 "For God sent the Son": John 3:17.

Chapter 2

35 "Truly, I say to you": Luke 23:43.

36 "Are you not the Christ": Luke 23:39.

36 "Jesus, remember me": Luke 23:40–43.

38 "All things are possible": Mark 9:23–24.

38 faith no greater than a mustard seed: Matthew 17:20.

39 every knee will bow: Philippians 2:10.

41 the Lord placed an angel: Genesis 3:24.

41 "I am the way": John 14:6.

41 "Greater love": John 15:13.

41 "You did not chose me": John 15:16.

42 "And I": John 12:32.

44 "desires all to be saved": 1 Timothy 2:4.

45 "In him we have redemption": Ephesians 1:7–10.

45 "He is the image": Colossians 1:15–20.

47 "Wilt thou indeed destroy": Genesis 18:23–24, 32.

48 "I have seen this people": Exodus 32:9–10, 11–14.

48 "to the effect that": Luke 18:1.

49 "Will not God": Luke 18:7.

49 "to reconcile to himself": Colossians 1:20.

49 "one mediator": 1 Timothy 2:5.

49 The sheep will be separated: Matthew 25:31–46; 13:36–40; 7:13–14; 18:23–35.

50 we will see face to face: 1 Corinthians 13:12.

51 "the image of the invisible God": Colossians 1:15.

51 "He who has seen me": John 14:9.

51 "When all things": 1 Corinthians 15:28.

52 "Otherwise, what do people mean": 1 Corinthians 15:29.

52 "it is appointed": Hebrews 9:27.

53 "O the depth": Romans 11:33.

53 "Enter by the narrow gate": Matthew 7:13–14.

53 Be constantly awake: Matthew 25:1–30.

54 "new heavens": 2 Peter 3:13.

54 "He will wipe away": Revelation 21:4–5.

54 "For the creation waits": Romans 8:19–23.

55 "And there is salvation": Acts 4:12.

56 "What therefore you worship": Acts 17:23.

56 "For he has made known": Ephesians 1:9–10.

57 "Take what belongs": Matthew 20:14–16.

58 "Truly, I say to you": Mark 10:28–31.

59 "For my thoughts": Isaiah 55:8–9.

62 "The fear of the Lord": Psalm 111:10.

62 "But with me it is": 1 Corinthians 4:3.

62 "I am not aware": 1 Corinthians 4:4–5.

63 "God, I thank thee": Luke 18:11.

63 "Work out your salvation": Philippians 2:12–13.

65 "Beloved, never avenge yourselves": Romans 12:19.

65 "But the free gift": Romans 5:15.

65 "For God has consigned": Romans 11:32.

66 "Therefore you have no excuse": Romans 2:1–4.

67 "If it is my will": John 21:22.

69 "Now faith is the assurance": Hebrews 11:1.

Chapter 3

71 "When Jesus saw his mother": John 19:26–27.

71 "The hour is coming": John 16:32.

71 "Father, the hour has come": John 17:1.

72 "I will put enmity": Genesis 3:15.

73 "Behold, this child": Luke 2:34–35.

74 "Mary kept all these things": Luke 2:19.

75 "They have no wine": John 2:1–5

76 "How is it that you sought me": Luke 2:49.

77 "Who are my mother": Mark 3:33–34.

77 "Blessed is the womb": Luke 11:27–28.

79 "Have this mind": Philippians 2:5–7.

80 "We preach Christ crucified": 1 Corinthians 1:23–25.

83 "When the Spirit of truth comes": John 16:13.

90 "A woman in childbirth": John 16:21.

90 "A woman, crying out": Revelation 12:2.

90 "Joseph, son of David": Matthew 1:20.

91 "In your light": Psalm 36:9.

91 "We have beheld": John 1:14.

92 "For these things took place": John 19:36–37.

92 no bone of the paschal lamb: Exodus 12:46.

Chapter 4

133   "Hear, O Israel": Mark 12:29–30.

134   "But with me it is": 1 Corinthians 4:3–4.

136   "You did not choose me": John 15:16..

137   "What does it profit": Mark 8:36

137   "Rejoice and be glad": Matthew 5:12.

137   "O Jerusalem"": Matthew 23:37.

138   "And the Lord said to Samuel": 1 Samuel 8:7–8.

140   "anyone who has seen me": John 14:9.

142   "Saul, Saul": Acts 9:4.

142   "the least of these": Matthew 25:40.

Chapter 5

145   "I thirst": John 19:28.

145   "If any one thirst": John 7:37.

147   "After this Jesus": John 19: 28–30.

147   "Wait, let us see": Mark 15:36.

148   "I am poured out": Psalm 22:14–15.

148   Jesus says he lays down his life: John 10:17–18.

149   "The cup the Father has given me": John 18:11.

149   "I am never alone": John 16:32.

150   "Behold, the Lamb of God": John 1:29.

150   "Truly, truly, I say to you": John 6:53–54.

150   "This is a hard saying": John: 6:60, 67–68.

151   "the lamb slain": Revelation 13:8.

151   "what has been hidden": Matthew 13:35, quoting Psalm 78.

151   "Come, O blessed": Matthew 25:34.

151   "shed from the foundation": Luke 11:50.

151   "like that of a lamb": 1 Peter 1:19–20.

151   "Father, I desire": John 17:24.

151   "Blessed be the God": Ephesians 1:3–4.

151   "Go therefore": Matthew 28:19–20.

152   "he would have had to suffer": Hebrews 9:26.

152   "I tell you": Matthew 26:29.

153   "The cup of blessing": 1 Corinthians 10:16.

153   "And you shall be my witnesses": Acts 1:8.

Chapter 6

190   "I am the Alpha": Revelation 22:13.

191   all things are subjected to him: 1 Corinthians 15:28.

191   "the knowledge of the Son of God": Ephesians 4:13.

191   "it does not yet appear": 1 John 3:2.

192   "O the depth": Romans 11:25–26, 33, 36.

193   "In the world you will": John 16:33.

200   "Their idols are silver": Psalm 115:4–8.

201   "Would you betray": Luke 22:48.

204   "Lord, to whom shall we go": John 6:68.

204   "Greater love": John 15:13.

205   "Then he poured water": John 13:5–7.

205   "Now I rejoice": Colossians 1:24.

208   "How much more": Hebrews 9:14; 10:12–14.

208   "whom God put forward": Romans 3:25.

208   "gave himself up": Ephesians 5:2.

208   "the expiation for our sins": 1 John 2:2.

208   "by the precious blood": 1 Peter 1:19.

208   "every tribe and tongue": Revelation 5:9.

208   "to give his life": Matthew 20:28; Mark 10:45.

209   "the Lamb of God": John 1:29.

209   "I am the living bread": John 6:51.

209   "No one takes [my life]": John 10:18.

212   "Therefore, if any one": 2 Corinthians 5:17.

215   "We preach Christ crucified": 1 Corinthians 1:23.

219   "Be merciful": Luke 6:36.

219   "Beloved, never avenge yourselves": Romans 12:19.

221   "Receive the Holy Spirit": John 20:22.

221   "For those whom [God]": Romans 8:29.

222   "He is the head": Colossians 1:18.

223   "Was it not necessary": Luke 24:26.

225   "For we have not a high priest": Hebrews 4:15–16.

Chapter 7

229   "Father, into your hands": Luke 23:46.

229   "Jesus uttered a loud cry": Mark 15:7.

Select Bibliography

Augustine, St., Bishop of Hippo. *The City of God (De civitate Dei)*. New York: Modern Library, 1950.

Balthasar, Hans Urs von. *Dare We Hope "That All Men Be Saved"?* Translated by David Kipp and Lothar Krauth. San Francisco: Ignatius Press, 1988.

Bloom Harold. *The American Religion: The Emergence of the Post-Christian Nation*. New York: Simon & Schuster, 1992.

Bonhoeffer, Dietrich. *The Cost of Discipleship*. Translated by R. H. Fuller with revisions by Irmgard Booth. New York: Macmillan, 1963, c. 1959.

Brown, Raymond E. S. S. *The Death of the Messiah: From Gethsemane to the Grave: A Commentary on the Passion Narratives in the Four Gospels*. Anchor Bible Reference Library. New York: Doubleday, 1994.

Cantalamessa, Raniero. *Mary, Mirror of the Church*. Collegeville, Minn.: Liturgical Press, 1992.

De Vries, Peter. *The Blood of the Lamb*. Boston: Little, Brown, 1961.

"Evangelicals and Catholics Together: The Gift of Salvation." *First Things* 79 (January 1998): 20–23.

Fry, Christopher. *A Sleep of Prisoners: A Play.* New York: Oxford University Press, 1951.

Jenson, Robert. *Systematic Theology: The Triune God.* Vol. 1. New York: Oxford University Press, 1997.

Oakes, Edward. *Pattern of Redemption: The Theology of Hans Urs von Balthasar.* New York: Continuum, 1994.

Sayers, Dorothy. *The Man Born to Be King: A Play-Cycle on the Life of Our Lord and Savior Jesus Christ.* New York: Harper, 1949.

Schaff and Wace, eds. *Ante-Nicene Fathers. Nicene and Post-Nicene Fathers.* Peabody, Mass.: Hendrickson, 1995.

Wyschogrod, Michael. "A Jewish Perspective on Incarnation." *Modern Theology* 12 (April 1996): 195–209. German version in *Evangelische Theologie* (München) 55, no. 1 (1995): 13–28.

Yalom, Irvin D. *Love's Executioner and Other Tales of Psychotherapy.* New York: Basic Books, 1995.

A Note About the Author

Richard John Neuhaus is acclaimed as one of the foremost authorities on the role of religion in the contemporary world. He is president of the Institute on Religion and Public Life and the editor in chief of *First Things: A Monthly Journal of Religion and Public Life*. He is the author of numerous books including *The Naked Public Square: Religion and Democracy in America* and *Freedom for Ministry*. With Charles Colson, he is the editor of *Evangelicals & Catholics Together*. He lives in New York City.

A Note on the Type

Death on a Friday Afternoon has been composed in a digitized version of Weiss, a typeface designed by German typographer Emil Rudolph Weiss (1875–1943). Issued in metal in 1931 by the Bauer Foundry of Frankfurt, Weiss is an exemplar of Renaissance-influenced type. Its crisp serifs and chancery-based italic give Weiss a distinct beauty and render it a serviceable typeface for books.